Goodness Grows in North Carolina

Goodness Grows in North Carolina

This cookbook is a collection of our favorite recipes which are not necessarily original recipes.

Published by Favorite Recipes Press P.O. Box 305142
Nashville, Tennessee 37230

© North Carolina Department of Agriculture
Marketing Division
P.O. Box 27647
1 West Edenton Street
Raleigh, N.C. 27611

ISBN 0-87197-262-X
Library of Congress Number: 89-38869

All rights reserved. No part of this book may be reproduced in any form or by any means without prior written permission of the Publisher excepting brief quotes in connection with reviews written specifically for inclusion in a magazine or newspaper.

Manufactured in the United States of America
First Printing: 1989, 12,500 copies

State of North Carolina
Department of Agriculture
Raleigh

OFFICE OF
THE COMMISSIONER OF AGRICULTURE

You have just opened, in my opinion, the best cookbook you'll ever use. Why? Because it brings together the very best recipes North Carolina has to offer. Recipes containing ingredients produced by the best farmers in the country—the farmers of North Carolina.

I want to dedicate this **Goodness Grows in North Carolina Cookbook** to those farmers who give us the high quality, clean, safe, and healthy food we eat every day. Without such dedicated producers, we couldn't sing the high praises of our state's number one industry—agriculture.

I thank each commodity group and Goodness Grows company for their recipe contributions. Thanks also to each cookbook committee member from the Marketing Division who made this book a reality. As with any successful project, it could not have been accomplished without teamwork.

From the elegance of **Roast Duckling Milano** to the down-home flavor of **Hush Puppies**, you'll soon know why we proudly say that "Goodness Grows in North Carolina."

Jim Graham

James A. Graham
Commissioner of Agriculture

Goodness Grows in North Carolina

When you see this *Goodness Grows In North Carolina* logo on food products from our state, it signifies that the product is guaranteed to be of the finest quality available. Through the purchase of these products, you, as a consumer, are contributing to the economic growth of North Carolina and to our farmers. Your continued support of this program helps to strengthen the tradition of Agriculture as the number one industry in our state. So remember, look for this symbol on quality products from North Carolina and support your neighbor, the farmer, with your purchase.

Acknowledgements

The *Goodness Grows in North Carolina Cookbook* is a result of the cooperative efforts of the fine agricultural commodity organizations, the *Goodness Grows in North Carolina* member companies, and the North Carolina Department of Agriculture.

The recipes represented were selected from the promotional recipe files of all these participating parties and are among the finest to be found in our great state.

We are proud to present a cookbook which represents the number one industry in our state—AGRICULTURE.

Listed below are the participating Commodity Associations

American Dairy Association of North Carolina

North Carolina Apple Growers Association

North Carolina Corn Growers Association

North Carolina Corn Miller's Association

North Carolina Cotton Promotion Association

North Carolina Grape Growers Association

North Carolina Herb Association

North Carolina Peach Growers Society

North Carolina Peanut Growers Association

North Carolina Pork Producers Association

North Carolina Poultry Federation

North Carolina Soybean Producers Association

North Carolina Strawberry and Pick-Your-Own Operations Association

North Carolina Sweet Potato Commission

North Carolina Watermelon Association

*Enjoy the **Goodness Grows in North Carolina** recipes
and experience the diversity of North Carolina agriculture.*

Table of Contents

Nutritional Analysis Guidelines 8
Appetizers and Beverages 9
Soups, Salads and Salad Dressings 27
Main Dishes 45
    Meats 47
    Poultry 67
    Seafood 87
Vegetables and Side Dishes 95
Breads 113
Desserts 131
    Cakes 141
    Candy 151
    Cookies 154
    Pies 159
North Carolina Celebrity Selections 173
Informational Tables 191
    Wine Selections 193
    Wine and Cheese Complements 195
    Herb Chart 196
    Equivalent Chart 198
    Substitution Chart 200
    Quantities to Serve 100 201
Index 202
Mail Order Information 207

Nutritional Analysis Guidelines

The editors have attempted to present these family recipes in a form that allows approximate nutritional values to be computed. Persons with dietary or health problems or whose diets require close monitoring should not rely solely on the nutritional information provided. They should consult their physicians or a registered dietitian for specific information.

Abbreviations for Nutritional Analysis

Cal — Calories
Prot — Protein
T Fat — Total Fat
Chol — Cholesterol
Carbo — Carbohydrates
Sod — Sodium
Potas — Potassium
gr — gram
mg — milligram

Nutritional information for recipes is computed from values furnished by the United States Department of Agriculture Handbook. Many specialty items and new products now available on the market are not included in this handbook. However, producers of new products frequently publish nutritional information on each product's packaging and that information may be added, as applicable, for a more complete analysis. If the nutritional analysis notes the exclusion of a particular ingredient, check the package information.

Unless otherwise specified, the nutritional analysis of these recipes is based on the following guidelines.

- All measurements are level.
- Artificial sweeteners vary in use and strength so should be used "to taste," using the recipe ingredients as a guideline.
- Artificial sweeteners using aspartame (NutraSweet and Equal) should not be used as a sweetener in recipes involving prolonged heating which reduces the sweet taste. For further information on the use of these sweeteners, refer to package information.
- Alcoholic ingredients have been analyzed for the basic ingredients, although cooking causes the evaporation of alcohol thus decreasing caloric content.
- Buttermilk, sour cream, and yogurt are the types available commercially.
- Chicken, cooked for boning and chopping, has been roasted; this method yields the lowest caloric values.
- Cottage cheese is cream-style with 4.2% creaming mixture. Dry-curd cottage cheese has no creaming mixture.
- Eggs are all large.
- Flour is unsifted all-purpose flour.
- Garnishes, serving suggestions and other optional additions and variations are not included in the analysis.
- Margarine and butter are regular, not whipped or presoftened.
- Milk is whole milk, 3.5% butterfat. Lowfat milk is 1% butterfat. Evaporated milk is produced by removing 60% of the water from whole milk.
- Oil is any type of vegetable cooking oil. Shortening is hydrogenated vegetable shortening.
- Salt to taste as noted in the method has not been included in the nutritional analysis.
- If a choice of ingredients has been given, the nutritional analysis reflects the first option.

Appetizers and Beverages

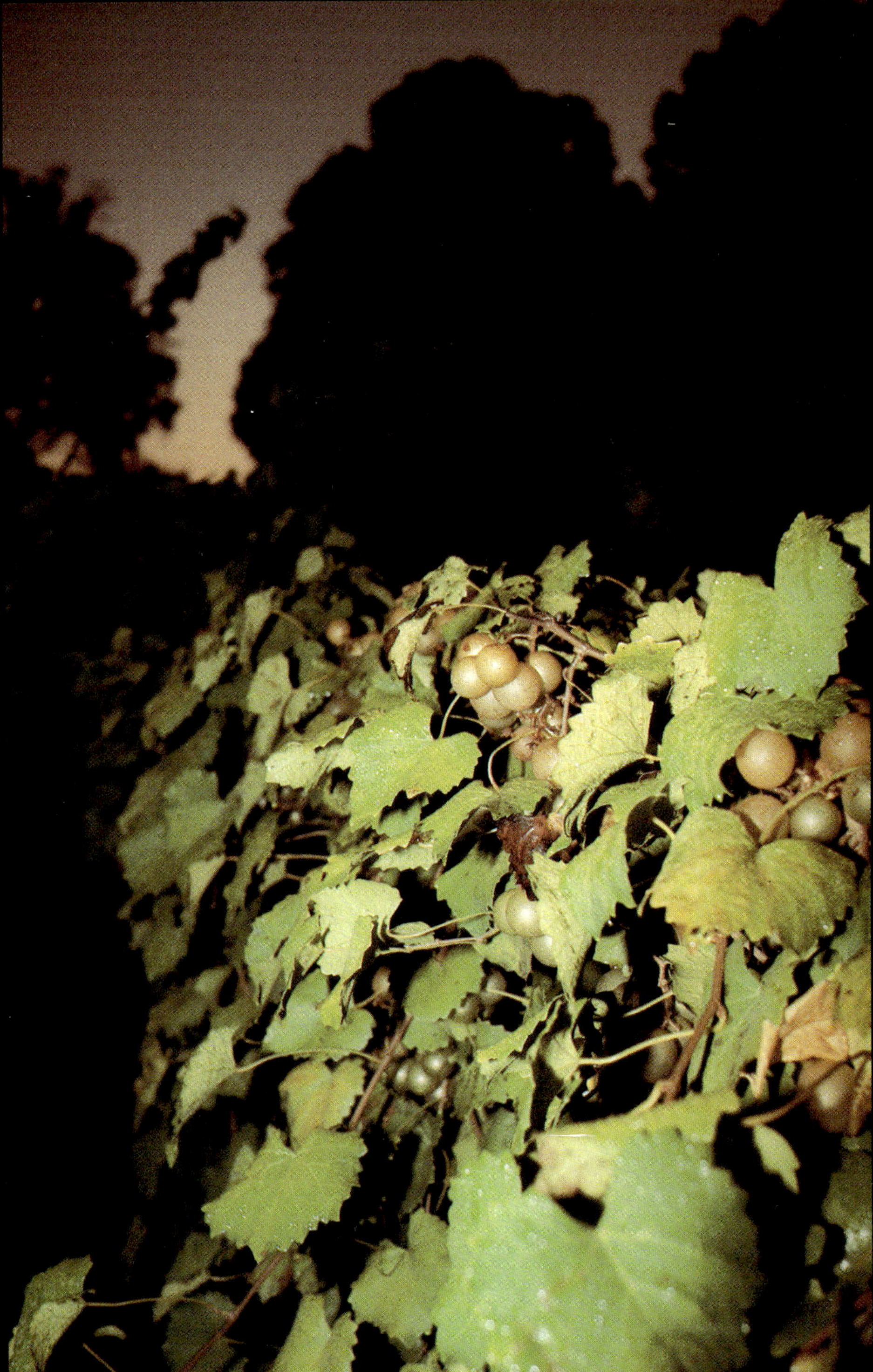

ANGELS ON HORSEBACK

1 cup select oysters
1 cup select scallops
12 slices bacon
1/2 teaspoon salt
1/8 teaspoon pepper
1/8 teaspoon paprika
2 tablespoons chopped parsley

Drain oysters and scallops. Cut bacon slices into halves. Place each oyster or scallop on 1 bacon slice; sprinkle with salt, pepper, paprika and parsley. Roll bacon to enclose seafood; fasten with toothpick. Place on rack in shallow baking pan. Bake at 450 degrees for 10 minutes or until bacon is crisp. Remove toothpicks.
Yield: 6 servings.

Approx Per Serving: Cal 144; Prot 15.4 g; Carbo 2.9 g; T Fat 7.6 g; Chol 50.0 mg; Potas 311.0 mg; Sod 501.0 mg.

North Carolina Department of Agriculture

BACON PIZZA SNACKS

1 loaf party rye bread
1 cup shredded sharp Cheddar cheese
1 cup shredded mozzarella cheese
1 cup Lundy's crumbled crisp-fried bacon
1/2 cup plus 1 tablespoon tomato sauce
1/2 cup chopped onion
1 tablespoon Worcestershire sauce
1/2 teaspoon minced garlic
1/4 to 1/2 teaspoon oregano

Place bread slices on baking sheet. Bake at 350 degrees for 10 minutes. Combine cheeses, bacon, tomato sauce, onion, Worcestershire sauce, garlic and oregano in bowl; mix well. Spoon 1 tablespoon cheese mixture onto each bread slice. Bake for 10 minutes longer. Yield: 36 appetizers.

Approx Per Appetizer: Cal 49; Prot 2.6 g; Carbo 3.2 g; T Fat 2.9 g; Chol 7.5 mg; Potas 60.0 mg; Sod 122.0 mg.

Lundy Packing Company
MEMBER

CHA-CHOS

1 (7-ounce) bag tortilla chips
8 ounces cheese, shredded
1/4 cup Texas Pete hot sauce

Spread chips in single layer on glass plate. Sprinkle with cheese. Season with hot sauce. Microwave on High for 30 to 60 seconds or just until cheese is melted. May bake at 350 degrees for 3 to 5 minutes. Yield: 4 servings.

Approx Per Serving: Cal 471; Prot 18.1 g; Carbo 30.2 g; T Fat 31.9 g; Chol 59.7 mg; Potas 112.0 mg; Sod 627.0 mg.

T. W. Garner Food Company
MEMBER

QUICK AND ZESTY CHEESE BALL

8 ounces cream cheese, softened
8 ounces Cheddar cheese, shredded
2 teaspoons Carolina Treet barbecue sauce
1 cup finely chopped walnuts

Blend first 3 ingredients in bowl until mixed well. Shape into ball; roll in walnuts. Chill in refrigerator until firm. Serve with crackers. Yield: 32 tablespoons.

Approx Per Tablespoon: Cal 78; Prot 2.8 g; Carbo 1.0 g; T Fat 7.2 g; Chol 15.2 mg; Potas 34.8 mg; Sod 68.0 mg.

Carolina Treet, Inc.
MEMBER

LIVER-CHEESE BALL

1 pound Neese's liver pudding
8 ounces cream cheese, softened
1/2 cup drained crushed pineapple
1/4 cup chopped olives
1/4 cup minced onion
1 cup finely chopped pecans
Parsley to taste

Crumble Neese's liver pudding into bowl. Add cream cheese, pineapple, olives and onion; mix well. Shape into ball. Roll in pecans and parsley. Yield: 64 tablespoons.

Approx Per Tablespoon: Cal 51; Prot 1.4 g; Carbo 0.9 g; T Fat 4.8 g; Chol 14.9 mg; Potas 27.3 mg; Sod 74.7 mg.

Neese's Country Sausage Company
MEMBER

MILDRED GARNER'S CHEESE CRISPS

1 pound sharp Cheddar cheese, shredded
3/4 cup butter, softened
2 cups all-purpose flour
1/8 teaspoon salt
2 tablespoons Texas Pete hot sauce
2 cups crisp rice cereal, crushed

Combine all ingredients in bowl; mix well. Shape into small balls; place on baking sheet. Bake at 325 degrees for 17 minutes. The cheese crisps will brown while cooling. Cool. Store in airtight container. Yield: 24 cheese crisps.

Approx Per Cheese Crisp: Cal 174; Prot 6.0 g; Carbo 10.3 g; T Fat 12.1 g; Chol 35.4 mg; Potas 33.5 mg; Sod 210.0 mg.

T. W. Garner Food Company
MEMBER

OUR FAVORITE CHEESE RING

1 pound Cheddar cheese, shredded
1 cup mayonnaise
1 cup finely chopped pecans
2 tablespoons Texas Pete hot sauce
1 small onion, minced
1/8 teaspoon salt
Pepper to taste
Paprika to taste
1 cup strawberry or cherry preserves

Blend cheese and mayonnaise in bowl until well mixed. Add pecans, hot sauce, onion, salt, pepper and paprika; mix well. Shape into ring on serving plate. Chill, covered, overnight. Place preserves in small bowl in center of ring before serving. Yield: 24 servings.

Approx Per Serving: Cal 213; Prot 5.4 g; Carbo 11.1 g; T Fat 16.9 g; Chol 25.3 mg; Potas 61.7 mg; Sod 187.0 mg.

T. W. Garner Food Company
MEMBER

CAPSICANA WINGS

10 chicken wings
1/4 cup **Capsicana Zing sauce**
1/4 cup **Kikkoman soy sauce**
1/4 cup **honey**

Wash chicken wings; remove and discard wing tips. Combine Capsicana Zing sauce, soy sauce and honey in saucepan. Add chicken. Simmer, covered, for 3 minutes, stirring frequently. Marinate in sauce in refrigerator for 4 hours to overnight. Drain. Grill over hot coals or broil until brown on both sides. Serve hot. Yield: 10 servings.

Approx Per Serving: Cal 129; Prot 9.5 g; Carbo 7.6 g; T Fat 6.7 g; Chol 28.0 mg; Potas 73.1 mg; Sod 439.0 mg.
Nutritional information does not include Capsicana Zing sauce.

Home Industries, Inc.
MEMBER

BUFFALO-STYLE CHICKEN WINGS

5 pounds (25 to 30) chicken wings
6 ounces **Texas Pete hot sauce**
1/2 cup **melted margarine**

Wash chicken wings; remove and discard wing tips. Drain chicken on paper towels. Combine hot sauce and margarine in bowl; mix well. Coat chicken in mixture; place in single layer in baking pan. Bake at 450 degrees for 35 minutes or until chicken is brown. Serve with celery sticks and blue cheese dressing dip. May deep-fry chicken wings in hot 375-degree oil for 10 to 12 minutes or until crispy. Yield: 25 servings.

Approx Per Serving: Cal 152; Prot 11.1 g; Carbo 0.1 g; T Fat 11.8 g; Chol 43.5 mg; Potas 72.5 mg; Sod 93.3 mg.

T. W. Garner Food Company
MEMBER

CHICKEN MOUSSE PHYLLO TRIANGLES

2 cups cubed Holly Farms fully cooked roasted chicken breast
8 ounces cream cheese, softened
1/4 cup whipping cream
1/8 teaspoon salt
Pepper to taste
1 (8-ounce) package prepared phyllo pastry
1/2 cup melted butter

Process chicken and cream cheese in food processor for 30 seconds. Add cream. Process for 30 seconds or until smooth. Season with salt and pepper. Place 2 phyllo pastry leaves on cutting board; brush with butter. Cut lengthwise into 2-inch wide strips. Place 1 teaspoon chicken filling on end of each strip. Fold in 1 corner to form triangle, enclosing filling. Continue folding to end of strip, keeping triangle shape. Place on baking sheet. Repeat with remaining phyllo pastry and filling. Bake at 350 degrees for 15 to 20 minutes or until golden brown. Serve hot. May serve chicken mousse mixture in miniature pastry shells or as a spread. Yield: 42 appetizers.

Approx Per Appetizer: Cal 56; Prot 2.4 g; Carbo 0.2 g; T Fat 5.1 g; Chol 19.7 mg; Potas 24.4 mg; Sod 47.0 mg.
Nutritional information does not include phyllo pastry.

Holly Farms Foods, Inc.
MEMBER

BACON-HORSERADISH DIP

8 ounces sour cream
3 tablespoons mayonnaise
1 tablespoon horseradish
3/4 cup crumbled crisp-fried bacon
Dash of Worcestershire sauce
1/8 teaspoon salt

Combine all ingredients in bowl; mix well. Chill in refrigerator overnight. Serve with crisp vegetables. Yield: 24 tablespoons.

Approx Per Tablespoon: Cal 39; Prot 0.6 g; Carbo 0.5 g; T Fat 3.9 g; Chol 6.1 mg; Potas 21.2 mg; Sod 43.3 mg.

North Carolina Department of Agriculture

APPETIZERS

MEXICAN BEAN AND BACON DIP

2 (11-ounce) cans baked beans
2 cups shredded Cheddar cheese
3 tablespoons Worcestershire sauce
1 1/2 teaspoons minced onion
1 teaspoon chili powder
1/2 teaspoon minced garlic
1/2 teaspoon cumin
4 drops of hot pepper sauce
1 cup Lundy's crumbled crisp-fried bacon

Purée beans in blender container. Combine beans and next 7 ingredients in saucepan. Cook until heated through, stirring frequently. Stir in crumbled bacon. Spoon into chafing dish. Serve with tostados or corn chips. Yield: 64 tablespoons.

Approx Per Tablespoon: Cal 31; Prot 1.7 g; Carbo 2.0 g; T Fat 1.8 g; Chol 5.2 mg; Potas 40.1 mg; Sod 77.5 mg.

Lundy Packing Company
MEMBER

CHILI CHEESE DIP

1 (10-ounce) can Texas Pete chili without beans
1 (4-ounce) can chopped green chilies
1 (16-ounce) package shredded sharp Cheddar cheese
2 tablespoons Texas Pete hot sauce

Combine all ingredients in saucepan. Cook over low heat until cheese melts, stirring frequently. Serve warm with corn chips or taco chips. May microwave, covered, for 6 minutes, stirring every 2 minutes. Yield: 32 tablespoons.

Approx Per Tablespoon: Cal 40; Prot 2.4 g; Carbo 1.5 g; T Fat 2.8 g; Chol 8.9 mg; Potas 51.9 mg; Sod 94.2 mg.

T. W. Garner Food Company
MEMBER

CURRY DIP

1 cup soybean oil mayonnaise
1 teaspoon curry powder
1 teaspoon Worcestershire sauce
1 teaspoon horseradish sauce
1 teaspoon grated onion
1 teaspoon vinegar
1 teaspoon minced garlic

Beat all ingredients in mixer bowl until fluffy. Chill, covered, in refrigerator. Serve with crisp vegetables.
Yield: 24 tablespoons.

Approx Per Tablespoon: Cal 66; Prot 0.1 g; Carbo 0.4 g; T Fat 7.3 g; Chol 5.4 mg; Potas 6.5 mg; Sod 54.3 mg.

North Carolina Soybean Producers Association

EAST INDIAN DIP

1 teaspoon lemon juice
1/2 teaspoon curry powder
1/4 teaspoon salt
1/8 teaspoon dry mustard
1/8 teaspoon ginger
1/8 teaspoon garlic salt
1 cup sour cream

Combine lemon juice and seasonings in bowl; mix well. Fold in sour cream. Chill, covered, in refrigerator for 1 to 2 hours for flavors to blend. Serve with fresh fruit.
Yield: 16 tablespoons.

Approx Per Tablespoon: Cal 31; Prot 0.4 g; Carbo 0.6 g; T Fat 3.0 g; Chol 6.4 mg; Potas 21.1 mg; Sod 57.7 mg.

American Dairy Association of North Carolina

INCREDIBLE EGG DIP

1 package Knorr's garden vegetable soup mix
16 ounces sour cream
4 hard-boiled eggs, chopped

Stir soup mix into sour cream in bowl. Add chopped eggs; mix well. Chill in refrigerator for 2 hours. Serve with crackers, chips or fresh vegetables.
Yield: 40 tablespoons.

Approx Per Tablespoon: Cal 40; Prot 1.2 g; Carbo 2.0 g; T Fat 3.2 g; Chol 32.6 mg; Potas 45.2 mg; Sod 83.6 mg.

North Carolina Egg Association

SHRIMP CHIP DIP

1 (4½-ounce) can shrimp
¼ cup chili sauce
2 teaspoons lemon juice
1 teaspoon prepared
   horseradish
½ teaspoon salt
⅛ teaspoon pepper
Dash of hot pepper sauce
1 cup sour cream

Rinse shrimp; drain. Chop finely. Mix chili sauce, lemon juice, horseradish and seasonings in bowl. Fold in shrimp and sour cream. Chill, covered, for several hours. Serve with crackers or chips.
Yield: 32 tablespoons.

Approx Per Tablespoon: Cal 21; Prot 1.0 g; Carbo 0.9 g; T Fat 1.6 g; Chol 8.4 mg; Potas 25.4 mg; Sod 70.9 mg.

American Dairy Association of North Carolina

TURKEY MEATBALLS

1 pound ground raw
   turkey
1 package meatball
   seasoning
1 tablespoon
   Worcestershire sauce
1 (12-ounce) can tomato
   sauce

Mix first 3 ingredients in bowl. Shape into small balls; place in baking dish. Pour tomato sauce over meatballs. Bake at 300 degrees for 30 minutes. Serve hot.
Yield: 24 meatballs.

Approx Per Meatball: Cal 47; Prot 5.1 g; Carbo 1.1 g; T Fat 2.5 g; Chol 15.9 mg; Potas 102.0 mg; Sod 114.0 mg.
Nutritional information does not include meatball seasoning.

House of Raeford, Inc.
MEMBER

MELON CUP

2 cups watermelon balls
2 cups cantaloupe balls
2 cups honeydew melon
   balls
1 cup pineapple juice

Combine melon balls in bowl; mix gently. Pour in pineapple juice. Chill in refrigerator. Serve as fruit cup. Yield: 6 servings.

Approx Per Serving: Cal 79; Prot 1.2 g; Carbo 19.2 g; T Fat 0.5 g; Chol 0.0 mg; Potas 436.0 mg; Sod 11.8 mg.

Murfreesboro Farms, Inc.
MEMBER

DIX MIX

½ cup butter
1¼ teaspoons seasoned salt
4½ teaspoons Worcestershire sauce
2⅔ cups square corn cereal
2⅔ cups square rice cereal
2⅔ cups square wheat cereal
1 (10-ounce) jar Dixie's Pride red peppered peanuts

Melt butter in 10x15-inch shallow baking dish in 325-degree oven. Stir in seasoned salt and Worcestershire sauce. Add cereal gradually, stirring to coat. Bake at 325 degrees for 20 to 25 minutes or until golden, stirring every 10 minutes. Cool. Stir in peanuts. Store in airtight container. May substitute Dixie's Pride salted, sugared, sugar and spice or parched peanuts for peppered peanuts. Yield: 10 cups.

Approx Per Cup: Cal 352; Prot 10.0 g; Carbo 28.4 g; T Fat 24.0 g; Chol 24.8 mg; Potas 285.0 mg; Sod 755.0 mg.

Dixie's Pride Peanuts
MEMBER

FAN-TASTIC CHEESE POPCORN

3 tablespoons oil
1 teaspoon caraway, comino or mustard seed
⅓ cup unpopped popcorn
1 cup shredded Cheddar, Monterey Jack or Swiss cheese
Salt to taste

Combine oil, desired seasoning seed and popcorn in popper. Pop according to manufacturer's instructions. Spread popped popcorn in buttered baking pan. Sprinkle with desired cheese. Bake at 350 degrees for 3 to 5 minutes. Season with salt. Stir; serve immediately. Yield: 12 cups.

Approx Per Cup: Cal 98; Prot 3.3 g; Carbo 6.1 g; T Fat 6.9 g; Chol 9.9 mg; Potas 29.3 mg; Sod 58.9 mg.

Carolina's Best Popcorn
MEMBER

TEX MEX MIX

2 teaspoons chili powder
2 teaspoons paprika
2 teaspoons cumin
2 quarts (popped in oil) popcorn
1 cup cubed Monterey Jack cheese

Mix chili powder, paprika and cumin in large bowl; mix well. Pour in hot popped popcorn; toss to mix. Add cheese cubes; mix well. Yield: 8 servings.

Approx Per Serving: Cal 131; Prot 5.5 g; Carbo 6.1 g; T Fat 9.8 g; Chol 13.0 mg; Potas 31.5 mg; Sod 76.4 mg.

Carolina's Best Popcorn
MEMBER

SCUPPERNONG SPICED PECANS

1 cup sugar
1/4 cup Scuppernong wine
1/8 teaspoon cream of tartar
1 teaspoon cinnamon
1 teaspoon vanilla extract
2 cups pecan halves

Cook sugar, wine and cream of tartar in saucepan to 230 to 234 degrees on candy thermometer, thread stage. Remove from heat. Add cinnamon and vanilla; mix well. Add pecans; stir until cooled. Pour onto buttered baking sheet. Separate pecans with fork. Bake at 350 degrees for several minutes. Remove to waxed paper to cool, separating pecans.
Yield: approximately 240 pecan halves.

Approx Per Pecan: Cal 10; Prot 0.1 g; Carbo 1.0 g; T Fat 0.7 g; Chol 0.0 mg; Potas 4.2 mg; Sod 0.0 mg.

North Carolina Grape Growers Association

PIZZA SQUARES

Anne's frozen flat dumplings
Pizza sauce
Pepperoni slices
Shredded mozzarella cheese

Cut dumplings into halves; place on baking sheet sprayed with nonstick cooking spray. Bake at 425 degrees until light brown. Place in glass baking pan. Spread with pizza sauce. Add pepperoni slices; top with cheese. Microwave on High until cheese is melted. Baked dumplings may also be eaten as crackers and topped with cheese spread or chicken salad.

Nutritional information for this recipe is not available.

Anne's Old Fashioned Dumplings
MEMBER

TINY CUCUMBER OPEN-FACED SANDWICHES

8 ounces cream cheese, softened
1/3 cup mayonnaise
20 slices sandwich bread
2 large cucumbers, sliced
Paprika to taste

Combine cream cheese and mayonnaise in bowl; mix well. Cut center of each bread slice with biscuit cutter. Spread with cream cheese mixture. Add slice of cucumber; sprinkle with paprika.
Yield: 20 sandwiches.

Approx Per Sandwich: Cal 107; Prot 2.2 g; Carbo 8.1 g; T Fat 7.4 g; Chol 14.5 mg; Potas 75.3 mg; Sod 127.0 mg.

Murfreesboro Farms, Inc.
MEMBER

CHEESE-BACON PICKLEWICHES

1/4 cup process cheese-bacon spread, softened
24 sweet fresh cucumber pickle slices

Spread 1 tablespoon cheese spread on half the pickle slices. Top with remaining pickle slices. Chill in refrigerator until set.
Yield: 12 servings.

Nutritional information for this recipe is not available.

Mt. Olive Pickle Company
MEMBER

HAM AND CHEESE PICKLEWICHES

12 large dill pickles
6 (1-ounce) slices American cheese
12 (1-ounce) slices ham

Cut each pickle into halves lengthwise. Cut cheese and ham slices to shape of pickle. Arrange 1 piece cheese and 2 pieces ham between each pickle half, sandwich style. Chill until serving time. Yield: 12 servings.

Approx Per Serving: Cal 109; Prot 8.6 g; Carbo 2.5 g; T Fat 7.5 g; Chol 29.5 mg; Potas 247.0 mg; Sod 1317.0 mg.

Mt. Olive Pickle Company
MEMBER

PIMENTO CHEESE PICKLEWICHES

5 teaspoons process pimento cheese spread
20 sweet pickle chips

Spread 1/2 teaspoon pimento cheese spread on half the pickle chips; top with remaining pickle chips. Chill in refrigerator until serving time. Yield: 10 servings.

Approx Per Serving: Cal 15; Prot 0.4 g; Carbo 2.8 g; T Fat 0.4 g; Chol 1.4 mg; Potas 17.3 mg; Sod 73.7 mg.

Mt. Olive Pickle Company
MEMBER

ZINGY SPARERIBS

3 pounds pork spareribs
3/4 cup Capsicana Zing gourmet sauce
1/4 cup Kikkoman soy sauce
3/4 cup water

Combine spare ribs, Capsicana Zing gourmet sauce and soy sauce in saucepan. Bring to a boil. Cook for 5 to 10 minutes, stirring and turning ribs frequently. Add water. Bring to a boil. Simmer, covered, for 40 minutes or until pork is tender, stirring frequently. May serve with rice as main dish. Yield: 6 servings.

Approx Per Serving: Cal 627; Prot 45.0 g; Carbo 4.0 g; T Fat 46.5 g; Chol 183.0 mg; Potas 559.0 mg; Sod 1082.0 mg.
Nutritional information does not include Capsicana Zing sauce.

Home Industries, Inc.
MEMBER

SAUSAGE BALLS

1 pound Neese's sausage, softened
1 (10-ounce) package shredded Cheddar cheese, softened
3 cups buttermilk baking mix
1 teaspoon paprika

Crumble sausage into bowl. Add cheese; mix well. Stir in baking mix and paprika, mixing well. Shape into small balls; place on baking sheet. Bake at 350 degrees for 15 to 20 minutes or until brown and sausage is cooked through. Yield: 100 sausage balls.

Approx Per Sausage Ball: Cal 47; Prot 1.5 g; Carbo 2.6 g; T Fat 3.3 g; Chol 6.1 mg; Potas 17.5 mg; Sod 95.5 mg.

Neese's Country Sausage Company
MEMBER

BEVERAGES 23

SAUSAGE POPPY ROLLS

1 1/2 pounds Neese's
   sausage
1 small onion, finely
   chopped (optional)
3/4 cup margarine
1 tablespoon poppy seed
1 tablespoon mustard
2 (8-ounce) packages tea
   biscuits or finger rolls
8 ounces Swiss cheese,
   shredded

Brown sausage in skillet, stirring until crumbly; drain well. Sauté onion in margarine in skillet until tender. Add poppy seed and mustard; mix well. Remove or slice top half from each pan of rolls. Spread bottom half with margarine mixture. Spread sausage over margarine mixture; sprinkle with cheese. Replace top halves. Bake, covered with foil, at 350 degrees for 10 to 15 minutes or until cheese melts. Yield: 48 rolls.

Approx Per Roll: Cal 132; Prot 3.7 g; Carbo 5.2 g; T Fat 10.5 g; Chol 14.0 mg; Potas 51.8 mg; Sod 196.0 mg.

Neese's Country Sausage Company
MEMBER

DUPLIN CHAMPAGNE FLOAT

1 scoop pineapple sherbet
1/2 cup crushed pineapple
1 cup Duplin non-
   alcoholic sparkling
   Scuppernong
1 maraschino cherry

Place pineapple sherbet in stemmed dessert glass; spoon crushed pineapple over sherbet. Pour in Scuppernong. Garnish with cherry. This makes a great holiday or summer dessert. Yield: 1 serving.

Approx Per Serving: Cal 389; Prot 2.9 g; Carbo 93.0 g; T Fat 2.2 g; Chol 7.0 mg; Potas 565.0 mg; Sod 53.5 mg.

Duplin Winery
MEMBER

COFFEE COOLER

3 cups cold milk
1 tablespoon instant coffee powder
1 pint coffee ice cream, softened

Blend milk and instant coffee in blender container. Add ice cream. Blend until of desired consistency. Serve immediately. Yield: 5 cups.

Approx Per Cup: Cal 198; Prot 6.7 g; Carbo 19.8 g; T Fat 10.6 g; Chol 43.4 mg; Potas 325.0 mg; Sod 108.0 mg.

American Dairy Association of North Carolina

ORANGE DREAM SHAKE

1 cup orange sherbet
1 (6-ounce) can frozen orange juice concentrate, thawed
3 cups cold milk
4 scoops orange sherbet
Mint leaves

Process 1 cup orange sherbet and orange juice concentrate in blender container. Add milk; blend well. Pour into four 12-ounce glasses. Top each with 1 scoop orange sherbet. Garnish with mint. Serve immediately. May substitute limeade and lime sherbet. Yield: 4 servings.

Approx Per Serving: Cal 383; Prot 8.7 g; Carbo 68.8 g; T Fat 9.1 g; Chol 35.2 mg; Potas 680.0 mg; Sod 144.0 mg.

American Dairy Association of North Carolina

PARTY GRAPE PUNCH

1 (12-ounce) can frozen lemonade concentrate
1 quart grape juice
1 teaspoon whole cloves
1 cup sugar
4 cinnamon sticks

Prepare lemonade using concentrate directions. Combine all ingredients in saucepan. Bring to a boil, stirring frequently; strain. Serve hot. Yield: 12 cups.

Approx Per Cup: Cal 167; Prot 0.5 g; Carbo 42.6 g; T Fat 0.1 g; Chol 0.0 mg; Potas 131.0 mg; Sod 4.1 mg.

North Carolina Grape Growers Association

MINTED PUNCH

1½ cups sugar
2 cups water
1 cup dry mint leaves
1 teaspoon grated orange rind
2 cups orange juice
1¼ cups lemon juice
1½ (67.6-ounce) bottles of ginger ale

Add sugar to boiling water in saucepan, stirring until sugar dissolves. Place mint leaves and orange rind in medium bowl. Pour in hot sugar syrup. Steep, covered, for 20 minutes. Stir in orange juice and lemon juice. Chill, covered, in refrigerator for 1½ hours to overnight. Strain. Pour over minted ice mold in punch bowl; add ginger ale. Serve in punch cups. Add ice cubes. Garnish with fresh mint. Yield: 16 servings.

Approx Per Serving: Cal 119; Prot 0.3 g; Carbo 30.7 g; T Fat 0.1 g; Chol 0.0 mg; Potas 80.6 mg; Sod 9.4 mg.

Rasland Herb Farm
MEMBER

PUNCH MELON

1 large watermelon
4 cups watermelon juice
1 (6-ounce) can frozen orange juice concentrate, thawed
1 (6-ounce) can frozen lemonade concentrate, thawed
1 (16-ounce) can pineapple juice
4 cups sugar

Stand watermelon on end; cut thin slice from 1 side to make level. Stand watermelon on level side; remove and discard top third of watermelon. Trace scallops around top of watermelon with sharp knife using jar ring for guide. Carve out scalloped edge. Scoop out pulp, reserving 4 cups watermelon juice. Chill carved watermelon in refrigerator. Combine watermelon juice, orange juice and lemonade concentrates, pineapple juice and sugar in large container. Add enough water to measure 2 gallons. Chill in refrigerator. Pour into watermelon bowl. Garnish with mint. Yield: 32 cups.

Approx Per Cup: Cal 151; Prot 0.7 g; Carbo 37.8 g; T Fat 0.4 g; Chol 0.0 mg; Potas 164.0 mg; Sod 3.0 mg.

North Carolina Watermelon Association

STRAWBERRY ROSÉ

3 ounces cracked ice
4 ounces Duplin Rosé
   wine
6 strawberries
1 teaspoon lemon juice
½ teaspoon sugar

Combine ice with remaining ingredients in blender container; process until smooth. Pour into chilled wine glasses. Yield: 2 servings.

Approx Per Serving: Cal 62; Prot 0.5 g; Carbo 6.0 g; T Fat 0.2 g; Chol 0.0 mg; Potas 152.0 mg; Sod 3.3 mg.

Duplin Winery
MEMBER

COUNTRY SYLLABUB (North Carolina Style)

½ cup sugar
½ cup Scuppernong wine
1 quart whipping cream
½ cup Brandy
Nutmeg

Mix sugar and wine in bowl until sugar is dissolved. Add a small amount of cream; mix well. Whip remaining cream in large bowl until thickened. Add wine mixture and Brandy gradually, beating well. Pour into large pitcher; pour back into bowl. Repeat process until mixture is frothy. Garnish with nutmeg. Yield: 10 servings.

Approx Per Serving: Cal 403; Prot 2.0 g; Carbo 17.0 g; T Fat 35.2 g; Chol 130.5 mg; Potas 86.5 mg; Sod 36.9 mg.

North Carolina Grape Growers Association

RUSSIAN TEA

1 gallon water
2 cinnamon sticks
2 tablespoons whole
   cloves
20 teaspoons tea leaves
2 cups grape juice
Juice of 6 lemons

Bring water, cinnamon and cloves to a boil in saucepan. Pour over tea leaves in pitcher. Steep until of desired strength; strain into saucepan. Stir in grape juice and lemon juice. Heat to serving temperature. Yield: 20 servings.

Approx Per Serving: Cal 19; Prot 0.2 g; Carbo 5.0 g; T Fat 0.1 g; Chol 0.0 mg; Potas 50.4 mg; Sod 0.9 mg.

North Carolina Grape Growers Association

Soups, Salads and Salad Dressings

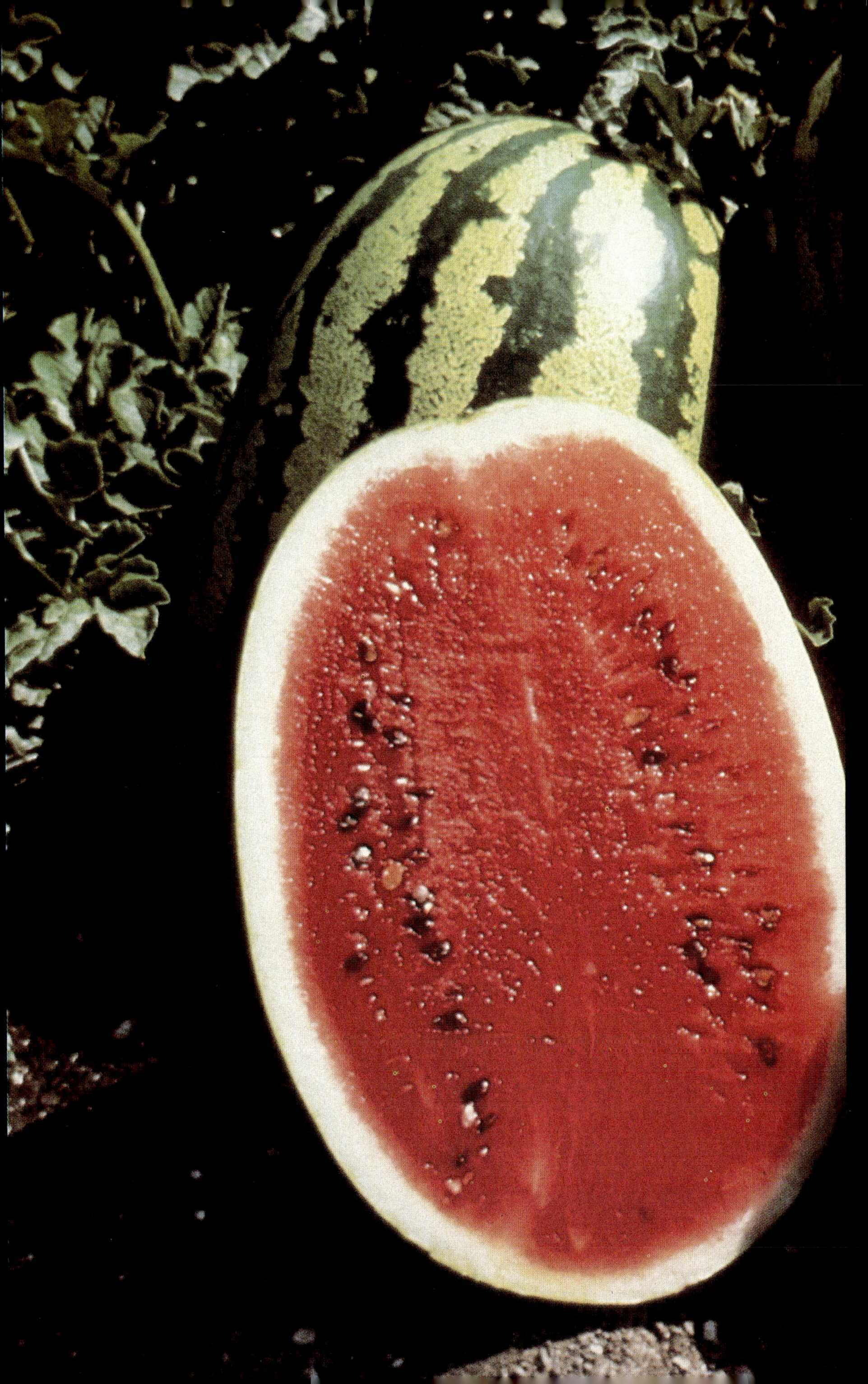

CREAM OF BROCCOLI SOUP

2 cups water
1 (16-ounce) package frozen broccoli cuts
1/2 cup chopped onion
1/2 cup melted butter
1/2 cup all-purpose flour
6 cups milk
4 chicken bouillon cubes
1 teaspoon white pepper

Bring water to a boil in medium saucepan; add broccoli. Cover; reduce heat. Simmer for 5 minutes; remove from heat. Sauté onion in butter in saucepan over low heat for 10 minutes or until tender. Add flour, stirring until smooth. Cook for 1 minute, stirring constantly. Add milk gradually. Add bouillon cubes. Cook over medium heat until thickened, stirring constantly. Add undrained broccoli and white pepper. Simmer for 20 to 30 minutes, stirring occasionally. Ladle into serving bowls. Yield: 9 cups.

Approx Per Cup: Cal 237; Prot 8.2 g; Carbo 16.7 g; T Fat 15.9 g; Chol 49.6 mg; Potas 416.0 mg; Sod 678.0 mg.

North Carolina Department of Agriculture

CATFISH AND SHRIMP SOUP

2 cups chopped onions
2 cloves of garlic, crushed
2 tablespoons oil
1 large (16-ounce) can tomatoes
3 tablespoons tomato paste
1/2 teaspoon salt
1/4 teaspoon freshly ground black pepper
1 bay leaf
3 cups water
1 cup dry white wine
1 cup chicken broth
4 catfish fillets, cut into 1-inch pieces
1/2 pound shelled shrimp
2 tablespoons chopped fresh parsley

Sauté onions and garlic lightly in oil in saucepan. Stir in tomatoes, tomato paste, salt, pepper and bay leaf. Simmer, covered, for 15 minutes. Add water, wine and broth. Simmer, uncovered, for 45 minutes. Add catfish and shrimp. Cook for 10 minutes or until fish flakes easily. Remove bay leaf. Ladle into soup bowls. Sprinkle with parsley. Yield: 8 servings.

Approx Per Serving: Cal 246; Prot 28.5 g; Carbo 7.1 g; T Fat 9.0 g; Chol 121.0 mg; Potas 744.0 mg; Sod 464.0 mg.

Carolina Classics Catfish
MEMBER

GAZPACHO SOUP

1 medium cucumber, minced
4 ripe tomatoes
1/3 cup minced onion
1 clove of garlic, minced
1/2 cup chopped green bell pepper
1/4 cup chopped fresh basil
1/4 cup olive oil
1/4 cup vinegar
2 cups vegetable juice cocktail
1 teaspoon salt

Place all ingredients in blender container. Process on High until puréed. Chill, covered, for 4 hours to overnight. Ladle into serving bowls. Serve cold with sandwiches for lunch or as a first course at dinner. May substitute canned tomatoes for fresh tomatoes. Yield: 4 servings.

Approx Per Serving: Cal 186; Prot 2.6 g; Carbo 15.8 g; T Fat 14.1 g; Chol 0.0 mg; Potas 664.0 mg; Sod 987.0 mg.

North Carolina Herb Association

HEARTY HAMBURGER SOUP

2 tablespoons butter
1 cup chopped onion
1 cup sliced carrot
1/2 cup chopped green bell pepper
1 pound ground beef
2 cups tomato juice
1 cup chopped potatoes
1 1/2 teaspoons salt
1 teaspoon seasoned salt
1/8 teaspoon pepper
1 cup milk
1/3 cup all-purpose flour
3 cups milk

Melt butter in saucepan. Add onion, carrot and green pepper. Sauté just until onion is tender. Brown ground beef in skillet, stirring until crumbly; drain. Add to vegetable mixture. Stir in tomato juice, potatoes and seasonings. Cook, covered, over low heat for 20 minutes or until vegetables are tender. Stir 1 cup milk into flour gradually to make smooth paste. Stir flour mixture into soup mixture gradually. Add remaining 3 cups milk. Cook until thickened, stirring frequently; do not boil. Ladle into serving bowls. Yield: 8 cups.

Approx Per Cup: Cal 276; Prot 15.4 g; Carbo 18.8 g; T Fat 15.7 g; Chol 60.8 mg; Potas 566.0 mg; Sod 1002.0 mg.

American Dairy Association of North Carolina

SEAFOOD GUMBO

1 pound okra, sliced
1/4 cup shortening
2 tablespoons all-purpose flour
1 onion, chopped
1 bunch green onions, chopped
1/2 cup chopped celery
1 (16-ounce) can tomatoes
2 sprigs of parsley, chopped
1 bay leaf
1 sprig of thyme
8 cups water
Salt and pepper to taste
1 pound fresh shrimp, peeled
8 ounces crab meat
1 teaspoon filé

Fry okra in 2 tablespoons shortening in skillet until okra no longer "ropes." Melt remaining 2 tablespoons shortening in heavy skillet. Stir in flour. Cook over medium heat until dark brown, stirring constantly. Add onions and celery. Cook for 5 minutes or until tender. Stir in okra, tomatoes, parsley, bay leaf, thyme and water. Simmer for 30 minutes. Add seasonings, shrimp and crab. Simmer for 30 minutes longer; remove from heat. Stir in filé just before serving. Never cook filé. Gumbo is best cooked early in the morning and refrigerated for several hours. Reheat and serve with cooked rice. Yield: 6 servings.

Approx Per Serving: Cal 258; Prot 26.1 g; Carbo 14.6 g; T Fat 11.0 g; Chol 153.0 mg; Potas 787.0 mg; Sod 354.0 mg.

North Carolina Department of Agriculture

SWEET POTATO AND PEPPER SOUP

1 hot pepper, roasted, finely minced
2 pounds sweet potatoes, cooked, puréed
1 teaspoon garlic powder
5 cups chicken stock, skimmed
2 red bell peppers, roasted, chopped
1/4 teaspoon cinnamon
1 cup skim milk

Combine hot pepper, sweet potato purée, garlic powder, chicken stock, red peppers and cinnamon in saucepan. Bring to a boil; reduce heat. Simmer for 30 minutes. Stir in milk. Heat to serving temperature. Ladle into serving bowls. Yield: 6 servings.

Approx Per Serving: Cal 216 ; Prot 8.6 g; Carbo 42.3 g; T Fat 1.58 g; Chol 1.5 mg; Potas 865.0 mg; Sod 686.0 mg.

North Carolina Sweet Potato Commission

HEARTY VEGETABLE CHOWDER

1 (10-ounce) can chicken broth
2/3 cup water
4 cups frozen mixed vegetables
1/4 cup minced onion
1/4 cup minced green bell pepper
3 tablespoons butter, melted
1/4 cup all-purpose flour
1/2 teaspoon paprika
1/2 teaspoon dry mustard
2 cups milk
1/8 teaspoon pepper
2 cups (8 ounces) shredded Cheddar cheese

Combine broth and water in saucepan. Bring to a boil. Add mixed vegetables. Cook for 15 minutes or until tender. Sauté onion and green pepper in butter in saucepan until tender. Stir in flour, paprika and dry mustard. Add milk and vegetable mixture gradually. Bring to a boil over medium heat, stirring constantly. Remove from heat. Add pepper and cheese; stir until cheese melts. Ladle into serving bowls. Garnish with carrot curl and parsley. Yield: 7 cups.

Approx Per Cup: Cal 304; Prot 14.8 g; Carbo 21.4 g; T Fat 18.5 g; Chol 56.9 mg; Potas 360.0 mg; Sod 446.0 mg.

North Carolina Department of Agriculture

TANGY WATERCRESS SOUP

6 tablespoons butter
2 cups watercress leaves
1 cup sliced green onions
3 tablespoons all-purpose flour
1 teaspoon basil
1/4 teaspoon salt
1/8 teaspoon pepper
2 cups chicken broth
1 1/2 cups milk
2 cups yogurt

Melt butter in large heavy saucepan. Add watercress and onions. Cook for 5 minutes or until onions are tender. Stir in flour and seasonings until smooth; remove from heat. Stir in broth and milk gradually. Bring to a boil, stirring constantly; reduce heat. Simmer, covered, for 15 minutes. Cool slightly. Pour 1/3 of the soup into blender container. Process until smooth; pour into large bowl. Repeat with remaining soup. Stir in yogurt. Chill, covered, for 5 hours or longer. Serve in chilled bowls. Garnish with additional watercress. Yield: 6 cups.

Approx Per Cup: Cal 218; Prot 7.4 g; Carbo 10.7 g; T Fat 16.5 g; Chol 49.5 mg; Potas 357.0 mg; Sod 510.0 mg.

American Dairy Association of North Carolina

FRESH FRUIT AMBROSIA

4 oranges, peeled
2 unpeeled apples, chopped
2 cups fresh pineapple chunks
1 cup seedless green grape halves
1 cup orange juice
1/3 cup sugar
2 tablespoons cream Sherry
1/4 teaspoon vanilla extract
1/4 teaspoon almond extract
2 cups sliced strawberries
1 cup flaked coconut

Slice oranges crosswise; cut each slice into quarters. Combine with apples, pineapple and grapes in bowl; mix well. Combine orange juice and sugar in small bowl, stirring until sugar dissolves. Add Sherry and flavorings; pour over fruit. Chill, covered, for 2 to 3 hours. Add strawberries. Spoon into serving dishes. Top with coconut. Yield: 8 servings.

Approx Per Serving: Cal 188; Prot 1.7 g; Carbo 39.6 g; T Fat 3.6 g; Chol 0.0 mg; Potas 388.0 mg; Sod 26.4 mg.

North Carolina Department of Agriculture

BLUEBERRY DESSERT SALAD

2 (3-ounce) packages blackberry gelatin
2 cups boiling water
1 (16-ounce) can crushed pineapple
1 (16-ounce) can blueberries
8 ounces cream cheese, softened
8 ounces sour cream
1/2 cup plus 1 teaspoon sugar
1 teaspoon vanilla extract
1/2 cup chopped pecans

Dissolve gelatin in boiling water in bowl. Drain pineapple and blueberries, reserving 1/2 cup of each juice. Stir pineapple and blueberries into gelatin. Add reserved juices; mix well. Pour into 9x13-inch dish. Chill until firm. Combine cream cheese, sour cream, sugar and vanilla in bowl; mix well. Spread over congealed layer. Sprinkle pecans over cream cheese layer. Yield: 12 servings.

Approx Per Serving: Cal 278; Prot 4.1 g; Carbo 36.7 g; T Fat 14.1 g; Chol 29.0 mg; Potas 125.0 mg; Sod 113.0 mg.

North Carolina Department of Agriculture

FRUIT TOWER SALAD

1½ cups cottage cheese
⅓ cup chopped salted cashews
1 tablespoon honey
1 teaspoon grated lime rind
4 honeydew melon rings (½ inch thick), chilled
4 cantaloupe rings (½ inch thick), chilled
4 slices pineapple, chilled

Place cottage cheese in blender container. Process at High speed for 5 minutes or until almost smooth. Stir in cashews, honey and lime rind. Chill, covered, for 1 to 2 hours. Remove rind from melon rings. Place honeydew rings on chilled lettuce-lined salad plates. Spoon about ¼ cup cottage cheese mixture onto each honeydew ring. Place cantaloupe ring on top of each. Reserve 4 small scoops cottage cheese mixture. Spoon remaining mixture over cantaloupe ring. Top each with pineapple slice. Add scoop of reserved cottage cheese mixture in center. Garnish with lime slice. Yield: 4 servings.

Approx Per Serving: Cal 236; Prot 12.8 g; Carbo 28.9 g; T Fat 9.0 g; Chol 11.6 mg; Potas 648.0 mg; Sod 402.0 mg.

American Dairy Association of North Carolina

ON-THE-GO FRUIT SALAD

1 (10-ounce) package frozen strawberries with juice
1 (21-ounce) can peach pie filling
1 (16-ounce) can pineapple tidbits, drained
1 (12-ounce) can mandarin oranges, drained
3 bananas, sliced

Combine all ingredients in bowl; mix well. Chill until serving time. Serve on lettuce-lined salad plates or in fruit cups. Yield: 6 servings.

Approx Per Serving: Cal 237; Prot 1.6 g; Carbo 61.9 g; T Fat 0.4 g; Chol 0.0 mg; Potas 498.0 mg; Sod 35.4 mg.

North Carolina Strawberry and Pick-Your-Own Association

SALADS & DRESSINGS

FROSTY MELON SALAD

1 (3-ounce) package fruit-flavored gelatin
1 cup boiling water
1/2 cup cold water
2 tablespoons lemon juice
1/2 cup mayonnaise
1/4 teaspoon salt
1 cup crushed pineapple
1 cup watermelon cubes

Dissolve gelatin in boiling water in mixer bowl. Add cold water, lemon juice, mayonnaise and salt; beat well. Chill, covered, for 25 minutes or until partially set. Beat until thick and fluffy. Fold in pineapple and watermelon gently. Pour into molds. Chill for 45 to 60 minutes or until firm. Unmold onto serving plates. Yield: 4 servings.

Approx Per Serving: Cal 340; Prot 2.8 g; Carbo 35.9 g; T Fat 22.1 g; Chol 16.3 mg; Potas 132.0 mg; Sod 492.0 mg.

North Carolina Watermelon Association

SIX-CUP FRUIT SALAD

1 cup shredded coconut
1 cup drained pineapple chunks
1 cup miniature marshmallows
1 cup mandarin oranges
1 cup sour cream
1 cup chopped Carolina Nut Cracker pecans

Combine all ingredients in bowl; mix well. Press into molds. Chill in refrigerator overnight. Serve as side dish with dinner or as dessert. Yield: 8 servings.

Approx Per Serving: Cal 263; Prot 2.7 g; Carbo 23.4 g; T Fat 19.1 g; Chol 12.7 mg; Potas 187.0 mg; Sod 47.6 mg.

Carolina Nut Cracker
MEMBER

QUEEN PEACH SALAD

1 (20-ounce) can crushed pineapple, drained
1 cup shredded coconut
1 cup cottage cheese
1 cup sour cream
4 medium unpeeled fresh peaches, chopped
8 large fresh peaches

Combine first 4 ingredients in bowl; mix well. Chill until serving time. Fold in 4 chopped peaches gently. Cut 8 whole peaches into quarters to about 1/2-inch from bottom. Twist out seeds. Spread sections apart to form cups. Serve cottage cheese mixture in peach cups.
Yield: 8 servings.

Approx Per Serving: Cal 210; Prot 5.4 g; Carbo 26.6 g; T Fat 10.3 g; Chol 16.6 mg; Potas 347.0 mg; Sod 146.0 mg.

North Carolina Peach Growers Association

SALADS & DRESSINGS

STRAWBERRY PRETZEL SALAD

2 cups pretzels, crushed
1/4 cup sugar
3/4 cup margarine, melted
8 ounces cream cheese, softened
1 cup sugar
16 ounces whipped topping
1 (6-ounce) package strawberry gelatin
2 cups boiling water
2 (10-ounce) packages frozen strawberries

Combine crushed pretzels, 1/4 cup sugar and melted margarine in bowl; mix well. Press into 9x13-inch baking dish. Bake at 400 degrees for 5 minutes. Cool. Combine cream cheese and 1 cup sugar in bowl. Beat until smooth. Fold in whipped topping. Spread over cooled pretzel layer. Dissolve gelatin in boiling water. Add frozen strawberries, stirring until thawed. Pour over cream cheese mixture. Chill overnight. Yield: 12 servings.

Approx Per Serving: Cal 476; Prot 4.4 g; Carbo 54.4 g; T Fat 27.9 g; Chol 20.6 mg; Potas 116.0 mg; Sod 398.0 mg.

North Carolina Strawberry and Pick-Your-Own Association

CALIFORNIAN WALDORF SALAD

1 1/2 cups chopped unpeeled apples
1 (15-ounce) can pineapple chunks, drained
1 cup green grape halves
1 cup chopped walnuts
1 1/2 cups thinly sliced celery
1 cup miniature marshmallows
1 tablespoon pineapple juice
1/2 cup soybean oil mayonnaise

Combine apples, pineapple, grapes, walnuts, celery and marshmallows in bowl. Mix pineapple juice and mayonnaise in small bowl. Pour over fruit; toss gently. Chill until serving time. Serve in large bowl lined with lettuce or in half a hollowed fresh pineapple. Garnish with fresh parsley. Yield: 6 servings.

Approx Per Serving: Cal 368; Prot 3.9 g; Carbo 31.7 g; T Fat 27.3 g; Chol 10.8 mg; Potas 352.0 mg; Sod 142.0 mg.

North Carolina Soybean Producers Association

BLACK-EYED PEA SALAD

3 (16-ounce) cans black-eyed peas, rinsed
1 (2-ounce) jar chopped pimento, drained
1/2 cup chopped purple onion
1/4 cup cider vinegar
6 tablespoons red wine vinegar
6 tablespoons sugar
6 tablespoons oil
3/4 teaspoon red pepper
1/4 teaspoon salt

Combine black-eyed peas, pimento and onion in bowl; toss gently. Combine cider vinegar, red wine vinegar, sugar, oil, red pepper and salt in small bowl; mix well. Pour over black-eyed pea mixture. Chill, covered, for 3 hours. Yield: 6 servings.

Approx Per Serving: Cal 350; Prot 10.9 g; Carbo 46.0 g; T Fat 14.9 g; Chol 0.0 mg; Potas 432.0 mg; Sod 760.0 mg.

North Carolina Department of Agriculture

FRESH BROCCOLI SALAD

1 bunch fresh broccoli, chopped
1/2 cup raisins
1/2 cup Spanish peanuts
2 stalks celery, chopped
1 carrot, grated
1 tablespoon Parmesan cheese
1/2 jar real bacon bits
1 cup mayonnaise-type salad dressing
2 tablespoons sugar
1 tablespoon vinegar

Combine broccoli, raisins, peanuts, celery, carrot, Parmesan cheese and bacon bits in bowl; toss to mix. Combine salad dressing, sugar and vinegar in small bowl; mix until sugar dissolves. Pour over broccoli mixture. Marinate for 12 hours or longer before serving. Yield: 6 servings.

Approx Per Serving: Cal 332; Prot 7.6 g; Carbo 31.6 g; T Fat 21.6 g; Chol 14.2 mg; Potas 483.0 mg; Sod 447.0 mg.

Albemarle Pride Broccoli
MEMBER

SALADS & DRESSINGS

FRESH BROCCOLI AND BACON SALAD

1 bunch fresh broccoli
1/2 jar real bacon bits
1 onion, chopped
1 cup grated sharp cheese
1/2 cup mayonnaise
1/4 cup sugar
2 tablespoons vinegar

Chop broccoli into bite-sized pieces. Combine broccoli, bacon bits, onion and cheese in bowl. Combine mayonnaise, sugar and vinegar in small bowl; mix well. Pour over broccoli mixture. Chill overnight before serving. Yield: 6 servings.

> Approx Per Serving: Cal 322; Prot 8.2 g; Carbo 22.5 g; T Fat 23.1 g; Chol 34.1 mg; Potas 283.0 mg; Sod 310.6 mg.

Albemarle Pride Broccoli
MEMBER

CAULIFLOWER SALAD

1 small head cauliflower
1 (10-ounce) package peas, cooked
1 cup chopped celery
1/4 cup chopped onion
1 1/2 teaspoons seasoning salt
1/8 teaspoon pepper
3/4 cup soybean oil mayonnaise

Cut cauliflower into flowerets. Combine peas, celery and onion in bowl. Add seasonings and mayonnaise; toss gently to coat vegetables. Chill in refrigerator. Yield: 8 servings.

> Approx Per Serving: Cal 185; Prot 2.7 g; Carbo 7.6 g; T Fat 16.6 g; Chol 12.2 mg; Potas 199.0 mg; Sod 574.0 mg.

North Carolina Soybean Producers Association

OVERNIGHT COLESLAW

1 medium head cabbage
1 cup chopped onion
1/2 cup chopped green bell pepper
1 cup vinegar
3/4 cup soybean oil
1 teaspoon salt
1 tablespoon celery seed
1 tablespoon dry mustard

Shred cabbage. Alternate layers of onion, cabbage and green pepper in bowl. Combine remaining ingredients in sauce-pan. Bring to a boil. Pour over cabbage. Chill, covered, overnight or for several days. Yield: 12 servings.

> Approx Per Serving: Cal 134; Prot 0.5 g; Carbo 3.6 g; T Fat 13.7 g; Chol 0.0 mg; Potas 106.0 mg; Sod 182.0 mg.

North Carolina Soybean Producers Association

SALADS & DRESSINGS

HYDROPONIC WILTED LETTUCE

4 slices bacon
1/3 cup sugar
1/2 teaspoon salt
1/2 cup vinegar
1/4 cup water
4 heads hydroponic Boston lettuce, torn
2 hard-boiled eggs

Fry bacon in skillet until crisp. Remove bacon to drain. Add sugar, salt, vinegar and water to drippings; mix well. Bring to a boil. Pour over lettuce in salad bowl; toss gently. Sprinkle with coarsely chopped eggs and crumbled bacon; toss lightly. Yield: 4 servings.

Approx Per Serving: Cal 202; Prot 10.8 g; Carbo 29.1 g; T Fat 6.9 g; Chol 142.0 mg; Potas 1260.0 mg; Sod 425.0 mg.

Elkridge, Inc.
MEMBER.

TOSSED HYDROPONIC GREEN SALAD

2 teaspoons minced parsley
1/3 cup French dressing
4 cups torn assorted hydroponic salad greens
3 tablespoons Parmesan cheese

Combine parsley and French dressing in small bowl; mix well. Pour over greens in salad bowl; toss to mix. Sprinkle with cheese. Yield: 4 servings.

Approx Per Serving: Cal 137; Prot 2.4 g; Carbo 3.5 g; T Fat 12.9 g; Chol 2.9 mg; Potas 158.0 mg; Sod 318.0 mg.

Elkridge, Inc.
MEMBER

SWEET FRENCH DRESSING

3/4 cup sugar
1 teaspoon salt
1 teaspoon mustard
1 1/2 cups vinegar
1/4 cup chopped onion
1/2 cup chopped green bell pepper
1 (4-ounce) jar chopped pimentos
1 cup soybean oil

Combine sugar, salt and mustard in mixer bowl; mix well. Add vinegar, onion, green pepper and pimentos. Add oil gradually, beating constantly with electric mixer. Store in covered container in refrigerator. Shake well before serving. Yield: 48 tablespoons.

Approx Per Tablespoon: Cal 54; Prot 0.0 g; Carbo 3.8 g; T Fat 4.6 g; Chol 0.0 mg; Potas 11.1 mg; Sod 46.0 mg.

North Carolina Soybean Producers Association

SALADS & DRESSINGS

CHAMPIONSHIP POTATO SALAD

15 large potatoes, cooked
1 1/2 cups chopped celery
6 hard-boiled eggs, chopped
1 teaspoon salt
1 tablespoon chopped fresh parsley
1 cup sugar
1 egg, beaten
2 tablespoons cornstarch
1/2 teaspoon salt
1 cup water
1/3 cup vinegar
1 tablespoon mustard
3 tablespoons mayonnaise

Peel cooled potatoes; slice. Place in large bowl. Add celery, hard-boiled eggs, 1 teaspoon salt and parsley. Combine sugar, beaten egg, cornstarch, 1/2 teaspoon salt, water, vinegar and mustard in saucepan. Bring to a boil. Cook until thickened, stirring constantly. Remove from heat; cool. Add mayonnaise; beat well with mixer. Pour over potatoes; toss gently to mix. Chill in refrigerator. Yield: 15 servings.

Approx Per Serving: Cal 335; Prot 7.6 g; Carbo 66.4 g; T Fat 5.1 g; Chol 129.0 mg; Potas 918.0 mg; Sod 301.0 mg.

North Carolina Egg Association

MISS IDA'S DILLED POTATO SALAD

7 medium potatoes, cooked
1/3 cup Cates dill pickle juice
2 tablespoons olive oil
1/2 cup chopped Cates dill pickles
1/3 cup sliced green onions
4 hard-boiled eggs
1 cup mayonnaise
1/2 cup sour cream
2 teaspoons Dijon-style mustard
Garlic salt to taste
Celery seed to taste
Pepper to taste
12 lettuce leaves

Peel and slice warm potatoes. Place in large bowl. Pour mixture of pickle juice and olive oil over warm potatoes. Chill for 2 hours. Add pickles, onions and chopped egg whites. Sieve yolks into small bowl. Add mayonnaise, sour cream and mustard; mix well. Fold into potato mixture. Add garlic salt, celery seed and pepper; mix gently. Chill for 2 hours. Scoop into lettuce leaves with ice cream scoop. Garnish with Cates Kosher Icebergs. Yield: 12 servings.

Approx Per Serving: Cal 340; Prot 6.5 g; Carbo 34.3 g; T Fat 21.1 g; Chol 106.0 mg; Potas 834.0 mg; Sod 1636.0 mg.

Cates Pickles, Inc.
MEMBER

SALADS & DRESSINGS

SPINACH SALAD

1 pound fresh spinach
¼ cup sugar
¼ cup vinegar
⅓ cup catsup
1 teaspoon salt
¼ cup finely chopped onion
1 teaspoon Worcestershire sauce
1 cup soybean oil
2 hard-boiled eggs, chopped
1 cup sliced fresh mushrooms
¼ cup soy protein bacon bits
4 tomatoes, cut into wedges
1 cup croutons

Wash spinach, discarding stems; pat dry. Tear into bite-sized pieces; chill. Combine sugar, vinegar, catsup, salt, onion and Worcestershire sauce in bowl; mix well. Add oil gradually, beating constantly with electric mixer until blended. Pour into covered container. Chill in refrigerator. Place spinach in salad bowl. Add eggs, mushrooms and bacon bits. Shake dressing well; drizzle over salad. Serve on chilled plates. Garnish with tomato wedges and croutons.
Yield: 8 servings.

Approx Per Serving: Cal 354; Prot 4.7 g; Carbo 18.9 g; T Fat 30.0 g; Chol 68.5 mg; Potas 560.0 mg; Sod 590.0 mg.

North Carolina Soybean Producers Association

MARINATED FRESH VEGETABLE SALAD

1 cup thinly sliced cucumber
1 cup thinly sliced squash
1 cup thinly sliced carrots
1 cup chopped celery
1 medium onion, sliced into rings
¾ cup sugar
1 cup vinegar
½ cup soybean oil
1 teaspoon celery seed
1 teaspoon salt
½ teaspoon pepper
½ teaspoon mustard

Combine cucumber, squash, carrots, celery and onion in large bowl. Combine sugar, vinegar, oil, celery seed, salt, pepper and mustard in blender container. Process until blended. Pour over vegetable mixture; mix well. Chill, covered, in refrigerator for 4 hours to overnight. Other seasonal vegetables such as zucchini, broccoli, cauliflower or bell peppers may be added.
Yield: 4 servings.

Approx Per Serving: Cal 445; Prot 1.9 g; Carbo 52.5 g; T Fat 27.8 g; Chol 0.0 mg; Potas 456.0 mg; Sod 599.0 mg.

North Carolina Soybean Producers Association

SUMMER GARDEN SALAD WITH BACON

1/2 head iceberg lettuce
1/2 head curly endive
1/2 head leaf lettuce
1/2 bunch fresh spinach
2 cups cubed Lundy's fully cooked ham
6 slices Lundy's bacon, crisp-fried, crumbled
1 small onion, sliced into rings
3/4 cup sliced stuffed green olives
1/2 cup Parmesan cheese
1/3 cup Vinaigrette Dressing

Wash and drain greens. Combine ham, bacon, greens, onion and olives in large bowl. Add 3 tablespoons Parmesan cheese; toss well. Pour Vinaigrette Dressing over salad; toss to mix. Sprinkle with remaining Parmesan cheese. Yield: 8 servings.

> Approx Per Serving: Cal 197; Prot 12.2 g; Carbo 3.2 g; T Fat 15.4 g; Chol 29.4 mg; Potas 319.0 mg; Sod 800.0 mg.

VINAIGRETTE DRESSING

1/2 cup oil
1/2 cup white vinegar
1/2 teaspoon sugar
1/4 teaspoon Worcestershire sauce
2 to 3 drops of Tabasco sauce
1/4 teaspoon coarsely ground black pepper
1/4 teaspoon salt
1/4 teaspoon salad herbs
1/4 teaspoon minced garlic

Combine oil, vinegar, sugar, Worcestershire sauce, Tabasco sauce, pepper, salt, herbs and garlic in covered container. Shake well to mix. Store in refrigerator. Yield: 20 tablespoons.

> Approx Per Tablespoon: Cal 49; Prot 0.0 g; Carbo 0.5 g; T Fat 5.4 g; Chol 0.0 mg; Potas 6.7 mg; Sod 28.1 mg.

Lundy Packing Company
MEMBER

SWEET POTATO SALAD

3 1/2 pounds sweet potatoes
1 medium onion, sliced into thin rings
1 green bell pepper, cut into thin strips
Honey Vinaigrette

Cook sweet potatoes in boiling salted water to cover in saucepan for 20 minutes or until just fork tender; do not overcook. Peel and cut into halves lengthwise. Cut into 1/4-inch slices. Combine with onion and green pepper in large bowl. Pour Honey Vinaigrette over mixture; toss lightly. Marinate for 3 hours. Remove garlic and bay leaves before serving. Yield: 6 servings.

Approx Per Serving: Cal 472; Prot 4.1 g; Carbo 73.4 g; T Fat 19.1 g; Chol 0.0 mg; Potas 610.0 mg; Sod 215.0 mg.

HONEY VINAIGRETTE

1 cup tarragon vinegar
1/2 cup oil
1 tablespoon honey
2 cloves garlic
2 bay leaves
1/2 teaspoon salt
1/4 teaspoon pepper
1/4 teaspoon oregano
1/4 teaspoon thyme

Combine vinegar, oil, honey, garlic, bay leaves, salt, pepper, oregano and thyme in covered container. Shake vigorously until well mixed. Yield: 1 1/2 cups.

Nutritional information is included in recipe above.

North Carolina Sweet Potato Commission

SAVORY TOFU MIX

1 pound tofu, drained, mashed
1/2 cup chopped green onions
1/2 cup grated carrots
1/2 cup soybean oil mayonnaise
2 tablespoons mustard
1 teaspoon garlic powder
1/2 teaspoon salt
1/4 teaspoon turmeric

Combine tofu, green onions, carrots, mayonnaise, mustard, garlic powder, salt and turmeric in bowl; mix well. Chill in refrigerator. Serve on bed of lettuce or as sandwich filling or dip. Yield: 3 servings.

Approx Per Serving: Cal 401; Prot 13.7 g; Carbo 8.0 g; T Fat 36.9 g; Chol 21.7 mg; Potas 322.0 mg; Sod 712.0 mg.

North Carolina Soybean Producers Association

HERB GARDEN TUNA SALAD

2 (12-ounce) cans tuna
1 tablespoon dried basil
1 tablespoon marjoram
1 pinch dried thyme
1/2 cup salad pickles
3/4 cup mayonnaise
8 ounces spiral noodles
6 hard-boiled eggs
4 tomatoes, chopped
1 pound mild cheese
1 head lettuce, torn
Fresh herbs, minced
Herbed Honey Dressing

Combine first 6 ingredients in large bowl; mix well. Set aside to develop flavor. Cook noodles using package directions. Drain and cool. Add noodles, chopped hard-boiled eggs, tomatoes, cubed cheese, lettuce and herbs to tuna mixture. Pour dressing over all; toss gently to mix. Assorted herbs for dressing and salad may include basil, burnet, chives, garlic, lovage, marjoram, mint, parsley and thyme. Yield: 8 servings.

Approx Per Serving: Cal 1039; Prot 47.9 g; Carbo 47.4 g; T Fat 73.9 g; Chol 292.0 mg; Potas 513.0 mg; Sod 909.0 mg.

HERBED HONEY DRESSING

1/2 cup herbal vinegar
1 cup olive oil
2 tablespoons minced fresh herbs
1/2 cup honey
1 clove garlic, crushed

Combine vinegar, olive oil, herbs, honey and garlic in jar. Cover; shake to mix well. Yield: 1 1/2 cups.

Nutritional information is included in recipe above.

Rasland Herb Farm
MEMBER

ZESTY ITALIAN DRESSING

1 cup soybean oil
1/3 cup vinegar
1 teaspoon sugar
1/2 teaspoon salt
1/2 teaspoon celery salt
1/4 teaspoon dry mustard
1/4 teaspoon cayenne pepper
1 clove of garlic, minced

Combine oil, vinegar, sugar, salt, celery salt, dry mustard, cayenne pepper and garlic in blender container. Process until blended. Yield: 20 tablespoons.

Approx Per Tablespoon: Cal 98; Prot 0.0 g; Carbo 0.5 g; T Fat 10.9 g; Chol 0.0 mg; Potas 5.3 mg; Sod 107.0 mg.

North Carolina Soybean Producers Association

Main Dishes

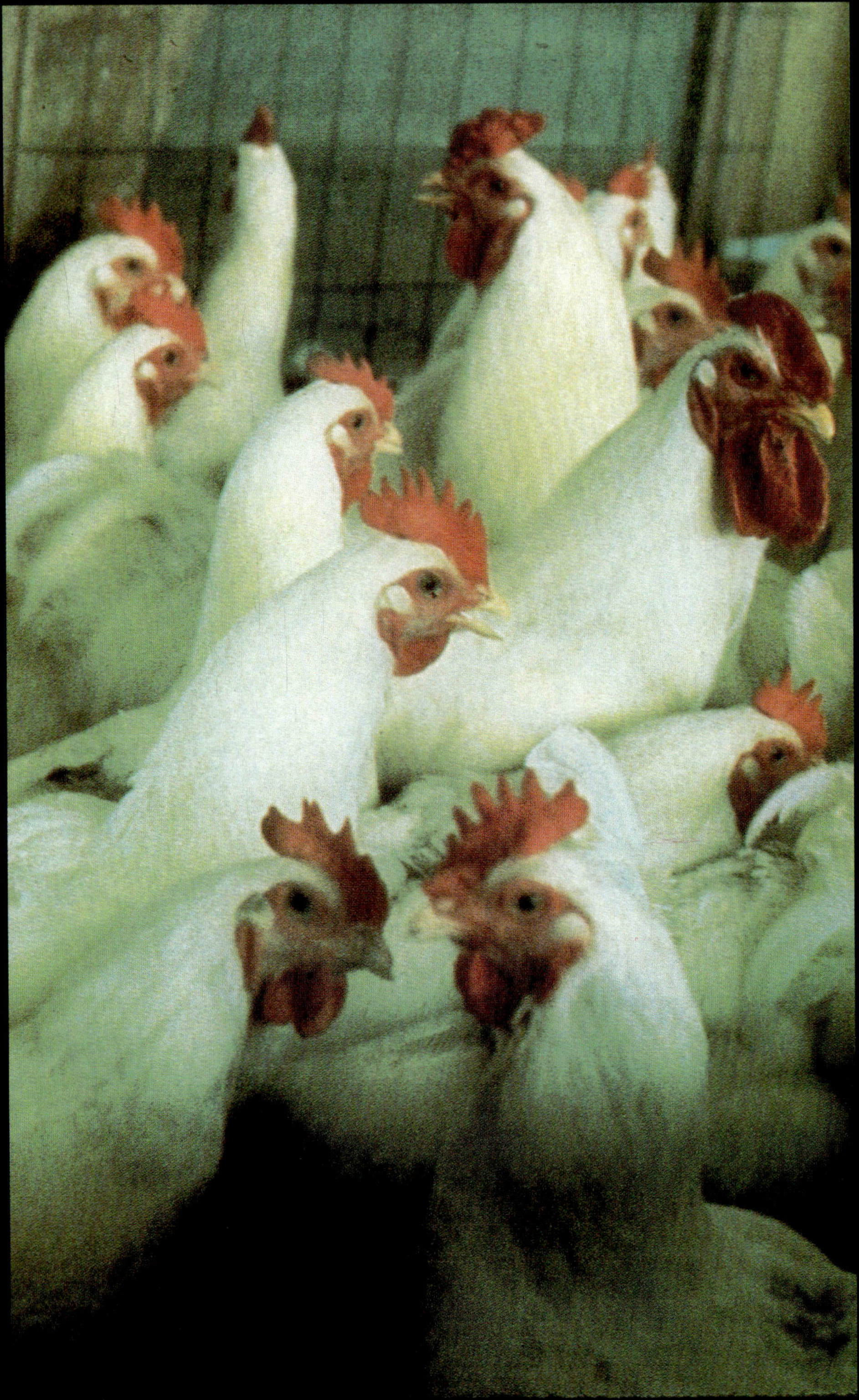

BEEF AND BROCCOLI WITH CHIVE GRAVY

1 pound top round steak, partially frozen
1½ pounds fresh broccoli
3 tablespoons boiling water
1 tablespoon oil
8 ounces fresh mushrooms, sliced
1 tablespoon oil
8 ounces sour cream
1 tablespoon minced chives
½ teaspoon salt
⅛ teaspoon pepper

Slice steak diagonally cross grain into ⅛ to ¼-inch strips. Cut broccoli into 1x2-inch pieces. Add to boiling water in saucepan. Cook for 8 to 10 minutes or until tender-crisp; drain. Heat 1 tablespoon oil in skillet over medium heat. Add mushrooms. Sauté until tender. Remove from skillet. Add 1 tablespoon oil to skillet. Heat over medium heat. Add steak. Sauté for 2 to 3 minutes. Add broccoli and mushrooms; reduce heat. Stir in sour cream, chives, salt and pepper. Cook until heated through.
Yield: 4 servings.

Approx Per Serving: Cal 457; Prot 28.0 g; Carbo 14.1 g; T Fat 33.8 g; Chol 90.5 mg; Potas 1134.0 mg; Sod 392.0 mg.

Albemarle Pride Broccoli
MEMBER

BEEF MALAYA

5 pounds round steak
2 tablespoons olive oil
2 medium onions, chopped
1 clove of garlic, chopped
2 peaches, mashed
2 cups sour cream
8 ounces Cheddar cheese, shredded
½ cup dry red wine
1 bay leaf
1 cup mushroom soup
Kitchen Bouquet to taste

Cut steak into 1-inch cubes. Brown in olive oil in skillet over low heat. Place in large baking dish. Add onions, garlic, peaches, sour cream, cheese, wine and bay leaf; mix well. Bake, covered, at 325 degrees for 1½ hours. Stir in soup and Kitchen Bouquet. Bake for 30 minutes longer. Remove bay leaf. Yield: 12 servings.

Approx Per Serving: Cal 575; Prot 40.0 g; Carbo 7.2 g; T Fat 41.4 g; Chol 146.0 mg; Potas 647.0 mg; Sod 386.0 mg.
Nutritional information does not include Kitchen Bouquet.

North Carolina Grape Growers Association

BEEF AND WINE CASSEROLE

2 pounds round steak
All-purpose flour
Salt and pepper to taste
1 cup hot water
1/2 cup dry North Carolina red wine
1 (3-ounce) can mushrooms
1 envelope dry onion soup mix

Cut steak into serving pieces; trim off fat. Rub fat in skillet to grease. Coat steak with flour; sprinkle with salt and pepper. Brown slowly on both sides in greased skillet. Place in baking dish. Add water, wine, mushrooms and soup mix to skillet, stirring to deglaze. Pour over steak. Bake, covered, at 350 degrees for 1 hour. Bake, uncovered, for 15 minutes longer. Yield: 4 servings.

> **Approx Per Serving:** Cal 460; Prot 40.6 g; Carbo 2.6 g; T Fat 28.7 g; Chol 131.0 mg; Potas 645.0 mg; Sod 343.0 mg.
> Nutritional information does not include flour.

North Carolina Grape Growers Association

CHINESE BEEF

1 pound beef cubes
2 green onions, sliced
2 tablespoons peanut oil
2 tablespoons Duplin Rosé wine
2 tablespoons soy sauce
1 tablespoon sugar
1/2 teaspoon salt
1 cup cold water
1 medium carrot, chopped

Brown beef with green onions in peanut oil in saucepan. Stir in wine, soy sauce, sugar and salt. Bring to a boil. Add water. Bring to a boil; reduce heat to medium. Cook for 30 minutes. Add carrot. Cook for 15 minutes longer. Yield: 2 servings.

> **Approx Per Serving:** Cal 780; Prot 41.3 g; Carbo 12.4 g; T Fat 61.3 g; Chol 160.0 mg; Potas 547.0 mg; Sod 1674.0 mg.

Duplin Winery
MEMBER

BEEF AND GREEN PEPPER

2 pounds sirloin steak
1 large green bell pepper
3/4 cup butter
2 tablespoons soy sauce
2 tablespoons dry North Carolina red wine

Cut steak and green pepper into strips. Melt butter in large skillet. Stir in soy sauce and wine. Add green pepper. Sauté just until heated through. Remove with slotted spoon. Add steak. Cook to desired degree of doneness. Return green peppers to skillet. Heat to serving temperature.
Yield: 4 servings.

Approx Per Serving: Cal 956; Prot 59.5 g; Carbo 2.3 g; T Fat 77.3 g; Chol 272.0 mg; Potas 882.0 mg; Sod 950.0 mg.

North Carolina Grape Growers Association

HONEY-GLAZED RIBS

2 cups Carolina Treet barbecue sauce
1 cup honey
1 cup catsup
8 pounds beef ribs

Combine barbecue sauce, honey and catsup in bowl; mix well. Add ribs. Marinate in refrigerator overnight. Drain, reserving marinade. Grill ribs to desired degree of doneness, basting occasionally with marinade. Yield: 8 servings.

Approx Per Serving: Cal 1502; Prot 76.1 g; Carbo 49.5 g; T Fat 110.0 g; Chol 288.0 mg; Potas 1255.0 mg; Sod 1083.0 mg.
Nutritional information includes entire amount of marinade.

Carolina Treet, Inc.
MEMBER

BARBECUE STEAK SPECIAL

2 pounds (1-inch thick) steak
Garlic salt and onion salt to taste
Pepper and cayenne pepper to taste
1 cup Duplin red wine

Place steak in shallow dish. Pierce with ice pick or fork with large tines. Sprinkle with seasonings and half the wine. Pierce steak again to season well. Turn steak; repeat seasoning process with remaining ingredients. Marinate in refrigerator for 4 hours or longer. Grill over medium coals to desired degree of doneness.
Yield: 4 servings.

Approx Per Serving: Cal 471 ; Prot 40.1 g; Carbo 1.0 g; T Fat 28.5 g; Chol 131.0 mg; Potas 638.0 mg; Sod 97.0 mg.

Duplin Winery
MEMBER

MARINATED BEEF AND BACON KABOBS

1 pound boneless lean sirloin steak
1 (8-ounce) bottle of Russian salad dressing
2 tablespoons lemon juice
1 tablespoon Worcestershire sauce
1/8 teaspoon garlic powder
1/4 teaspoon pepper
10 slices bacon, cut into halves
2 medium green bell peppers, cut into 1-inch squares
1 large onion, cut into 2-inch pieces
8 ounces fresh mushrooms
1 pint cherry tomatoes

Trim fat from beef; cut beef into 1 1/2-inch cubes. Combine salad dressing, lemon juice, Worcestershire sauce, garlic powder and pepper in bowl; mix well. Add beef. Marinate, covered, in refrigerator for 8 hours. Drain, reserving marinade. Wrap 1/2 bacon slice around each beef cube. Alternate beef and vegetables on 4 skewers. Grill over medium-hot coals for 15 minutes or to desired degree of doneness, turning and basting frequently with reserved marinade. Serve with rice, salad and bread.
Yield: 4 servings.

Approx Per Serving: Cal 621; Prot 26.0 g; Carbo 19.6 g; T Fat 50.1 g; Chol 103.0 mg; Potas 998.0 mg; Sod 838.0 mg.
Nutritional information includes entire amount of marinade.

North Carolina Department of Agriculture

SWEET AND SPICY KABOBS

1 pound round steak
1 cup Carolina Treet barbecue sauce
1/2 cup honey
1/2 cup catsup
1 onion, coarsely chopped
1 green bell pepper, coarsely chopped
2 zucchini, thickly sliced
16 cherry tomatoes
16 large mushrooms

Cut steak into cubes. Mix with barbecue sauce in bowl. Marinate in refrigerator overnight. Drain, reserving marinade. Stir honey and catsup into marinade. Alternate steak and vegetables on skewers. Grill to desired degree of doneness, turning and basting frequently with marinade.
Yield: 4 servings.

Approx Per Serving: Cal 462; Prot 23.9 g; Carbo 58.4 g; T Fat 16.4 g; Chol 65.4 mg; Potas 971.0 mg; Sod 922.0 mg.
Nutritional information includes entire amount of marinade.

Carolina Treet, Inc.
MEMBER

GREEN PEPPER STEAK (Duplin Style)

1 pound round steak
1/4 cup all-purpose flour
1/8 teaspoon salt
1/4 cup oil
2 tablespoons soy sauce
1 cup chopped celery
3 green bell peppers, chopped
1 clove of garlic, minced
1 cup water
1/2 cup North Carolina red wine

Cut steak into cubes. Coat with mixture of flour and salt. Brown in oil in saucepan. Combine soy sauce, celery, green peppers, garlic and water in bowl; mix well. Pour over steak. Add wine. Simmer for 1 hour and 15 minutes or until tender. Yield: 3 servings.

Approx Per Serving: Cal 543; Prot 29.3 g; Carbo 15.0 g; T Fat 37.7 g; Chol 87.1 mg; Potas 705.0 mg; Sod 881.0 mg.

North Carolina Grape Growers Association

MARINATED STEAK TERIYAKI

1/4 cup oil
2 tablespoons soy sauce
1 tablespoon cider vinegar
1 tablespoon honey
1 tablespoon finely chopped green onion
1 small clove of garlic, minced
1 teaspoon ginger
3/4 pound sirloin steak

Combine oil, soy sauce, vinegar, honey, green onion, garlic and ginger in shallow dish; mix well. Add beef, turning to coat well. Marinate, covered, in refrigerator for 24 hours, turning occasionally; drain. Broil 6 inches from heat source for 5 to 7 minutes on each side or to desired degree of doneness. Yield: 2 servings.

Approx Per Serving: Cal 607; Prot 30.4 g; Carbo 12.0 g; T Fat 48.7 g; Chol 89.4 mg; Potas 470.0 mg; Sod 1102.0 mg.
Nutritional information includes entire amount of marinade.

North Carolina Department of Agriculture

BEEF STEW ROSÉ

5 medium onions, chopped
2 tablespoons bacon drippings
3 pounds lean stew beef
1½ tablespoons all-purpose flour
Salt and pepper to taste
½ cup beef bouillon
½ cup Duplin Rosé wine
½ cup (about) water

Sauté onions in bacon drippings in large skillet until brown. Remove onions. Brown beef in drippings in skillet. Sprinkle with flour and salt and pepper. Add bouillon, wine and enough water to barely cover beef. Add onions; mix well. Simmer for 1 hour. May add mushrooms to taste with onions. Yield: 6 servings.

Approx Per Serving: Cal 501; Prot 47.1 g; Carbo 11.6 g; T Fat 27.1 g; Chol 148.0 mg; Potas 682.0 mg; Sod 145.0 mg.

Duplin Winery
MEMBER

EASY BAKED STEW

2 pounds lean stew beef
2 tablespoons dry onion soup mix
½ teaspoon salt
Paprika and pepper to taste
6 medium potatoes
8 white onions
3 carrots, cut into quarters
1 can cream of celery soup
½ cup Duplin Rosé wine
½ cup water

Place beef in baking dish. Sprinkle with dry soup mix, salt, paprika and pepper. Add potatoes, onions and carrots. Mix celery soup, wine and water in bowl. Pour over beef. Bake, covered, at 250 to 300 degrees for 5 hours. Yield: 6 servings.

Approx Per Serving: Cal 467; Prot 27.5 g; Carbo 57.2 g; T Fat 13.4 g; Chol 71.8 mg; Potas 1341.0 mg; Sod 666.0 mg.

Duplin Winery
MEMBER

VINEYARD BEEF STEW

2 pounds stew beef
1/2 cup North Carolina red wine
2 cans condensed consommé
1 large onion, sliced
1/2 teaspoon garlic salt
1 teaspoon salt
1/4 teaspoon pepper
1/2 cup sifted all-purpose flour
1/2 cup fine dry bread crumbs
1/4 cup North Carolina red wine

Combine beef, 1/2 cup wine, consommé, onion, garlic salt, salt and pepper in heavy baking dish. Mix flour with crumbs in small bowl. Stir into beef mixture. Bake, covered, at 300 degrees for 3 hours or until beef is tender. Stir in 1/4 cup wine just before serving. Yield: 4 servings.

Approx Per Serving: Cal 735; Prot 43.6 g; Carbo 23.9 g; T Fat 47.4 g; Chol 156.0 mg; Potas 547.0 mg; Sod 1359.0 mg.

North Carolina Grape Growers Association

BEEF STROGANOFF

3 pounds (1/2-inch thick) round steak, partially frozen
1/4 cup all-purpose flour
1 large onion, thinly sliced
1/4 cup butter
1 can consommé
1 can tomato soup
1 (4-ounce) can sliced mushrooms, drained
1/4 cup white wine
1/2 teaspoon salt
1/4 teaspoon pepper
1/2 cup sour cream
1 (16-ounce) package egg noodles, cooked

Slice steak cross grain into 1/4x2-inch strips. Coat with flour. Brown with onion in butter in large skillet. Stir in consommé, soup, mushrooms, wine, salt and pepper. Reduce heat. Simmer, covered, for 30 to 45 minutes or until steak is tender. Stir in sour cream. Cook just until heated through. Serve over hot noodles. Yield: 8 servings.

Approx Per Serving: Cal 669; Prot 39.4 g; Carbo 50.5 g; T Fat 33.1 g; Chol 117.0 mg; Potas 596.0 mg; Sod 713.0 mg.

North Carolina Department of Agriculture

MARINATED BEEF TENDERLOIN

1 cup catsup
2 teaspoons prepared mustard
1/2 teaspoon Worcestershire sauce
1 1/2 cups water
2 envelopes Italian salad dressing mix
1 (6-pound) beef tenderloin, trimmed

Combine catsup, mustard, Worcestershire sauce, water and salad dressing mix in bowl; mix well. Pierce beef in several places. Combine with marinade in heavy-duty sealable plastic bag; seal. Marinate in refrigerator for 8 hours, turning occasionally. Drain, reserving marinade. Place beef on rack in baking pan; insert meat thermometer. Bake at 425 degrees for 30 to 45 minutes or to 140 degrees on meat thermometer for rare, 150 degrees for medium-rare or 160 degrees for medium, basting occasionally with reserved marinade. Place on serving plate. Garnish with watercress and grapes. Serve with remaining marinade. Yield: 12 servings.

Approx Per Serving: Cal 420; Prot 45.5 g; Carbo 5.8 g; T Fat 22.5 g; Chol 144.0 mg; Potas 527.0 mg; Sod 326.0 mg.
Nutritional information includes entire amount of marinade.

North Carolina Department of Agriculture

WINEMAKER'S BEEF

1 (4-pound) beef roast
1/4 cup oil
2 1/2 cups water
1 envelope dry onion soup mix
1/2 cup sugar
2 cinnamon sticks
1/2 cup North Carolina red wine
3 tablespoons all-purpose flour

Brown roast on all sides in oil in heavy saucepan. Combine water, soup mix, sugar and cinnamon in small bowl; mix well. Pour over roast. Simmer for 2 to 3 hours. Add wine. Simmer for 1 hour longer. Remove roast to serving platter. Reserve 2 1/3 cups cooking liquid, discarding cinnamon sticks. Blend flour with a small amount of reserved liquid in saucepan. Stir in remaining liquid and enough water to make gravy of desired consistency. Cook until thickened, stirring constantly. Yield: 8 servings.

Approx Per Serving: Cal 532; Prot 45.2 g; Carbo 15.7 g; Fat 30.3 g; Chol 121.0 mg; Potas 627.0 mg; Sod 177.0 mg.

North Carolina Grape Growers Association

SKILLET BARBECUED BURGERS

1 1/2 pounds lean ground beef
1 egg, beaten
1 (8-ounce) can tomato sauce
1/2 teaspoon salt
1/4 teaspoon pepper
1 small onion, sliced
1 tablespoon oil
1/2 lemon, thinly sliced
1/4 cup finely chopped celery
1 (18-ounce) bottle of Carolina Treet barbecue sauce

Combine ground beef, egg, tomato sauce, salt and pepper in bowl; mix well. Shape into patties. Press 1 onion slice into top of each patty. Brown onion side down in oil in skillet. Drain and turn patties. Add lemon slices and celery. Pour barbecue sauce over top. Simmer, covered, for 15 minutes. Yield: 6 servings.

Approx Per Serving: Cal 346; Prot 24.7 g; Carbo 13.6 g; T Fat 21.8 g; Chol 121.0 mg; Potas 624.0 mg; Sod 1183.0 mg.

Carolina Treet, Inc.
MEMBER

BARBECUE AND CHEESE CORN BREAD CASSEROLE

1 cup Carolina Treet barbecue sauce
1 cup self-rising cornmeal
1 egg
1 (16-ounce) can whole kernel corn, drained
1/2 cup water
1 pound ground beef
1 cup finely chopped onion
2 cups coarsely chopped green bell peppers
2 cups shredded cheese
1 teaspoon garlic salt
1 teaspoon pepper

Combine barbecue sauce, cornmeal, egg, corn and water in bowl; mix well. Pour half the mixture into greased 10x13-inch baking pan. Combine ground beef, onion, green peppers, cheese, garlic salt and pepper in bowl; mix well. Spoon over corn bread layer. Top with remaining corn bread mixture. Bake at 325 degrees for 1 hour. Turn off oven. Let stand in oven for 15 minutes longer. Cool for 15 minutes before serving. Yield: 6 servings.

Approx Per Serving: Cal 500; Prot 28.3 g; Carbo 37.6 g; T Fat 27.7 g; Chol 134.0 mg; Potas 546.0 mg; Sod 1162.0 mg.

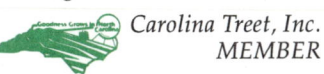

Carolina Treet, Inc.
MEMBER

CHILI BURRITOS

2 (10-ounce) cans Texas Pete chili without beans
1 (10-ounce) can refried beans
Texas Pete hot sauce to taste
1/2 cup shredded cheese
8 flour tortillas

Combine chili, refried beans, hot sauce and cheese in saucepan or glass dish; mix well. Heat or microwave until heated through, stirring occasionally. Warm tortillas according to package directions. Spoon filling onto tortillas. Roll to enclose filling. Serve immediately. Yield: 8 servings.

Approx Per Serving: Cal 263; Prot 10.2 g; Carbo 37.5 g; T Fat 9.0 g; Chol 14.4 mg; Potas 464.0 mg; Sod 886.0 mg.

T. W. Garner Food Company
MEMBER

CHINESE BEEF AND TOFU

1 pound fresh spinach
1 pound tofu
2 tablespoons soybean oil
2 cloves of garlic, minced
4 green onions, chopped
1/4 teaspoon crushed red pepper flakes
4 ounces ground beef
1/4 cup soy sauce

Tear spinach into bite-sized pieces. Cut tofu into 1/2-inch cubes. Heat oil to 350 degrees in wok or 10-inch skillet. Add garlic, onions and red pepper. Stir-fry for several seconds. Add ground beef. Stir-fry for 3 minutes or until brown. Add soy sauce, tofu and spinach. Stir-fry until spinach is wilted and mixture is heated through. Serve hot. Yield: 4 servings.

Approx Per Serving: Cal 244; Prot 18.4 g; Carbo 8.8 g; T Fat 16.9 g; Chol 18.3 mg; Potas 899.0 mg; Sod 1144.0 mg.

North Carolina Soybean Producers Association

HAMBURGER AND BISCUIT CASSEROLE

1 pound ground beef
1/4 cup chopped onion
3/4 cup Carolina Treet barbecue sauce
1 tablespoon brown sugar
2 (8-count) cans refrigerator biscuits
3/4 cup shredded Cheddar cheese

Brown ground beef with onion in skillet, stirring until ground beef is crumbly; drain. Add barbecue sauce and brown sugar; mix well. Press each biscuit over bottom and side of greased muffin cup. Spoon ground beef mixture into biscuit cups. Top with cheese. Bake at 400 degrees for 10 minutes. Yield: 8 servings.

Approx Per Serving: Cal 200; Prot 13.4 g; Carbo 6.8 g; T Fat 13.1 g; Chol 47.9 mg; Potas 199.5 mg; Sod 353.5 mg.

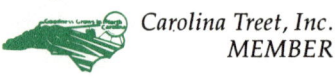

Carolina Treet, Inc.
MEMBER

CHEESY LASAGNA

1½ pounds ground beef
1 cup chopped onion
1 cup chopped green bell pepper
1 (28-ounce) can tomatoes, chopped
3 (8-ounce) cans tomato sauce
½ teaspoon garlic powder
1 tablespoon basil
2 tablespoons oregano
4 bay leaves
½ teaspoon seasoned salt
8 ounces fresh mushrooms, sliced
2 tablespoons butter
9 lasagna noodles
1 egg, beaten
2 cups cottage cheese
2 cups shredded mozzarella cheese
1 (14-ounce) can artichoke hearts, drained, cut into quarters
1 (6-ounce) can sliced black olives, drained
1 cup shredded Swiss cheese
½ cup Parmesan cheese

Brown ground beef with onion and green pepper in heavy saucepan, stirring until ground beef is crumbly; drain. Stir in undrained tomatoes, tomato sauce, garlic powder, basil, oregano, bay leaves and seasosned salt; reduce heat. Simmer for 1 hour or until thickened to desired consistency, stirring occasionally. Remove bay leaves. Sauté mushrooms in butter in skillet; drain. Cook noodles according to package directions; drain. Combine egg and cottage cheese in bowl; mix well. Layer ⅓ of the tomato sauce and 3 noodles in lightly greased 9x13-inch baking dish. Layer 1 cup mozzarella cheese and all the cottage cheese mixture over noodles. Add 3 noodles and ⅓ of the tomato sauce. Layer mushrooms, artichoke hearts and olives over sauce. Add layers of remaining noodles, Swiss cheese, remaining mozzarella cheese and remaining sauce. Bake, covered, at 350 degrees for 45 minutes. Top with Parmesan cheese. Bake, uncovered, for 10 to 15 minutes longer. Let stand for 15 minutes before serving. Yield: 8 servings.

Approx Per Serving: Cal 756; Prot 47.6 g; Carbo 65.8 g; T Fat 35.1 g; Chol 136.0 mg; Potas 1275.0 mg; Sod 1576.0 mg.

North Carolina Department of Agriculture

HERBED MEAT LOAF

1 pound lean ground beef
1 green bell pepper, chopped
1 onion, chopped
1 egg
1 cup oats
1 (8-ounce) can tomato sauce
1 tablespoon dry vegetable soup mix
1 1/2 teaspoons Italian seasoning

Combine ground beef, green pepper, onion, egg, oats, tomato sauce, soup mix and Italian seasoning in bowl; mix well. Shape into meat loaf. Place in loaf pan sprayed with nonstick cooking spray. Bake at 350 degrees for 1 1/2 hours. Let stand for 5 minutes. Slice to serve. Yield: 8 servings.

Approx Per Serving: Cal 166; Prot 12.9 g; Carbo 8.3 g; T Fat 9.2 g; Chol 71.4 mg; Potas 324.0 mg; Sod 380.0 mg.

North Carolina Herb Association

MEAT LOAF

2 pounds ground beef
1 envelope dry onion soup mix
1/2 cup North Carolina red wine
1/2 cup tomato juice
4 slices bacon
1/4 cup North Carolina red wine
1/2 cup tomato juice

Combine ground beef, soup mix, 1/2 cup wine and 1/2 cup tomato juice in bowl; mix well. Shape into loaf. Place in baking pan; top with bacon slices. Bake at 350 degrees for 45 minutes; drain. Add 1/4 cup wine and 1/2 cup tomato juice. Bake for 15 minutes longer, basting occasionally. Yield: 8 servings.

Approx Per Serving: Cal 277; Prot 20.6 g; Carbo 2.2 g; T Fat 18.7 g; Chol 75.7 mg; Potas 351.0 mg; Sod 307.0 mg.

North Carolina Grape Growers Association

CHILI-STUFFED PEPPERS

4 large green bell peppers
1/4 cup chopped green onions
1 medium tomato, chopped
3/4 cup shredded cheese
1 (10-ounce) can Texas Pete chili without beans
Texas Pete hot sauce to taste
1 (8-ounce) can corn, drained
1 (8-ounce) can tomato sauce
1/2 cup shredded cheese

Cut thin slice from stem end of each green pepper; discard seed and membrane. Combine green onions, tomato, 3/4 cup cheese, chili, hot sauce and corn in bowl; mix well. Spoon into peppers. Place in 8-inch baking pan. Pour tomato sauce over top. Bake at 350 degrees for 30 minutes. Sprinkle with 1/2 cup cheese. Bake for 10 minutes longer or until peppers are tender. Yield: 4 servings.

Approx Per Serving: Cal 329; Prot 15.9 g; Carbo 34.0 g; T Fat 16.5 g; Chol 44.2 mg; Potas 894.0 mg; Sod 1262.0 mg.

T. W. Garner Food Company
MEMBER

CHILI PIZZA

1 recipe pizza dough
2 (10-ounce) cans Texas Pete chili without beans
1 medium green bell pepper, sliced
1 small onion, chopped
Shredded mozzarella cheese
Texas Pete hot sauce to taste

Press pizza dough into baking pan. Top with chili, green pepper and onion. Sprinkle with cheese and hot sauce. Bake according to directions for pizza dough. Yield: 6 servings.

Approx Per Serving: Cal 235; Prot 8.4 g; Carbo 36.5 g; T Fat 6.4 g; Chol 9.3 mg; Potas 493.0 mg; Sod 937.0 mg.
Nutritional information does not include cheese.

T. W. Garner Food Company
MEMBER

APPLE AND SWEET POTATO FRANKFURTERS

2½ cups sliced peeled apples
3 large sweet potatoes, cooked, peeled and sliced
1 pound frankfurters, split, cut into halves
¼ cup packed light brown sugar
⅛ teaspoon cinnamon
¼ teaspoon salt
1 teaspoon fresh lemon juice
½ cup buttered soft bread crumbs

Alternate layers of apples, sweet potatoes and frankfurters in shallow baking dish until half of each is used. Combine brown sugar, cinnamon and salt in small bowl. Sprinkle half over layers. Add alternating layers of remaining apples, sweet potatoes and frankfurters. Sprinkle with remaining brown sugar mixture and lemon juice. Top with crumbs. Bake, covered, at 375 degrees for 45 minutes. Bake, uncovered, for 10 minutes longer. Yield: 6 servings.

Approx Per Serving: Cal 409; Prot 10.0 g; Carbo 41.3 g; T Fat 23.0 g; Chol 35.8 mg; Potas 362.0 mg; Sod 897.0 mg.

North Carolina Sweet Potato Commission

DIXIE-STYLE HAM AND YAMS

1 (17-ounce) can yams
1 cup packed brown sugar
6 tablespoons melted margarine
1 cup chopped pecans
1 (1½-pound) slice Lundy's fully cooked ham (1 inch thick)

Drain yams, reserving ½ can liquid. Combine yam liquid with brown sugar and margarine in large skillet; blend well. Add yams and pecans. Cook over low heat for 35 to 45 minutes or until sauce is thick and yams are coated, turning yams frequently. Slash edges of ham slice to prevent curling. Place on broiler pan. Broil 3 inches from heat source for 5 to 8 minutes on each side. May bake ham on rack in shallow pan at 325 degrees for 25 to 30 minutes.
Yield: 4 servings.

Approx Per Serving: Cal 1111; Prot 41.0 g; Carbo 91.8 g; T Fat 65.9 g; Chol 104.0 mg; Potas 1255.0 mg; Sod 2253.0 mg.

Lundy Packing Company
MEMBER

HAM CASSEROLE WITH BISCUITS

2/3 cup chopped onion
1/3 cup butter
1/3 cup all-purpose flour
Dash of pepper
2 cups milk
1 tablespoon prepared mustard
1 teaspoon Worcestershire sauce
1 cup shredded Cheddar cheese
1 (10-ounce) package frozen mixed vegetables, cooked
1 1/2 cups cubed cooked ham
1 (10-ounce) can refrigerator buttermilk biscuits
2 tablespoons melted butter
1/8 teaspoon garlic powder

Sauté onion in 1/3 cup butter in large skillet for 3 minutes or until tender. Stir in flour and pepper. Remove from heat. Add milk gradually. Bring to a boil, stirring constantly. Cook for 1 minute, stirring constantly. Add mustard, Worcestershire sauce and cheese; stir until cheese melts. Stir in mixed vegetables and ham. Spoon into buttered 9x13-inch baking dish. Arrange biscuits around edge of ham mixture. Brush tops of biscuits with mixture of melted butter and garlic powder. Bake at 400 degrees for 20 to 25 minutes or until hot and bubbly and biscuits are golden brown. Yield: 6 servings.

Approx Per Serving: Cal 550; Prot 20.8 g; Carbo 40.0 g; T Fat 34.1 g; Chol 92.4 mg; Potas 399.0 mg; Sod 1330.0 mg.

American Dairy Association of North Carolina

HERBED PORK CHOPS

4 (1-inch thick) pork chops
1 cup unsweetened pineapple juice
2/3 cup dry Sherry
2 tablespoons brown sugar
1/2 teaspoon rosemary
1 clove of garlic, minced

Place pork chops in mixture of pineapple juice, Sherry, brown sugar, rosemary and garlic in shallow dish. Marinate, covered, in refrigerator overnight, turning occasionally. Drain, reserving marinade. Grill pork chops for 5 to 6 minutes on each side, basting once with reserved marinade.
Yield: 4 servings.

Approx Per Serving: Cal 734; Prot 46.5 g; Carbo 16.0 g; T Fat 47.5 g; Chol 175.0 mg; Potas 727.0 mg; Sod 118.0 mg.
Nutritrional information includes entire amount of marinade.

North Carolina Pork Producers Association

SPECIAL CHOPS

4 (1½-inch thick) boneless loin chops
1 (8-ounce) bottle of Italian dressing

Combine chops with salad dressing in shallow dish. Marinate, covered, in refrigerator for 2 to 4 hours. Bake on preheated 350-degree nonstick griddle or grill over medium-hot coals for 6 to 7 minutes on each side. Yield: 4 servings.

Approx Per Serving: Cal 890; Prot 46.6 g; Carbo 5.8 g; T Fat 81.5 g; Chol 175.0 mg; Potas 595.0 mg; Sod 388.0 mg.

North Carolina Department of Agriculture

NORTH CAROLINA PORK CHOPS

4 pork chops
¼ cup catsup
¼ cup steak sauce
¼ cup honey

Place pork chops in 9x13-inch baking dish. Mix catsup, steak sauce and honey in small bowl. Pour over pork chops. Bake, covered with foil, at 400 degrees for 1 hour or until pork chops are tender. Yield: 4 servings.

Approx Per Serving: Cal 879; Prot 58.6 g; Carbo 24.4 g; T Fat 59.4 g; Chol 219.0 mg; Potas 806.0 mg; Sod 317.0 mg.

E. Lester Selph Bee Farm
MEMBER

MISS IDA'S BAKED DILL PORK CHOPS

4 (1-inch thick) pork chops
Salt and pepper to taste
3 tablespoons all-purpose flour
1 tablespoon oil
4 medium potatoes, cut into quarters
2 medium onions, chopped
1 cup chopped Cates dill pickles
½ cup pickle juice
1 cup water

Sprinkle pork chops with salt and pepper; coat with flour. Brown on both sides in oil in skillet. Arrange pork chops and potato quarters in casserole. Sauté onions and pickles in pan drippings. Add pickle juice and water; mix well. Pour over pork chops and potatoes. Bake, covered, at 350 degrees for 30 minutes. Remove cover. Bake for 30 minutes longer. Yield: 4 servings.

Approx Per Serving: Cal 887; Prot 51.4 g; Carbo 54.1 g; T Fat 51.4 g; Chol 175.0 mg; Potas 1440.0 mg; Sod 500.0 mg.

Cates Pickles, Inc.
MEMBER

MUSHROOM AND BEER CHOPS

4   (1 1/2-inch thick) boneless loin chops
1 tablespoon butter
1/2 cup chopped green onions
2 cloves of garlic, minced
8 ounces mushrooms, sliced
1/2 teaspoon thyme
1   (12-ounce) can beer

Brown loin chops on both sides in butter in skillet. Remove to platter. Sauté onions and garlic in pan drippings for 2 minutes. Add mushrooms and thyme. Sauté for 1 minute longer. Return chops to skillet. Add beer. Bring to a boil; reduce heat. Simmer, covered, for 8 to 10 minutes or until tender. Serve with noodles or rice. Yield: 4 servings.

Approx Per Serving: Cal 706; Prot 48.0 g; Carbo 7.10 g; T Fat 50.6 g; Chol 183.0 mg; Potas 859.0 mg; Sod 142.0 mg.

North Carolina Pork Producers Association

SOUTHERN PORK CHOP BAKE

6 Lundy's pork chops
1/2 teaspoon salt
1/2 teaspoon pepper
1   (10-ounce) package frozen green beans, thawed, drained
1/2 cup sliced fresh mushrooms
1/4 cup chopped green bell pepper
1/4 cup chopped onion
2 tablespoons butter
1 can cream of mushroom soup
2 tablespoons milk
1/2 to 1 teaspoon basil
1/2 teaspoon Worcestershire sauce
2 to 3 drops Tabasco sauce
1   (3-ounce) can chow mein noodles

Brown pork chops on both sides in skillet; sprinkle with salt and pepper. Place in baking dish. Top with green beans. Sauté mushrooms, green pepper and onion in butter in skillet until tender. Spoon over green beans. Combine soup, milk, basil, Worcestershire sauce and Tabasco sauce in small bowl; mix well. Pour over vegetables. Bake at 350 degrees for 30 minutes. Sprinkle with chow mein noodles. Bake for 10 minutes longer. Yield: 6 servings.

Approx Per Serving: Cal 802; Prot 50.1 g; Carbo 16.4 g; T Fat 58.9 g; Chol 188.0 mg; Potas 747.0 mg; Sod 887.0 mg.

Lundy Packing Company
MEMBER

MARMALADE AND GINGER RIBS

5 pounds Lundy's pork back ribs
1 cup lime juice
1 cup honey
3 tablespoons soy sauce
Pinch of ground ginger
1 cup orange marmalade

Cut ribs into serving pieces; place in large shallow dish. Mix lime juice, honey, soy sauce and ginger in bowl. Pour over ribs. Marinate, covered, in refrigerator for several hours to overnight, basting frequently with marinade. Drain, reserving marinade. Place ribs on rack in 9x13-inch baking pan. Bake at 325 degrees for 45 minutes. Drain. Mix marmalade with reserved marinade. Bake for 45 minutes longer, basting frequently with marmalade mixture. Yield: 6 servings.

Approx Per Serving: Cal 1201; Prot 69.2 g; Carbo 87.3 g; T Fat 65.1 g; Chol 224.0 mg; Potas 1425.0 mg; Sod 826.0 mg.

Lundy Packing Company
MEMBER

CAJUN PORK ROAST

1 (2-pound) boneless pork loin roast
2 tablespoons oil
3 tablespoons paprika
1/2 teaspoon cayenne pepper
1 tablespoon garlic powder
2 teaspoons oregano
2 teaspoons thyme
1/2 teaspoon salt
1/2 teaspoon white pepper
1/2 teaspoon cumin
1/4 teaspoon nutmeg

Rub surface of roast with oil. Mix paprika, cayenne pepper, garlic powder, oregano, thyme, salt, white pepper, cumin and nutmeg in small bowl. Rub over surface of roast. Place roast in shallow pan. Bake at 350 degrees for 1 hour to 1 hour and 15 minutes or to 155 degrees on meat thermometer. Let rest for 5 to 10 minutes before slicing. Yield: 4 servings.

Approx Per Serving: Cal 608; Prot 44.7 g; Carbo 5.9 g; T Fat 44.7 g; Chol 155.0 mg; Potas 722.0 mg; Sod 378.0 mg.

North Carolina Pork Producers Association

PORK AND SWEET POTATO STIR-FRY

1¼ pounds pork tenderloin
2 medium sweet potatoes
2 tablespoons oil
½ teaspoon salt
½ cup water
⅓ cup chopped green onions
2 tablespoons raisins
1½ teaspoons cornstarch
2 tablespoons cooking wine
2 cups thinly sliced apples

Cut pork diagonally into ¼-inch thick slices. Peel sweet potatoes; cut into ⅛x½x1-inch strips. Stir-fry pork, a small amount at a time, in hot oil in wok until pink color disappears. Remove to platter; sprinkle with salt. Add sweet potatoes and water to wok. Cook, covered, for 5 minutes, stirring occasionally. Add pork, onions and raisins; mix well. Stir in mixture of cornstarch and wine. Cook until thickened, stirring constantly. Fold in apples just before serving. Yield: 6 servings.

Approx Per Serving: Cal 391; Prot 20.0 g; Carbo 21.3 g; T Fat 24.4 g; Chol 72.3 mg; Potas 420.0 mg; Sod 231.0 mg.

North Carolina Sweet Potato Commission

TACOS DELICIOSOS

1 pound Lundy's ground pork
2 tablespoons tomato paste
1 teaspoon minced garlic
1 teaspoon chili powder
1 teaspoon salt
½ teaspoon cumin
½ cup water
6 taco shells
1 medium tomato, cut into thin wedges
6 mild Italian peppers
2 tablespoons chopped onion
6 tablespoons shredded lettuce
6 tablespoons shredded sharp Cheddar cheese
1 (4½-ounce) can taco sauce

Brown ground pork in skillet, stirring until crumbly; drain. Add tomato paste, garlic, chili powder, salt and cumin; mix well. Add water gradually, stirring constantly. Simmer until heated through. Spoon into taco shells. Add 1 or 2 tomato wedges, 1 Italian pepper, 1 teaspoon onion, 1 tablespoon lettuce, 1 tablespoon cheese and 1 or 2 teaspoons taco sauce to each serving.
Yield: 6 servings.

Approx Per Serving: Cal 316; Prot 19.2 g; Carbo 17.7 g; T Fat 19.8 g; Chol 67.0 mg; Potas 532.0 mg; Sod 544.0 mg.

Lundy Packing Company
MEMBER

PORK TENDERLOIN MEDALLIONS

8 (1½ pounds) Lundy's pork tenderloin medallions
1 egg, beaten
1 tablespoon milk
½ cup cornflake crumbs
2 tablespoons shortening
½ teaspoon salt
¼ teaspoon coarsely ground pepper
1 can tomato soup
3 tablespoons chili sauce
2 tablespoons shredded sharp Cheddar cheese
1 tablespoon Worcestershire sauce
¼ teaspoon basil

Pound pork with meat mallet; score. Mix egg and milk in small bowl. Dip pork into egg mixture; coat with crumbs. Brown on both sides in hot shortening in skillet. Sprinkle with salt and pepper. Place in 8x8-inch baking dish. Mix soup, chili sauce, cheese, Worcestershire sauce and basil in bowl. Spoon over pork. Bake at 350 degrees for 50 minutes or until pork is tender. Yield: 4 servings.

Approx Per Serving: Cal 664; Prot 39.6 g; Carbo 21.8 g; T Fat 45.9 g; Chol 204.0 mg; Potas 715.0 mg; Sod 1233.0 mg.

Lundy Packing Company
MEMBER

PORK AU VIN

1 pound boneless loin pork
1 tablespoon oil
8 small onions, peeled
8 ounces mushrooms, cut into halves
½ cup beef broth
1 cup dry red wine
1 tablespoon Dijon-style mustard
2 tablespoons chopped parsley
1 teaspoon cornstarch
1 teaspoon cold water

Cut pork into ¾-inch slices. Brown in hot oil in skillet. Remove to platter. Add onions to pan drippings. Cook until browned, stirring frequently. Remove to platter. Add mushrooms to pan drippings. Cook until lightly browned, stirring frequently. Return pork and onions to skillet. Add beef broth, wine and mustard. Bring to a boil; reduce heat. Simmer, covered, for 12 to 15 minutes. Stir in parsley. Remove pork and vegetables to serving platter. Stir mixture of cornstarch and water into wine mixture. Bring to a boil, stirring constantly. Pour over pork. Yield: 4 servings.

Approx Per Serving: Cal 430; Prot 25.0 g; Carbo 13.1 g; T Fat 26.7 g; Chol 84.0 mg; Potas 716.0 mg; Sod 216.0 mg.

North Carolina Pork Producers Association

SMOKED SAUSAGE AND MACARONI BAKE

1 (7-ounce) package macaroni
1 pound Lundy's smoked sausage
3 eggs, beaten
1 pound Cheddar cheese, shredded
1 small onion, chopped
2 cups milk, scalded
2 tablespoons melted butter
1 cup bread crumbs
1/2 cup shredded Cheddar cheese

Cook macaroni according to package directions; drain. Cut sausage into bite-sized pieces. Add macaroni to eggs in large bowl; mix well. Stir in cheese and onion. Add scalded milk; mix well. Spoon into 3-quart casserole. Top with sausage pieces. Mix butter, bread crumbs and cheese in bowl. Sprinkle over top of macaroni mixture. Bake at 325 degrees for 45 minutes or until hot and bubbly. Yield: 6 servings.

Approx Per Serving: Cal 977; Prot 42.3 g; Carbo 45.0 g; T Fat 69.4 g; Chol 300.0 mg; Potas 520.0 mg; Sod 1256.0 mg.

Lundy Packing Company
MEMBER

CHICKEN CASSEROLE

1 chicken, cut up
1 tablespoon oil
1 large onion, chopped
3 cloves of garlic, crushed
1/4 teaspoon oregano
1 bay leaf
1/2 cup water
1 (8-ounce) can tomato sauce
1 cup Duplin Carlos wine
3 potatoes, cut into quarters
1 stalk celery, chopped

Brown chicken in oil in skillet. Add onion, garlic, oregano, bay leaf and water. Simmer until chicken is tender. Add tomato sauce. Simmer for 7 minutes longer. Add wine, potatoes and celery. Simmer over low heat until vegetables are tender. Remove bay leaf. Serve with steamed rice. Yield: 4 servings.

Approx Per Serving: Cal 529; Prot 52.6 g; Carbo 31.7 g; T Fat 16.4 g; Chol 152.0 mg; Potas 1113.0 mg; Sod 336.0 mg.

Duplin Winery
MEMBER

CHICKEN AND VEGETABLE CASSEROLE

3 pounds chicken breast filets
1 clove of garlic, crushed
1 tablespoon oil
1 teaspoon salt
1/4 teaspoon pepper
1/4 teaspoon paprika
1 pound small red potatoes, unpeeled
8 ounces small white onions
1 cup dry white wine
1/4 cup water
2 teaspoons rosemary
8 ounces yellow squash
8 ounces fresh shiitake mushrooms, sliced
1 cup sliced red bell pepper

Cook chicken and garlic in hot oil in deep skillet for 3 minutes, turning chicken once. Season with salt, pepper and paprika. Add potatoes, onions, wine, water and rosemary. Simmer, covered, for 20 minutes. Add squash, mushrooms and red bell pepper. Simmer, covered, for 10 minutes. Simmer, uncovered, for 10 minutes longer to reduce pan juices. Yield: 6 servings.

Approx Per Serving: Cal 338; Prot 38.1 g; Carbo 22.2 g; T Fat 7.8 g; Chol 95.6 mg; Potas 718.0 mg; Sod 466.0 mg.

American Forest Foods
MEMBER

OLD-FASHIONED CHICKEN AND DUMPLINGS

1 (5-pound) chicken
1/2 cup chopped celery
1 medium onion, finely chopped
1/2 package Anne's frozen flat dumplings
1 cup all-purpose flour
2 cups milk

Place chicken in water to cover in large soup pot. Add celery, onion and salt and pepper to taste. Bring to a boil; reduce heat. Simmer until chicken is tender. Remove chicken from broth; bone. Add enough water to broth to measure 3 quarts. Bring to a boil. Drop dumplings 8 to 10 at a time into boiling broth. Cook, covered, for 10 to 12 minutes. Return chicken to broth. Season with salt and pepper to taste. Stir in mixture of flour and milk. Cook until thickened, stirring constantly. Yield: 6 servings.

Approx Per Serving: Cal 496; Prot 59.9 g; Carbo 22.0 g; T Fat 17.0 g; Chol 180.0 mg; Potas 657.0 mg; Sod 206.0 mg.
Nutritional information does not include dumplings.

Anne's Old Fashioned Dumplings
MEMBER

DUPLIN CHICKEN

6 chicken breasts
1/4 cup all-purpose flour
Salt and pepper to taste
1/4 cup butter
1/2 cup Duplin
  Scuppernong wine
1/3 cup water
1 cup catsup
2 tablespoons lemon juice
1 tablespoon
  Worcestershire sauce
1 medium onion, minced

Coat chicken with mixture of flour and salt and pepper. Brown on both sides in butter in skillet. Arrange chicken in 2-quart casserole. Combine wine, water, catsup, lemon juice, Worcestershire sauce and onion with pan drippings in skillet; mix well. Bring to a boil. Pour over chicken. Bake at 325 degrees for 1 hour and 15 minutes or until chicken is tender. Yield: 6 servings.

Approx Per Serving: Cal 307; Prot 28.2 g; Carbo 18.3 g; T Fat 11.8 g; Chol 92.4 mg; Potas 461.0 mg; Sod 631.0 mg.

Duplin Winery
MEMBER

FAMILY CHICKEN WITH BROWN SUGAR GLAZE

1 Holly Farms fully
  cooked roasted chicken
2 tablespoons butter
1 cup packed brown sugar
1/4 cup mustard
1/2 cup pork sausage
1/2 cup chopped onion
2 cups fresh bread crumbs
2 pears, chopped
1/2 cup chopped chestnuts
1/4 cup chicken broth
1 teaspoon sage
1/8 teaspoon thyme
1/4 teaspoon salt
1/8 teaspoon pepper

Place chicken on rack in roasting pan. Melt butter in small saucepan. Stir in brown sugar and mustard. Simmer for 3 minutes over medium heat. Brush on chicken. Brown sausage with onion in skillet, stirring until sausage is crumbly; drain. Add bread crumbs, pears, chestnuts, broth, sage, thyme, salt and pepper; mix well. Spoon into shallow 1-quart baking dish. Place chicken and stuffing in oven. Bake at 375 degrees for 15 minutes or until heated through, brushing chicken frequently with glaze. Yield: 4 servings.

Approx Per Serving: Cal 871; Prot 56.6 g; Carbo 88.9 g; T Fat 32.3 g; Chol 187.0 mg; Potas 962.0 mg; Sod 902.0 mg.

Holly Farms Foods, Inc.
MEMBER

GOURMET STUFFED CHICKEN BREASTS

4 whole boneless chicken breasts
1/2 teaspoon salt
Pepper to taste
1 cup shredded Swiss cheese
4 ounces turkey ham, coarsely chopped
1 tablespoon melted margarine
2 tablespoons butter
3 tablespoons all-purpose flour
1 1/2 cups chicken broth
1/2 cup evaporated milk
Juice of 1/2 lemon
Cayenne pepper to taste

Split chicken breasts, leaving skin intact; remove small fillet layer from each breast half. Place small fillets and chicken breasts skin side down on smooth surface. Flatten with meat mallet to uniform thickness. Season with 1/2 teaspoon salt and pepper. Spoon an equal amount of cheese and ham in center of each chicken breast. Cover filling with small fillets. Fold sides and ends of breasts toward small fillets, enclosing filling completely. Arrange in greased baking dish. Brush with margarine. Heat baking dish briefly on stove top to seal on bottoms. Bake at 425 degrees for 30 minutes or until chicken is tender. Melt butter in saucepan over low heat. Add flour; mix well. Stir in broth. Simmer for 5 minutes or until thickened, stirring constantly. Add evaporated milk. Cook for 5 minutes longer, stirring constantly. Stir in lemon juice and cayenne pepper. Serve with chicken. Yield: 8 servings.

Approx Per Serving: Cal 297; Prot 35.4 g; Carbo 4.92 g; T Fat 14.3 g; Chol 105.0 mg; Potas 361.0 mg; Sod 575.0 mg.

North Carolina Poultry Federation

HONEYED CHICKEN AND SWEET POTATOES

4 whole chicken breasts
1 cup whipping cream
2 tablespoons honey
1 teaspoon salt
1/2 teaspoon nutmeg
1/2 teaspoon allspice
Pinch of cloves
2 tablespoons butter
4 large sweet potatoes

Bone and split chicken breasts, leaving skin intact. Arrange skin side up in shallow baking dish. Combine whipping cream, honey and seasonings in small bowl; mix well. Pour over chicken. Dot with butter. Bake at 350 degrees for 30 minutes, basting occasionally. Place sweet potatoes in water to cover in large saucepan. Bring to a boil. Cook for 20 minutes; drain. Cool slightly; peel. Arrange around chicken in baking dish. Bake for 30 minutes longer or until chicken is fork-tender. Yield: 8 servings.

Approx Per Serving: Cal 299; Prot 14.8 g; Carbo 23.9 g; T Fat 16.1 g; Chol 84.4 mg; Potas 272.0 mg; Sod 345.0 mg.

North Carolina Sweet Potato Commission

HONEY-MUSTARD DRUMSTICK WRAP-UPS

2 tablespoons mustard
2 teaspoons honey
1 (8-ounce) package refrigerator crescent rolls
8 Holly Farms fully cooked roasted drumsticks

Combine mustard and honey in small bowl; mix well. Separate crescent roll dough into triangles on baking sheet. Spoon small amount of sauce onto each triangle. Place meaty portion of drumstick on sauce. Wrap dough around drumstick, leaving end exposed. Bake for 15 minutes or until golden brown. Yield: 8 servings.

Approx Per Serving: Cal 264; Prot 24.7 g; Carbo 10.7 g; T Fat 13.0 g; Chol 79.0 mg; Potas 261.0 mg; Sod 317.0 mg.

Holly Farms Foods, Inc.
MEMBER

MICROWAVE CHEESE CHICKEN

4 chicken breast halves, skinned
1/4 cup melted butter
3 cups crushed cheese crackers

Brush chicken with butter; roll in cracker crumbs. Arrange in glass dish; cover with waxed paper. Microwave on High for 12 to 15 minutes, rotating dish 1/2 turn after 6 minutes. Let stand for 2 to 3 minutes before serving. Yield: 4 servings.

Approx Per Serving: Cal 354; Prot 28.4 g; Carbo 11.3 g; T Fat 21.7 g; Chol 115.0 mg; Potas 249.0 mg; Sod 398.0 mg.

North Carolina Department of Agriculture

NUGGETS SESAME

1 (8-ounce) package Holly Farms chicken nuggets
2 tablespoons oil
1 tablespoon sesame oil
1/4 cup thinly sliced green onions
1 tablespoon brown sugar
1 tablespoon soy sauce
1 tablespoon sesame seed, toasted

Stir-fry chicken in oils in wok. Add green onions, brown sugar and salt and pepper to taste. Reduce heat. Stir in soy sauce. Stir-fry over medium heat until chicken is cooked through. Remove to serving dish. Sprinkle with sesame seed. Yield: 4 servings.

Approx Per Serving: Cal 228; Prot 17.1 g; Carbo 4.6 g; T Fat 15.6 g; Chol 50.6 mg; Potas 184.0 mg; Sod 308.0 mg.

Holly Farms Foods, Inc.
MEMBER

CHICKEN AND SAUSAGE JAMBALAYA

1 pound chicken breast filets
1/4 teaspoon pepper
1/4 teaspoon red pepper
3 tablespoons oil-free Italian salad dressing
12 ounces turkey sausage
2 1/4 cups chopped celery
2 1/2 cups chopped onions
1 3/4 cups sliced green onions
1 cup chopped green bell pepper
2 cloves of garlic, minced
2 chicken bouillon cubes
3 cups hot water
1/2 teaspoon Kitchen Bouquet
1 1/2 cups long grain rice

Cut chicken into bite-sized pieces. Season with pepper and red pepper. Combine with Italian dressing in deep skillet. Cook over medium heat for 3 minutes, stirring frequently. Remove chicken. Brown sausage in skillet over medium heat, stirring until crumbly. Drain in colander; pat dry with paper towels. Sauté celery, onions, green onions, green pepper and garlic in large skillet sprayed with nonstick cooking spray until tender-crisp. Add chicken. Simmer, covered, for 15 minutes. Dissolve bouillon cubes in hot water; add Kitchen Bouquet. Stir into chicken mixture. Bring to a boil. Stir in rice and sausage. Simmer, covered, for 20 minutes or until rice is tender. Yield: 6 servings.

Approx Per Serving: Cal 377; Prot 28.7 g; Carbo 46.5 g; T Fat 7.6 g; Chol 71.2 mg; Potas 634.0 mg; Sod 722.0 mg.
Nutritional information does not include Kitchen Bouquet.

North Carolina Poultry Federation

CHICKEN WITH LIME BUTTER

6 chicken breast fillets
1/2 teaspoon salt
1/2 teaspoon pepper
1/3 cup oil
Juice of 1 lime
1/2 cup butter
1/2 teaspoon minced chives
1/2 teaspoon dillweed

Season chicken filets with salt and pepper. Cook in oil in skillet over medium heat for 4 minutes or until lightly browned. Turn filets. Cook, covered, over low heat for 10 minutes or until fork-tender. Remove fillets to warm platter; keep warm. Drain oil from skillet. Pour lime juice into skillet. Simmer briefly over low heat. Add butter, stirring constantly until butter becomes opaque. Stir in chives and dillweed. Spoon sauce over chicken. Yield: 6 servings.

Approx Per Serving: Cal 393; Prot 26.6 g; Carbo 1.4 g; T Fat 31.2 g; Chol 113.0 mg; Potas 232.0 mg; Sod 373.0 mg.

North Carolina Department of Agriculture

MEXICAN SUPER SUPPER

1 Holly Farms chicken
1 (7-ounce) package taco-flavored chips, crumbled
1 medium onion, minced
1 can chicken soup
1 can cream of mushroom soup
3 tablespoons minced jalapeño peppers
1 cup sour cream
1/2 cup sliced black olives
1/8 teaspoon garlic powder
1 cup shredded Cheddar cheese

Cut chicken into pieces. Simmer in water to cover in large saucepan until tender. Cool slightly. Bone chicken; cut into bite-sized pieces. Combine chicken, chips, onion, soups, peppers, sour cream, olives and garlic powder in 3-quart baking dish. Sprinkle with cheese. Bake at 350 degrees for 30 minutes or until hot and bubbly. Serve with crisp, green salad and Texas toast.
Yield: 6 servings.

Approx Per Serving: Cal 676; Prot 44.0 g; Carbo 31.6 g; T Fat 42.5 g; Chol 143.0 mg; Potas 505.0 mg; Sod 1414.0 mg.

Holly Farms Foods, Inc.
MEMBER

NORTH CAROLINA CHICKEN

3 tablespoons butter
1 cup chopped onion
1 cup chopped celery
1/2 cup chopped green bell pepper
1 clove of garlic, minced
1 chicken, cut up
1/2 cup honey
3/4 cup cream Sherry
1/2 cup orange juice
1/4 cup catsup
1 tablespoon vinegar
1 tablespoon Worcestershire sauce
1 tablespoon mustard
1 teaspoon salt
1/2 cup Parmesan cheese
1 tablespoon all-purpose flour

Melt butter in large casserole over medium heat. Add onion, celery, green pepper and garlic. Arrange chicken over top. Combine honey, Sherry, orange juice, catsup, vinegar, Worcestershire sauce, mustard and salt in bowl; mix well. Pour over chicken. Bake at 350 degrees for 1 1/2 hours or until chicken is tender. Sprinkle with Parmesan cheese. Bake for 5 minutes longer or until cheese melts. Remove chicken to warm platter. Stir flour into pan drippings. Cook over medium heat until thickened, stirring constantly. Serve with chicken.
Yield: 4 servings.

Approx Per Serving: Cal 705; Prot 55.6 g; Carbo 54.0 g; T Fat 24.8 g; Chol 183.0 mg; Potas 825.0 mg; Sod 1237.0 mg.

E. Lester Selph Bee Farm
MEMBER

CHICKEN PIE WITH SWEET POTATO CRUST

2 cups plus 3 tablespoons all-purpose flour
1 teaspoon baking powder
1/2 teaspoon salt
1/3 cup shortening
1 cup cold mashed sweet potatoes
1 egg, well beaten
6 small white onions, cooked
3 cups chopped cooked chicken
1 cup cooked sliced carrots
1 tablespoon chopped fresh parsley
1 cup milk
1 cup chicken broth

Mix 2 cups flour, baking powder and 1/2 teaspoon salt in bowl. Cut in shortening until crumbly. Add sweet potatoes and egg; mix well. Roll dough to 1/4-inch thickness on lightly floured surface. Cut onions into quarters. Layer chicken, carrots and onions in greased 2 1/2-quart casserole. Sprinkle with parsley. Combine 3 tablespoons flour and small amount of milk in saucepan; mix until smooth. Stir in remaining milk and chicken broth. Cook over low heat until thickened, stirring constantly. Add salt and pepper to taste; mix well. Pour over layers. Top with sweet potato pastry. Bake at 350 degrees for 45 minutes. Yield: 6 servings.

Approx Per Serving: Cal 517; Prot 29.8 g; Carbo 53.9 g; T Fat 19.6 g; Chol 114.0 mg; Potas 530.0 mg; Sod 552.0 mg.

North Carolina Sweet Potato Commission

SUPER CHEESE PIE

1 cup shredded Cheddar cheese
1 cup shredded mozzarella cheese
1 cup shredded Monterey Jack cheese
1 medium onion, chopped
1 cup chopped cooked chicken
2 tablespoons all-purpose flour
4 eggs, slightly beaten
1 cup half and half
1/2 teaspoon salt
1/2 teaspoon dry mustard
1/2 teaspoon Worcestershire sauce
2 medium tomatoes, sliced

Combine cheeses, onion, chicken and flour in bowl; mix well. Spoon into greased pie plate. Combine eggs, half and half, salt, dry mustard and Worcestershire sauce in small bowl; mix well. Pour over chicken mixture. Bake at 350 degrees for 35 to 40 minutes or until set. Let stand for 10 minutes. Arrange tomato slices, overlapping slightly, around edge of pie. Yield: 6 servings.

Approx Per Serving: Cal 440; Prot 25.6 g; Carbo 8.2 g; T Fat 33.7 g; Chol 299.0 mg; Potas 317.0 mg; Sod 554.0 mg.

North Carolina Department of Agriculture

PLUM GOOD CHICKEN

3 chicken breasts
3 chicken thighs
3 chicken drumsticks
1 (15-ounce) can plums, drained
1/4 cup chopped onion
1/2 cup cider vinegar
1/2 cup molasses
1/8 teaspoon garlic powder
1 to 2 dashes of hot sauce
Salt to taste

Arrange chicken in single layer in shallow dish. Purée plums in blender container until smooth. Combine with onion, vinegar, molasses, garlic powder, hot sauce and salt in bowl; mix well. Pour over chicken. Marinate in refrigerator for 2 to 3 hours. Place chicken in baking dish. Pour marinade over top. Bake at 400 degrees for 45 minutes or until tender, basting frequently. May grill chicken over hot coals to 180 to 185 degrees on meat thermometer, turning and basting frequently with marinade. Yield: 5 servings.

Approx Per Serving: Cal 447; Prot 44.1 g; Carbo 39.4 g; T Fat 12.3 g; Chol 138.0 mg; Potas 778.0 mg; Sod 155.0 mg.

Holly Farms Foods, Inc.
MEMBER

MISS IDA'S CAROLINA COAST CHICKEN SALAD

2 1/2 cups chopped cooked chicken
1/2 cup finely chopped celery
1/4 cup Cates sweet salad cubes
1/2 cup plain yogurt
2 teaspoons pickle juice
1 tablespoon honey

Combine chicken, celery and pickles in salad bowl. Add mixture of yogurt, pickle juice and honey; mix well. Chill in refrigerator for 30 minutes or longer. Serve on lettuce leaves with Cates Kosher Icebergs. Yield: 6 servings.

Approx Per Serving: Cal 147; Prot 17.7 g; Carbo 7.6 g; T Fat 5.0 g; Chol 54.5 mg; Potas 220.0 mg; Sod 135.0 mg.

Cates Pickles, Inc.
MEMBER

CHICKEN SALAD-STUFFED AVOCADO

2 cups chopped Holly Farms fully cooked roasted chicken
1/2 cup mayonnaise
1 tablespoon lemon juice
1/2 teaspoon ginger
1/2 cup chopped red bell pepper
1/4 cup chopped green onions
Salt and pepper to taste
2 avocados, cut into halves, seeded, peeled

Place chicken in salad bowl. Add mayonnaise, lemon juice, ginger, red pepper, green onions and salt and pepper; mix well. Chill in refrigerator for 1 hour. Spoon into avocado halves. Yield: 4 servings.

Approx Per Serving: Cal 502; Prot 22.9 g; Carbo 10.4 g; T Fat 42.6 g; Chol 78.7 mg; Potas 843.0 mg; Sod 229.0 mg.

Holly Farms Foods, Inc.
MEMBER

CHICKEN FRUIT SALAD

3 cups chopped cooked chicken
3/4 cup chopped celery
3/4 cup seeded red grape halves
1 (11-ounce) can mandarin oranges, drained
1 (15-ounce) can pineapple chunks, drained
3 tablespoons chopped pecans
1/4 cup soybean oil mayonnaise
1 tablespoon chopped pecans

Combine chicken, celery, grapes, mandarin oranges, pineapple and 3 tablespoons pecans in bowl; toss lightly. Add mayonnaise; toss to mix well. Chill until serving time. Serve on lettuce-lined plates. Top with remaining pecans. Yield: 6 servings.

Approx Per Serving: Cal 317; Prot 21.4 g; Carbo 23.2 g; T Fat 16.1 g; Chol 67.9 mg; Potas 388.0 mg; Sod 130.0 mg.

North Carolina Soybean Producers Association

HOT CHICKEN SALAD

2 cups chopped cooked chicken
1 1/2 cups finely chopped celery
1/2 cup slivered almonds, toasted
2 hard-boiled eggs, chopped
1 tablespoon chopped onion
1 cup soybean oil mayonnaise
1 1/2 teaspoons grated lemon rind
2 teaspoons lemon juice
1/2 teaspoon pepper
1 1/2 cups shredded Cheddar cheese
1 1/2 cups crushed potato chips

Place chicken in large bowl. Add celery, almonds, eggs, onion, mayonnaise, lemon rind, lemon juice and pepper; mix gently. Spoon into greased shallow 2-quart casserole. Sprinkle with cheese. Top with potato chips. Bake at 375 degrees for 25 minutes or until heated through. Yield: 6 servings.

Approx Per Serving: Cal 663; Prot 26.5 g; Carbo 15.2 g; T Fat 56.5 g; Chol 185.0 mg; Potas 596.0 mg; Sod 564.0 mg.

North Carolina Soybean Producers Association

TORTELINI CHICKEN SALAD

1/2 cup olive oil
1/3 cup wine vinegar
1/2 teaspoon basil
Salt and pepper to taste
4 ounces spinach tortelini, cooked
4 ounces cheese tortelini, cooked
2 cups chopped Holly Farms fully cooked roasted chicken
1 1/2 cups chopped fresh vegetables

Combine olive oil, vinegar, basil and salt and pepper in salad bowl; mix well. Add tortelini, chicken and vegetables; toss to coat well. Chill, covered, in refrigerator for 2 hours. Yield: 4 servings.

Approx Per Serving: Cal 501; Prot 25.1 g; Carbo 22.5 g; T Fat 34.9 Chol 65.5; Potas 550.0 mg; Sod 355.0 mg.

Holly Farms Foods, Inc.
MEMBER

CHICKEN AND BROCCOLI STIR-FRY

1 whole chicken breast
2 teaspoons cornstarch
1/4 teaspoon ginger
1/4 cup soy sauce
2 tablespoons soybean oil
1 cup broccoli flowerets
1 medium onion, thinly sliced
8 ounces fresh mushrooms, sliced

Combine chicken with water to cover in saucepan. Bring to a boil; reduce heat. Simmer for 15 minutes or until tender. Drain, reserving 1/2 cup broth. Bone chicken; cut into 1/8-inch strips. Combine cornstarch, ginger and soy sauce in small bowl; mix well. Pour over chicken. Marinate in refrigerator for 30 minutes. Heat oil to 350 degrees in wok. Add broccoli and reserved broth. Simmer, covered, for 2 minutes. Add chicken, marinade, onion and mushrooms. Stir-fry until vegetables are tender-crisp. Serve over hot cooked rice.
Yield: 4 servings.

Approx Per Serving: Cal 182; Prot 16.4 g; Carbo 9.5 g; T Fat 9.2 g; Chol 35.8 mg; Potas 482.0 mg; Sod 1071.0 mg.

North Carolina Soybean Producers Association

SUCCULENT CHICKEN

6 chicken breasts
2 tablespoons Dijon-style mustard
1/4 cup honey
2 tablespoons chopped fresh rosemary

Place chicken skin side down on foil-lined baking sheet. Spread with mustard. Drizzle with honey. Sprinkle with rosemary. Bake at 350 degrees for 1 hour or until chicken is tender. Chicken skin will stick to foil when removed. Yield: 6 servings.

Approx Per Serving: Cal 194; Prot 26.6 g; Carbo 12.0 g; T Fat 4.1 g; Chol 71.7 mg; Potas 224.0 mg; Sod 132.0 mg.

North Carolina Herb Association

SKEWERED CHICKEN WITH SOUR CREAM DIP

1 pound Holly Farms fully cooked roasted chicken breast
1/3 cup tarragon vinegar
1/4 cup olive oil
1/4 teaspoon oregano
Salt and pepper to taste
1 cup sour cream
1/4 cup chopped cucumber
2 tablespoons chopped green onion

Cut chicken into 1-inch cubes. Skewer on toothpicks. Combine vinegar, olive oil, oregano and salt and pepper in shallow dish; mix well. Place chicken in marinade. Chill, covered, in refrigerator for 1 hour or longer. Combine sour cream, cucumber and green onion in bowl; mix well. Arrange chicken on platter around sour cream dip. Yield: 8 servings.

Approx Per Serving: Cal 232; Prot 17.4 g; Carbo 2.14 g; T Fat 17.0 g; Chol 63.4 mg; Potas 204.0 mg; Sod 64.3 mg.

Holly Farms Foods, Inc.
MEMBER

SUPER-FAST CHICKEN

1 1/2 cups instant rice
1 cup chopped cooked chicken
1/2 cup chopped onion
1 tablespoon butter
4 eggs, slightly beaten
3 tablespoons soy sauce
1 cup chopped fresh shiitake mushrooms

Cook rice using package directions. Sauté chicken and onion in butter in skillet over medium heat for 2 to 3 minutes. Add eggs. Cook for 3 minutes or until eggs are set, stirring occasionally. Stir in rice, soy sauce and mushrooms. Cook until heated through. Garnish with thinly sliced scallions. Yield: 3 servings.

Approx Per Serving: Cal 451; Prot 27.4 g; Carbo 50.6 g; T Fat 15.0 g; Chol 417.0 mg; Potas 360.0 mg; Sod 1196.0 mg.

American Forest Foods
MEMBER

CHICKEN TACOS

1 cup shredded Holly
    Farms fully cooked
    roasted chicken thighs
1/2 cup chopped onion
1 clove of garlic, minced
1 tablespoon oil
1/4 cup taco sauce
12 taco shells
1/2 cup shredded Cheddar
    cheese
1/2 cup shredded lettuce
1/4 cup chopped tomato
1 cup sour cream

Sauté chicken, onion and garlic in oil in skillet until onion is tender. Add taco sauce; mix well. Simmer until heated through. Heat taco shells using package directions. Spoon chicken mixture into taco shells. Top with cheese, lettuce, tomato and sour cream. Yield: 12 servings.

Approx Per Serving: Cal 188; Prot 6.3 g; Carbo 11.3 g; T Fat 14.2 g; Chol 24.3 mg; Potas 119.0 mg; Sod 118.0 mg.

Holly Farms Foods, Inc.
MEMBER

WINE CHICKEN

1 (3-pound) chicken,
    cut up
1/2 cup Duplin Carlos wine
1/4 cup soy sauce
1/4 cup oil
2 tablespoons water
1 clove of garlic, minced
1/2 teaspoon oregano
1 tablespoon brown sugar
1/2 cup mushroom pieces

Arrange chicken in baking dish. Combine wine, soy sauce, oil, water, garlic, oregano, brown sugar and mushrooms in bowl; mix well. Pour over chicken. Bake at 350 degrees for 1 to 1 1/2 hours or until chicken is tender, basting occasionally. Yield: 4 servings.

Approx Per Serving: Cal 651; Prot 75.0 g; Carbo 5.8 g; T Fat 32.6 g; Chol 228.0 mg; Potas 721.0 mg; Sod 1251.0 mg.

Duplin Winery
MEMBER

DUCKLING WITH MUSHROOM AND WINE SAUCE

1 Concord Farms frozen duckling, thawed
1 teaspoon pepper
1/2 cup finely chopped green onions
1/4 cup finely chopped carrot
1 teaspoon oil
1 tablespoon all-purpose flour
3/4 cup white wine
3/4 cup water
1/2 teaspoon instant chicken bouillon
1/2 teaspoon rosemary
1/4 teaspoon thyme
1/4 teaspoon garlic powder
1 bay leaf
8 ounces mushrooms, sliced

Cut duckling into quarters and remove skin. Season with pepper. Place in roasting pan sprayed with nonstick cooking spray. Sauté green onions and carrots in oil in skillet until tender-crisp. Add flour; mix well. Cook over medium heat for 1 minute, stirring constantly. Stir in wine, water, bouillon, rosemary, thyme, garlic powder, bay leaf and mushrooms. Bring to a boil; reduce heat. Simmer for 5 to 10 minutes, stirring frequently. Remove bay leaf. Spoon over duckling. Bake, covered, at 350 degrees for 1 hour and 10 minutes, basting frequently during last 30 minutes of cooking time. Yield: 4 servings.

Approx Per Serving: Cal 199; Prot 16.9 g; Carbo 6.6 g; T Fat 8.6 g; Chol 57.1 mg; Potas 490.0 mg; Sod 195.0 mg.

Concord Farms, Inc
MEMBER

ROAST DUCKLING MILANO

1 Concord Farms frozen duckling, thawed
1/4 teaspoon pepper
1 tablespoon oregano
1/2 tablespoon basil
1/4 cup Dijon-style mustard
1/3 cup Parmesan cheese
1/3 cup dry vermouth
1/4 cup chopped parsley

Cut duckling into quarters; score skin with sharp knife. Arrange skin side up on rack in roasting pan. Season with pepper, oregano and basil. Roast, uncovered, at 400 degrees for 1 hour. Remove duckling and rack from pan. Drain pan juices. Return duckling to pan without rack. Spread with mustard. Sprinkle with cheese. Pour vermouth into pan. Bake for 45 minutes longer or until tender. Garnish with parsley.
Yield: 4 servings.

Approx Per Serving: Cal 201; Prot 18.8 g; Carbo 3.8 g; T Fat 10.0 g; Chol 62.3 mg; Potas 256.0 mg; Sod 367.0 mg.

Concord Farms, Inc.
MEMBER

MEXITALIAN DUCKLING DINNER

1 Concord Farms frozen duckling, thawed
3 tablespoons olive oil
1 large onion, chopped
1 clove of garlic, minced
1 (4-ounce) can chopped green chilies, drained
8 ounces mushrooms, sliced
1 (16-ounce) jar salsa
1 cup white wine
1 teaspoon oregano
1/2 cup sliced black olives
1/4 cup Parmesan cheese
1 cup shredded Monterey Jack cheese

Cut duckling into quarters and remove skin. Brown on all sides in oil in skillet. Add onion, garlic, green chilies and mushrooms. Cook for 5 minutes. Stir in salsa, wine and oregano. Simmer, covered, for 45 to 50 minutes or until duckling is tender. Stir in olives and Parmesan cheese. Sprinkle with Monterey Jack cheese. Cook, covered, for 2 minutes or until cheese melts. Serve over hot cooked noodles. Yield: 4 servings.

Approx Per Serving: Cal 523; Prot 27.7 g; Carbo 15.8 g; T Fat 37.1 g; Chol 87.0 mg; Potas 824.0 mg; Sod 627.0 mg.

Concord Farms, Inc.
MEMBER

ONE-DAY-AHEAD BARBECUED TURKEY

1 (14-pound) frozen turkey, thawed, cut into quarters
2 (18-ounce) bottles of Carolina Treet barbecue sauce
1 (32-ounce) bottle of catsup
1 cup margarine
1 1/3 cups packed light brown sugar
1/3 cup molasses
3 tablespoons Worcestershire sauce
1/2 cup vinegar
Soy sauce and crushed red pepper to taste

Place turkey in roasting pan. Roast at 325 degrees until brown, but not fully cooked. Heat barbecue sauce, catsup and margarine in saucepan until margarine melts, stirring constantly. Add remaining ingredients; mix well. Drain half the pan drippings from turkey. Pour sauce over turkey. Cover with foil. Bake at 325 degrees until done, turning and basting every 30 minutes. Remove turkey; cool slightly. Carve into chunks; return to sauce. Chill in refrigerator overnight. Bake, covered, at 350 degrees for 30 minutes. Bake, uncovered, for 30 minutes longer. Serve over rice. Yield: 8 servings.

Approx Per Serving: Cal 1221; Prot 121.0 g; Carbo 77.6 g; T Fat 46.0 g; Chol 303.0 mg; Potas 2109.0 mg; Sod 2840.0 mg.

Carolina Treet, Inc.
MEMBER

GRILLED TURKEY FILLETS

1 1/2 pounds House of Raeford turkey fillets
1/2 cup dry white wine
1/2 cup corn oil
1/4 cup soy sauce
1 teaspoon garlic salt
1 teaspoon MSG
1/4 teaspoon garlic powder

Place turkey in shallow dish. Combine wine, oil, soy sauce, garlic salt, MSG and garlic powder in small bowl. Pour over turkey. Marinate in refrigerator for 24 to 48 hours. Drain, reserving marinade. Grill 6 inches from hot coals for 20 to 30 minutes or until turkey is white and solid in center, turning and basting frequently with marinade. Do not overcook.
Yield: 4 servings.

Approx Per Serving: Cal 470; Prot 39.2 g; Carbo 1.8 g; T Fat 31.4 g; Chol 88.4 mg; Potas 441.0 mg; Sod 2716.0 mg.

House of Raeford, Inc.
MEMBER

HERBED PEPPERCORN TURKEY BREAST

4 (6-ounce) turkey breast tenderloins
2/3 cup dry white wine
3 tablespoons olive oil
2 teaspoons minced garlic
2 tablespoons chopped parsley
2 green onions, chopped
1 1/2 teaspoons bottled green peppercorns, crushed
1 bay leaf, crushed
1/2 teaspoon rosemary
1/2 teaspoon thyme
1/2 teaspoon salt
1 1/2 teaspoons coarsely ground fresh pepper
1 tablespoon olive oil
1 cup chicken broth
4 teaspoons cornstarch
1/4 teaspoon salt

Pierce turkey with fork. Combine wine, 3 tablespoons olive oil, garlic, parsley, onions, green peppercorns, bay leaf, rosemary and thyme in shallow dish. Add turkey, turning to coat both sides. Marinate in refrigerator for 2 hours or longer, turning at least once. Drain, reserving marinade. Pat dry with paper towels. Season turkey with 1/2 teaspoon salt and pepper. Let stand for 15 minutes. Spray skillet with nonstick cooking spray. Add 1 tablespoon olive oil. Heat oil over medium-high heat until hot. Add turkey. Cook for 5 to 7 minutes on each side or until tender. Remove to warm platter; keep warm. Pour reserved marinade into skillet. Bring to a boil. Cook for 2 minutes. Add mixture of chicken broth, cornstarch and 1/4 teaspoon salt. Cook until thickened, stirring constantly. Remove bay leaf. Serve with turkey. Yield: 4 servings.

Approx Per Serving: Cal 370; Prot 39.7 g; Carbo 4.1 g; T Fat 18.0 g; Chol 88.6 mg; Potas 505.0 mg; Sod 678.0 mg.

North Carolina Turkey Federation

TURKEY LASAGNA

8 lasagna noodles
1 (10-ounce) package frozen chopped spinach, thawed
1 small onion, finely chopped
3 cloves of garlic, crushed
1 teaspoon oregano
1 teaspoon basil
1/4 cup olive oil
1 pound ground turkey
1 (15-ounce) can tomato sauce
1/2 teaspoon thyme
3 tablespoons minced parsley
1 pint ricotta cheese
1 egg, well beaten
1 1/2 cups shredded mozzarella cheese
1/2 cup grated Parmesan cheese

Cook noodles and spinach using package directions; drain. Sauté onion and garlic with oregano and basil in oil in skillet until onion is tender. Add ground turkey. Cook until cooked through, stirring until crumbly. Add salt to taste. Combine tomato sauce, thyme and parsley in small bowl; mix well. Mix ricotta cheese with egg in small bowl. Arrange half the noodles in lightly greased 8x10-inch baking dish. Layer turkey mixture, half the tomato sauce, ricotta cheese mixture, spinach and mozzarella cheese over noodles. Top with remaining noodles and tomato sauce. Sprinkle with Parmesan cheese. Bake, tightly covered with foil, at 350 degrees for 25 minutes or until hot and bubbly. Yields: 6 servings.

Approx Per Serving: Cal 757; Prot 46.8 g; Carbo 70.5 g; T Fat 31.6 g; Chol 154.0 mg; Potas 923.0 mg; Sod 819.0 mg.

House of Raeford, Inc.
MEMBER

TURKEY PARMIGIANA

1 pound (1/4-inch thick) turkey breast cutlets
2 egg whites
1 tablespoon skim milk
1/2 cup seasoned bread crumbs
2 tablespoons Parmesan cheese
1 cup bottled Italian cooking sauce
4 (1-ounce) slices mozzarella cheese

Dip turkey in mixture of egg whites and skim milk; coat with mixture of bread crumbs and Parmesan cheese. Arrange in greased 10x15-inch baking dish. Bake at 400 degrees for 4 to 5 minutes or until brown. Pour Italian sauce over turkey cutlets. Top each cutlet with slice of mozzarella cheese. Bake for 4 to 5 minutes longer or until sauce is heated through and cheese is melted. Yield: 4 servings.

Approx Per Serving: Cal 351; Prot 38.7 g; Carbo 20.4 g; T Fat 11.8 g; Chol 76.6 mg; Potas 576.0 mg; Sod 679.0 mg.

North Carolina Poultry Federation

BROCCOLI AND TURKEY PASTA PIE

6 ounces angel hair pasta
2 eggs, slightly beaten
2 tablespoons melted butter
1/3 cup Parmesan cheese
2 cups broccoli flowerets
1 red bell pepper, cut into julienne strips
1 medium onion, thinly sliced
2 cloves of garlic, minced
2 teaspoons basil
1 tablespoon butter
1 1/2 cups chopped cooked turkey
1/3 cup Parmesan cheese
2 eggs, slightly beaten
1/4 cup half and half
1/4 teaspoon salt
1/4 teaspoon pepper
1/4 cup Parmesan cheese

Cook pasta using package directions; drain. Combine 2 eggs, 2 tablespoons melted butter and 1/3 cup Parmesan cheese in bowl; mix well. Stir in pasta until well coated. Press over bottom and side of greased 9-inch deep-dish pie plate. Place weights inside shell. Bake, covered, at 350 degrees for 10 minutes. Remove weights. Cook broccoli in steamer over boiling water for 10 minutes. Sauté red pepper, onion, garlic and basil in 1 tablespoon butter in skillet until red pepper is tender-crisp. Add broccoli, turkey and 1/3 cup Parmesan cheese; mix well. Remove from heat. Stir in mixture of 2 eggs, half and half, salt and pepper; mix well. Spoon into pasta shell. Sprinkle with remaining 1/4 cup Parmesan cheese. Cover with foil. Bake at 350 degrees for 35 minutes. Bake, uncovered, for 10 minutes longer. Let stand for 5 minutes before slicing. Yield: 6 servings.

Approx Per Serving: Cal 361; Prot 24.8 g; Carbo 27.7 g; T Fat 16.7 g; Chol 238.0 mg; Potas 430.0 mg; Sod 451.0 mg.

Albemarle Pride Broccoli
MEMBER

FRIED TURKEY STEAKS WITH GRAVY

1 pound thinly sliced turkey steaks
1/2 teaspoon salt
Pepper to taste
1/4 cup all-purpose flour
3 tablespoons butter
2 tablespoons all-purpose flour
1 cup milk

Season turkey with 1/2 teaspoon salt and pepper. Coat with 1/4 cup flour. Brown in butter in large skillet for 5 minutes on each side or until tender. Remove to warm platter; keep warm. Sift 2 tablespoons flour evenly into pan drippings. Sprinkle with salt and pepper to taste. Stir in milk. Simmer until thickened, stirring constantly. Serve with turkey steaks. Yield: 4 servings.

Approx Per Serving: Cal 289; Prot 28.8 g; Carbo 11.8 g; T Fat 13.5 g; Chol 90.5 mg; Potas 355.0 mg; Sod 419.0 mg.

House of Raeford, Inc.
MEMBER

ORIENTAL TURKEY SALAD

1 (6-ounce) package frozen snow peas
3 cups cooked thin turkey strips
1 cup green grape halves
1 cup diagonally sliced celery
1 (8-ounce) can sliced water chestnuts, drained
1 cup sour cream
1 teaspoon instant minced onion
1 teaspoon salt
1 teaspoon vinegar
1/4 teaspoon ginger
1/8 teaspoon paprika
2 cups chow mein noodles

Cook pea pods using package directions. Soak in cold water for 5 minutes; drain. Combine with turkey, grapes, celery and water chestnuts in bowl; toss well. Chill, covered, for several hours. Combine sour cream, onion, salt, vinegar, ginger and paprika in small bowl; mix well. Chill, covered, for several hours. Toss salad with sour cream dressing just before serving. Serve over bed of chow mein noodles. Yield: 4 servings.

Approx Per Serving: Cal 525; Prot 38.0 g; Carbo 41.1 g; T Fat 23.2 g; Chol 108.0 mg; Potas 997.0 mg; Sod 901.0 mg.

American Dairy Association of North Carolina

POCKET SANDWICHES

2 cups chopped cooked turkey
1/2 cup chopped celery
1/4 cup chopped onion
2 hard-boiled eggs, chopped
1 tablespoon lemon juice
1/2 teaspoon salt
1/4 teaspoon pepper
2/3 cup mayonnaise
2 pita bread rounds, cut into halves

Combine chicken, celery, onion, eggs, lemon juice, salt, pepper and mayonnaise in bowl; mix well. Spoon mixture into pita bread pockets. Yield: 4 servings.

Approx Per Serving: Cal 522; Prot 27.0 g; Carbo 19.4 g; T Fat 37.4 g; Chol 221.0 mg; Potas 314.0 mg; Sod 751.0 mg.

North Carolina Poultry Federation

HOUSE OF RAEFORD LOW-FAT SPAGHETTI SAUCE

1 pound House of
  Raeford ground turkey
2 cloves of garlic, crushed
1/3 cup instant minced
  onion
2 (15-ounce) cans Italian
  tomato sauce
5 teaspoons instant beef
  bouillon
1 cup vegetable juice
  cocktail
5 tablespoons
  Worcestershire sauce

Brown turkey with garlic in skillet, stirring until crumbly; drain. Combine onion, tomato sauce, bouillon, vegetable juice cocktail and Worcestershire sauce in saucepan; mix well. Stir in turkey mixture. Simmer over low heat for 1 hour, stirring occasionally. Serve over spaghetti. Yield: 4 servings.

Approx Per Serving: Cal 242; Prot 28.8 g; Carbo 22.9 g; T Fat 4.7 g; Chol 65.0 mg; Potas 1339.0 mg; Sod 1771.0 mg.

House of Raeford, Inc.
MEMBER

BROILED CATFISH

1/3 cup soy sauce
1/4 teaspoon Tabasco sauce
3 tablespoons oil
1 clove of garlic, crushed
1/2 teaspoon ginger
1/2 teaspoon salt
1/4 teaspoon freshly
  ground pepper
6 (8-ounce) catfish fillets

Combine soy sauce, Tabasco sauce, oil, garlic, ginger, salt and pepper in bowl; mix well. Add fish. Marinate for 30 minutes. Drain, reserving marinade. Place fish on oiled broiler pan. Broil 4 inches from heat source for 8 to 10 minutes or until fish flakes easily with fork, basting occasionally with reserved marinade. Serve with lemon wedges. Yield: 6 servings.

Approx Per Serving: Cal 333; Prot 42.2 g; Carbo 1.7 g; T Fat 16.5 g; Chol 132.0 mg; Potas 825.0 mg; Sod 1227.0 mg.
Nutritional information includes entire amount of marinade.

Carolina Classics Catfish, Inc.
MEMBER

BLACKENED CATFISH

1 tablespoon paprika
1 teaspoon onion powder
1 teaspoon garlic powder
3/4 teaspoon freshly ground black pepper
1 teaspoon cayenne pepper
3/4 teaspoon white pepper
1/2 teaspoon thyme
1/2 teaspoon oregano
6 (8-ounce) skinless catfish fillets
6 tablespoons melted margarine

Combine paprika, onion powder, garlic powder, black pepper, cayenne pepper, white pepper, thyme and oregano in shallow dish. Dip fillets in margarine; coat well with seasoning mixture. Heat large cast-iron skillet over very high heat for 10 minutes or until it is beyond the smoking stage and has a white ash in the bottom. Place fillets in single layer in skillet. Cook over high heat for 2 minutes on each side or until fish is blackened and flakes easily with fork. Unless you have a very good exhaust fan for blackening fish, cook it outside. Yield: 6 servings.

Approx Per Serving: Cal 374; Prot 41.8 g; Carbo 2.1 g; T Fat 21.3 g; Chol 132.0 mg; Potas 846.0 mg; Sod 278.0 mg.

Carolina Classics Catfish, Inc.
MEMBER

CHARCOAL GRILLED CATFISH

6 (8-ounce) catfish fillets
1/4 cup oil
1/2 teaspoon garlic salt
1/2 teaspoon white pepper

Brush skinless side of fillets with oil; sprinkle with garlic salt and pepper. Place in oiled hinged fish basket. Place skin side down on grill 4 inches from medium coals. Grill for 5 minutes on each side or until fish flakes easily with fork. Yield: 6 servings.

Approx Per Serving: Cal 344; Prot 41.3 g; Carbo 0.1 g; T Fat 18.7 g; Chol 132.0 mg; Potas 792.0 mg; Sod 321.0 mg.

Carolina Classics Catfish, Inc.
MEMBER

CATFISH DIANE

1 1/2 cups all-purpose flour
1 teaspoon dry mustard
1 tablespoon salt
1 teaspoon pepper
1/4 cup butter
1/4 cup oil
2 pounds catfish fillets
3 tablespoons lemon juice
1 teaspoon Worcestershire sauce
2 tablespoons soy sauce
1 cup chicken broth
2 teaspoons frozen chives
1 (2 1/2-ounce) jar button mushrooms, drained

Sift flour, dry mustard, salt and pepper into shallow dish. Heat butter with oil to medium hot in 10-inch skillet. Coat fish with seasoning mixture. Place in skillet. Fry for 5 to 6 minutes on each side or until fish is golden brown and flakes easily with fork. Remove fish to warm platter. Add lemon juice, Worcestershire sauce, soy sauce, broth, chives and mushrooms to pan drippings in skillet. Bring to a boil. Pour over fish. Garnish with parsley. Yield: 6 servings.

Approx Per Serving: Cal 453; Prot 32.3 g; Carbo 25.9 g; T Fat 23.8 g; Chol 109.0 mg; Potas 641.0 mg; Sod 1759.0 mg.

Carolina Classics Catfish, Inc.
MEMBER

SPICY FRIED CATFISH

1 cup yellow cornmeal
1 1/2 teaspoons paprika
1/4 teaspoon dry mustard
1/2 teaspoon onion powder
1/2 teaspoon celery salt
1/2 teaspoon salt
1/2 teaspoon freshly ground pepper
6 (8-ounce) catfish fillets
Oil for frying

Combine cornmeal, paprika, dry mustard, onion powder, celery salt, salt and pepper in dish. Coat fish well with cornmeal mixture. Place in single layer in hot oil in large skillet. Fry over medium heat for 4 to 5 minutes on each side or until fillets are golden brown and flake easily with fork. Drain on paper towel. Serve with lemon wedges and tartar sauce. Yield: 6 servings.

Approx Per Serving: Cal 338; Prot 43.2 g; Carbo 15.6 g; T Fat 10.6 g; Chol 132.0 mg; Potas 867.0 mg; Sod 499.0 mg.
Nutritional information does not include oil for frying.

Carolina Classics Catfish, Inc.
MEMBER

CATFISH ROLL-UPS

2 tablespoons chopped green pepper
2 tablespoons chopped onion
2 tablespoons margarine
1/4 cup chopped toasted almonds
1/2 cup fresh bread crumbs
1 tablespoon lime juice
1/4 teaspoon oregano
1 tablespoon chopped fresh parsley
1/2 teaspoon salt
4 (8-ounce) catfish fillets
1 cup water
2 tablespoons chopped onion
2 cloves of garlic, crushed
3 tablespoons lime juice
1 bay leaf
1 teaspoon red pepper flakes

Sauté green pepper and 2 tablespoons onion lightly in margarine in skillet. Add almonds, bread crumbs, 1 tablespoon lime juice, oregano, parsley and salt; mix well. Spoon mixture down centers of catfish fillets. Roll fillets to enclose filling; secure with toothpicks. Place in shallow baking pan. Combine water, 2 tablespoons onion, garlic, 3 tablespoons lime juice, bay leaf and red pepper in small saucepan. Bring to a boil; reduce heat. Simmer for 15 minutes. Pour over catfish. Bake at 400 degrees for 30 to 35 minutes or until fish flakes easily with fork, basting occasionally. Remove bay leaf. Garnish with strips of lime rind. Yield: 4 servings.

Approx Per Serving: Cal 384; Prot 43.7 g; Carbo 6.7 g; T Fat 19.9 g; Chol 132.0 mg; Potas 918.0 mg; Sod 498.0 mg.

Carolina Classics Catfish, Inc.
MEMBER

ROLLED FISH FILLETS WITH HERBS

1 1/2 pounds fish fillets
1 teaspoon salt
Pepper and marjoram to taste
1 1/2 cups milk
2 tablespoons butter
2 tablespoons all-purpose flour
3/4 cup shredded Cheddar cheese
2 tablespoons Sherry

Sprinkle fish fillets with salt, pepper and marjoram. Roll and secure with toothpicks. Place in shallow baking dish. Pour milk over top. Bake at 350 degrees for 30 minutes. Melt butter in saucepan. Stir in flour. Drain fish, reserving cooking liquid. Stir reserved liquid into flour mixture in saucepan. Cook until thickened, stirring constantly. Stir in cheese until melted. Add Sherry. Place fish on serving plate. Pour sauce over fish. Yield: 6 servings.

Approx Per Serving: Cal 324; Prot 35.5 g; Carbo 5.1 g; T Fat 16.3 g; Chol 1.8 mg; Potas 644.0 mg; Sod 589.0 mg.

North Carolina Department of Agriculture

FLOUNDER KIEV

1/2 cup butter, softened
1 tablespoon fresh lemon juice
3/4 teaspoon Worcestershire sauce
1/4 teaspoon hot pepper sauce
1 clove of garlic, minced
2 tablespoons chopped parsley
2 pounds flounder fillets
1/2 teaspoon salt
Pepper to taste
1/2 cup all-purpose flour
2 eggs, beaten
2 tablespoons water
Bread crumbs
Oil for deep frying

Combine butter, lemon juice, Worcestershire sauce, hot sauce, garlic and parsley in bowl; mix well. Shape into roll on waxed paper. Chill until firm. Remove skin from fillets; cut fillets into twelve 2x6-inch strips. Sprinkle with salt and pepper. Cut butter roll into 12 pieces. Place 1 piece butter at end of each fish strip. Roll to enclose butter; secure with toothpicks. Coat well with flour. Dip in mixture of eggs and water. Roll in crumbs, coating well. Chill for 1 hour. Heat oil to 375 degrees. Deep-fry fish for 2 to 3 minutes or until fish is golden brown and flakes easily with fork. Drain on paper towel. Remove toothpicks.
Yield: 6 servings.

Approx Per Serving: Cal 340; Prot 31.8 g; Carbo 8.7 g; T Fat 19.1 g; Chol 205.0 mg; Potas 599.0 mg; Sod 460.0 mg.
Nutritional information does not include bread crumbs or oil.

North Carolina Department of Agriculture.

FLOUNDER SUPREME

2 pounds flounder fillets
1 teaspoon salt
Pepper to taste
1 (4-ounce) can sliced mushrooms
1/2 cup chopped onion
2 tablespoons butter
1/4 cup dry white wine
1 tablespoon chopped parsley
1 tablespoon all-purpose flour
3/4 cup half and half
White pepper to taste
1/4 cup shredded Cheddar cheese

Sprinkle fish fillets with salt and pepper. Roll fillets; secure with toothpicks. Drain mushrooms, reserving 1/4 cup liquid. Sauté mushrooms and onion in butter in large skillet. Add fish rolls, reserved liquid and wine. Sprinkle fish with parsley; cover. Bring to a boil; reduce heat. Simmer for 8 to 10 minutes or until fish flakes easily with fork. Remove fish to ovenproof platter. Blend flour and half and half in small bowl. Stir gradually into hot cooking liquid. Cook until thickened, stirring constantly. Add white pepper. Pour over fish. Sprinkle with cheese. Broil 5 inches from heat source for 2 to 3 minutes or until cheese is melted and light brown. Yield: 6 servings.

Approx Per Serving: Cal 250; Prot 31.2 g; Carbo 4.4 g; T Fat 10.8 g; Chol 99.0 mg; Potas 647.0 mg; Sod 633.0 mg.

North Carolina Department of Agriculture

CRAB MEAT ST. JACQUES

1/4 onion, chopped
1/2 green bell pepper, chopped
1 (4-ounce) can chopped mushrooms, drained
2 tablespoons butter
2 cups white sauce
1 pound canned crab meat
1 teaspoon Worcestershire sauce
Paprika to taste
Salt and pepper to taste
1 cup shredded Cheddar cheese
1 cup buttered bread crumbs

Sauté onion, green pepper and mushrooms in butter in saucepan until tender. Stir in white sauce, crab meat, Worcestershire sauce, paprika and salt and pepper. Spoon into greased baking dish. Sprinkle with cheese and bread crumbs. Top with additional paprika. Bake at 350 degrees until bubbly. Yield: 4 servings.

Approx Per Serving: Cal 430; Prot 36.8 g; Carbo 17.6 g; T Fat 23.5 g; Chol 163.0 mg; Potas 771.0 mg; Sod 1172.0 mg.

North Carolina Department of Agriculture

HOT CRAB MEAT PIE

1 (6 1/2-ounce) can crab meat, drained
6 ounces cream cheese, softened
2 tablespoons instant minced onion
1 tablespoon milk
1/2 teaspoon horseradish
1/4 teaspoon salt
Pepper to taste
1/3 cup sliced blanched almonds

Combine crab meat, cream cheese, onion, milk, horseradish, salt and pepper in bowl; mix well. Spoon into greased 8-inch pie plate. Sprinkle with almonds. Bake at 375 degrees for 15 to 20 minutes or until heated through. Yield: 8 servings.

Approx Per Serving: Cal 137; Prot 7.6 g; Carbo 2.5 g; T Fat 11.0 g; Chol 46.5 mg; Potas 163.0 mg; Sod 196.0 mg.

North Carolina Department of Agriculture

SEAFOOD EN CASSEROLE

1 cup dry white wine
1 small onion, sliced
1/2 bay leaf
6 sprigs parsley
1 teaspoon salt
1 (8-ounce) package frozen scallops, thawed, sliced
1 (8-ounce) can sliced mushrooms
2 teaspoons fresh lemon juice
1/4 cup butter
1/4 cup all-purpose flour
1 cup cooked crab meat
1 cup flaked, cooked mild fish
1 cup cooked shrimp
Pepper to taste
6 tablespoons shredded Swiss cheese
1/2 cup bread crumbs

Bring wine, onion, bay leaf, parsley and salt to a boil in saucepan. Add scallops. Simmer for 10 minutes. Drain, straining and reserving broth. Drain mushrooms, reserving liquid. Combine reserved broth, reserved mushroom liquid and lemon juice in measuring cup. Add enough water to measure 2 cups. Melt butter in saucepan. Blend in flour. Add 2 cups liquid gradually. Cook over very low heat for 10 minutes or until thickened, stirring constantly. Add scallops, crab meat, fish, shrimp, pepper and mushrooms; mix gently. Cook just until heated through. Spoon into 2-quart casserole or individual shells. Top with cheese and bread crumbs. Broil just until light brown. Yield: 8 servings.

Approx Per Serving: Cal 276; Prot 26.3 g; Carbo 11.7 g; T Fat 11.5 g; Chol 119.0 mg; Potas 521.0 mg; Sod 572.0 mg.

North Carolina Department of Agriculture

OYSTERS AND MACARONI AU GRATIN

3 tablespoons butter
3 tablespoons all-purpose flour
1 1/2 cups milk
1 cup cooked macaroni
1 pint oysters, drained
1 teaspoon salt
1/8 teaspoon pepper
1 cup shredded American cheese

Melt butter in double boiler. Blend in flour. Add milk gradually. Cook until thickened, stirring constantly. Layer half the macaroni and half the oysters in buttered baking dish. Sprinkle with half the salt, pepper and cheese. Repeat layers. Pour sauce over layers. Top with additional cheese. Bake at 350 degrees for 30 minutes or until light brown. Yield: 6 servings.

Approx Per Serving: Cal 256; Prot 13.3 g; Carbo 14.7 g; T Fat 15.9 g; Chol 87.1 mg; Potas 57.0 mg; Sod 792.0 mg.

North Carolina Department of Agriculture

SHRIMP DINNER CASSEROLE

1 cup chopped celery
1½ cups chopped green onions with tops
3 cloves of garlic, minced
⅓ cup butter
1 can cream of mushroom soup
½ cup water
3 cups cooked rice
2 slices bread, moistened
3 tablespoons minced parsley
1 teaspoon salt
¼ teaspoon pepper
1 pound peeled shrimp, cut into halves
¾ cup buttered bread crumbs

Sauté celery, green onions and garlic in butter in saucepan until tender. Add soup, water, rice, bread and parsley; mix well. Cook for 10 minutes. Add salt, pepper and shrimp. Spoon into greased 2½-quart casserole. Top with buttered bread crumbs. Bake at 375 degrees for 30 minutes.
Yield: 6 servings.

Approx Per Serving: Cal 376; Prot 20.6 g; Carbo 37.8 g; T Fat 15.5 g; Chol 175.0 mg; Potas 356.0 mg; Sod 1108.0 mg.

North Carolina Department of Agriculture

SHRIMP AND PEPPER COMBO

½ cup pineapple juice
2 teaspoons brown sugar
2 teaspoons fresh lemon juice
1 teaspoon soy sauce
1 pound fresh medium shrimp, cleaned
1 (6-ounce) jar red peppers, cut into 1-inch squares
1 green bell pepper, cut into 1-inch squares

Combine pineapple juice, brown sugar, lemon juice and soy sauce in bowl; mix well. Alternate shrimp with red peppers and green pepper on skewers. Brush with sauce. Place on lower rack of grill over medium coals. Grill for 8 to 10 minutes or until golden brown, turning one or more times and basting frequently with sauce.
Yield: 4 servings.

Approx Per Serving: Cal 156; Prot 24.5 g; Carbo 10.4 g; T Fat 1.6 g; Chol 221.0 mg; Potas 394.0 mg; Sod 344.0 mg.

North Carolina Department of Agriculture

Vegetables and Side Dishes

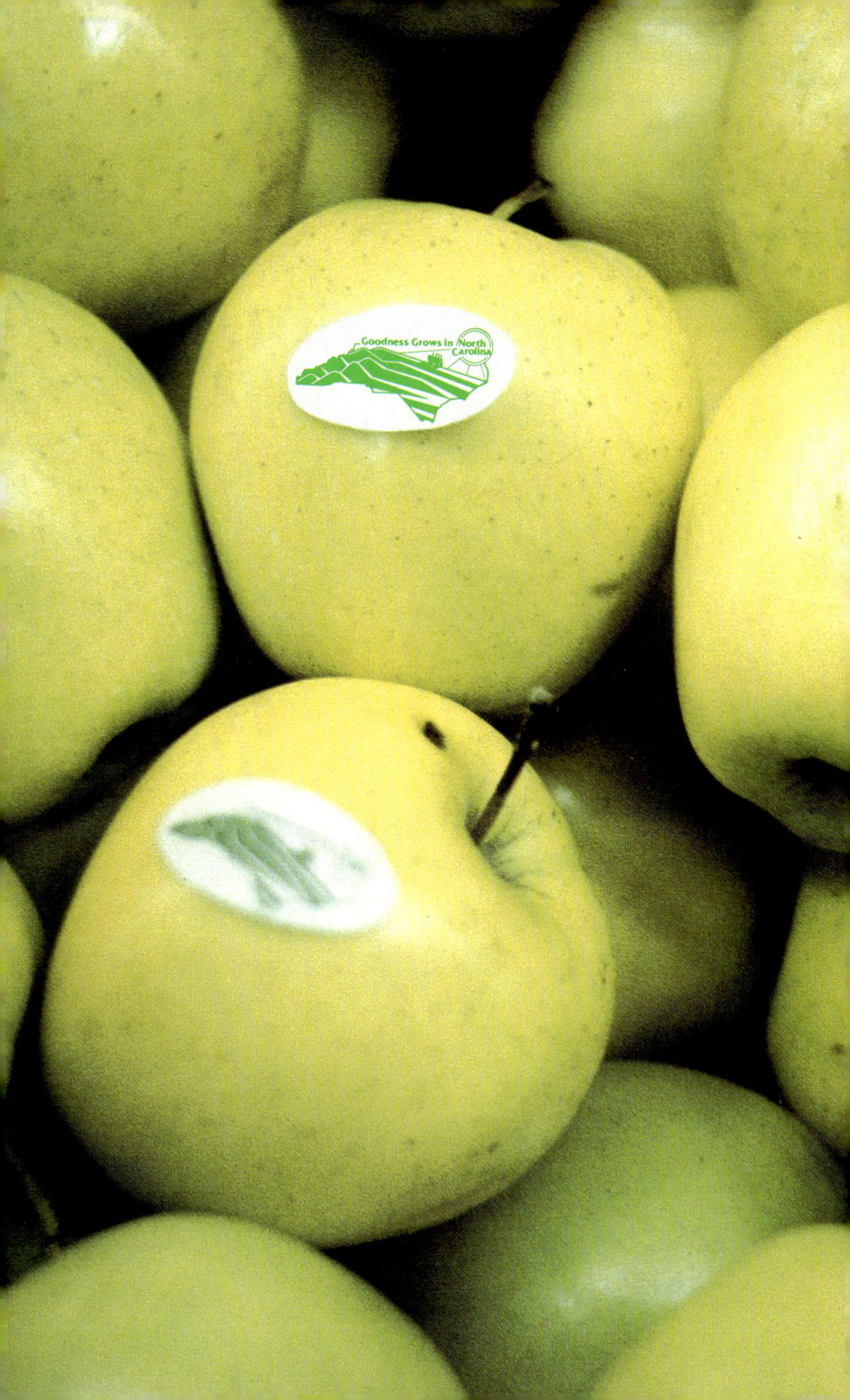
Goodness Grows In North Carolina

CAROLINA TREET BAKED BEANS

1 pound ground beef
½ medium green bell pepper, chopped
1 medium onion, chopped
½ cup Carolina Treet barbecue sauce
½ cup catsup
1 (31-ounce) can pork and beans
¼ cup packed brown sugar

Brown ground beef in skillet, stirring until crumbly; drain. Add green pepper, onion, barbecue sauce, catsup, pork and beans, brown sugar and salt and pepper to taste; mix well. Spoon into baking dish. Bake at 350 degrees for 35 minutes.
Yield: 6 servings.

Approx Per Serving: Cal 403; Prot 21.7 g; Carbo 49.7 g; T Fat 14.2 g; Chol 58.5 mg; Potas 756.0 mg; Sod 948.0 mg.

Carolina Treet, Inc.
MEMBER

GREEN BEAN AND CORN CASSEROLE

1 (16-ounce) can French-style green beans, drained
1 (12-ounce) can Mexican-style corn, drained
½ cup chopped celery
½ cup chopped onion
½ cup shredded sharp Cheddar cheese
½ cup sour cream
1 can cream of celery soup
¼ teaspoon white pepper
¼ cup melted butter
½ cup slivered almonds
1 cup herb-seasoned stuffing mix

Combine beans, corn, celery, onion, cheese, sour cream, soup and white pepper in bowl; mix well. Spoon into lightly greased 8x8-inch baking dish. Mix butter, almonds and stuffing mix in bowl; toss gently. Sprinkle over casserole. Bake at 350 degrees for 45 minutes. Yield: 6 servings.

Approx Per Serving: Cal 359; Prot 10.0 g; Carbo 30.6 g; T Fat 24.1 g; Chol 44.8 mg; Potas 410.0 mg; Sod 1004.0 mg.

North Carolina Department of Agriculture

ORIENTAL GREEN BEANS

8 ounces fresh green beans, trimmed, cut into halves
1 tablespoon oil
1/3 cup water
1/4 to 1/2 teaspoon ginger
1 teaspoon soy sauce

Sauté beans in oil in skillet over high heat for 4 minutes. Add mixture of water and ginger; reduce heat. Simmer, covered, for 15 minutes or until beans are tender-crisp. Toss with soy sauce. Yield: 2 servings.

Approx Per Serving: Cal 98; Prot 2.2 g; Carbo 8.5 g; T Fat 7.0 g; Chol 75.8 mg; Potas 245.0 mg; Sod 178.0 mg.

North Carolina Department of Agriculture

BROCCOLI GOURMET

2 (10-ounce) packages frozen chopped broccoli
2 eggs, beaten
1 can cream of mushroom soup
1 cup shredded sharp cheese
1/2 cup soybean oil mayonnaise
1/4 cup chopped onion
1 (2-ounce) jar chopped pimento
1 (8-ounce) can sliced water chestnuts
1/4 cup melted soybean oil margarine
3/4 cup fine dry bread crumbs
1/8 teaspoon garlic salt

Cook broccoli using package directions for 4 minutes; drain. Combine eggs with soup, cheese, mayonnaise, onion, pimento and water chestnuts in bowl; mix well. Add broccoli. Spoon into greased 2-quart baking dish. Mix margarine, bread crumbs and garlic salt in bowl. Sprinkle over casserole. Bake at 325 degrees for 30 to 40 minutes or until golden brown and bubbly. Yield: 8 servings.

Approx Per Serving: Cal 338; Prot 9.5 g; Carbo 18.4 g; T Fat 26.3 g; Chol 92.4 mg; Potas 348.0 mg; Sod 677.0 mg.

North Carolina Soybean Producers Association

VEGETABLES & SIDE DISHES

CANADIAN-STYLE BACON AND BROCCOLI

2 tablespoons butter
2 tablespoons all-purpose flour
1/2 teaspoon Worcestershire sauce
Tabasco sauce to taste
1/8 teaspoon salt
Coarsely ground pepper to taste
3/4 cup milk
2 tablespoons sour cream
2 tablespoons mayonnaise
1/2 teaspoon prepared mustard
1/2 cup shredded Cheddar cheese
1 (10-ounce) package frozen broccoli spears, partially cooked
8 slices Lundy's Canadian-style bacon
Paprika to taste

Melt butter in medium saucepan. Blend in flour, Worcestershire sauce, Tabasco sauce, salt and pepper. Add milk gradually. Cook until thickened, stirring constantly. Reduce heat. Stir in sour cream, mayonnaise, mustard and cheese. Cook until cheese melts, stirring constantly. Alternate layers of broccoli and bacon slices in small baking dish until all ingredients are used. Spoon sauce over layers. Sprinkle with paprika. Bake at 350 degrees for 25 to 30 minutes or until bubbly. Yield: 4 servings.

Approx Per Serving: Cal 321; Prot 19.3 g; Carbo 10.4 g; T Fat 23.0 g; Chol 70.8 mg; Potas 408.0 mg; Sod 1018.0 mg.

Lundy Packing Company
MEMBER

COUNTRY SWEET AND SOUR CABBAGE

2 apples, chopped
1 onion, chopped
1 1/2 tablespoons shortening
1/2 medium head red cabbage, shredded
1/2 cup water
1/2 cup packed brown sugar
1/2 cup vinegar
1 tablespoon butter
1/8 teaspoon salt

Sauté apples and onion in shortening in skillet for 10 minutes. Add cabbage and water gradually. Cook for 10 to 15 minutes or until cabbage is tender. Add brown sugar and vinegar. Cook to serving temperature. Stir in butter, salt and pepper to taste just before serving. Yield: 4 servings.

Approx Per Serving: Cal 247; Prot 1.6 g; Carbo 46.0 g; T Fat 8.2 g; Chol 7.8 mg; Potas 412.0 mg; Sod 115.0 mg.

North Carolina Department of Agriculture

STEAMED CABBAGE WITH CHEESE SAUCE

1 head cabbage, shredded
2 tablespoons butter
2 tablespoons all-purpose flour
1/4 teaspoon salt
White pepper to taste
1 1/4 cups milk
1 cup shredded cheese

Steam cabbage just until tender. Melt butter in saucepan over low heat. Blend in flour, salt and white pepper. Add milk at at once. Cook until thickened, stirring constantly. Stir in cheese until melted. Pour over cabbage in serving dish. Yield: 4 servings.

Approx Per Serving: Cal 258; Prot 11.7 g; Carbo 14.4 g; T Fat 18.0 g; Chol 55.6 mg; Potas 480.0 mg; Sod 413.0 mg.

North Carolina Department of Agriculture

ITALIAN CAULIFLOWER AND BROCCOLI TOSS

1 cup mayonnaise
1/2 cup sour cream
1 small onion, chopped
1 envelope Italian salad dressing mix
2 tablespoons minced parsley
Flowerets of 1 1/2 pounds fresh broccoli
Flowerets of 1 head cauliflower
1 cup shredded mozzarella cheese

Combine mayonnaise, sour cream, onion, salad dressing mix and parsley in bowl; mix well. Combine broccoli, cauliflower and cheese in serving bowl. Add dressing mixture; toss gently to mix. Chill for 3 hours or longer. Yield: 10 servings.

Approx Per Serving: Cal 248; Prot 5.8 g; Carbo 8.1 g; T Fat 22.6 g; Chol 26.9 mg; Potas 424.0 mg; Sod 198.0 mg.

Albemarle Pride Broccoli
MEMBER

PARMESAN CORN ON THE COB

4 ears of fresh corn
1/4 cup butter, softened
1/4 cup Parmesan cheese
1 1/2 teaspoons chopped fresh parsley
1/4 teaspoon dried whole salad herbs

Remove husks and silks from corn just before cooking. Combine butter, cheese, parsley and herbs in bowl; mix well. Spread on corn. Place each ear on sheet of heavy-duty plastic wrap. Roll wrap lengthwise around ear, twisting ends to seal. Arrange spoke fashion on microwave-safe plate. Microwave on High for 10 to 13 minutes or until tender, rearranging ears occasionally. Add salt to taste. Yield: 4 servings.

Approx Per Serving: Cal 224; Prot 6.0 g; Carbo 22.1 g; T Fat 14.4 g; Chol 35.0 mg; Potas 324.0 mg; Sod 209.0 mg.

North Carolina Corn Growers Association

TWO-CORN CASSEROLE

3/4 cup chopped green bell pepper
1/3 cup chopped onion
1/2 cup margarine
1 (17-ounce) can whole kernel corn
1 (17-ounce) can cream-style corn
3 eggs, beaten
1 (8-ounce) package corn muffin mix
1 cup shredded Cheddar cheese

Sauté green pepper and onion in margarine in skillet until tender. Combine corn, eggs and corn muffin mix in large bowl; mix well. Add onion mixture; mix well. Pour into greased 2-quart baking dish. Sprinkle with cheese. Bake at 350 degrees for 55 minutes to 1 hour or until set. Let stand for 5 minutes before serving. Yield: 12 servings.

Approx Per Serving: Cal 230; Prot 6.2 g; Carbo 22.9 g; T Fat 13.8 g; Chol 78.4 mg; Potas 173.0 mg; Sod 462.0 mg.

North Carolina Corn Growers Association

CORN PUDDING

1/2 cup butter
2 cups fresh whole kernel corn
4 eggs, beaten
2 tablespoons sugar
2 tablespoons all-purpose flour
1 teaspoon salt

Melt butter in 2-quart baking dish. Combine corn, eggs, sugar, flour and salt in bowl; mix well. Pour into baking dish. Bake at 350 degrees for 10 minutes. Stir mixture well. Bake for 35 minutes longer. Yield: 4 servings.

Approx Per Serving: Cal 387; Prot 9.2 g; Carbo 24.4 g; T Fat 29.5 g; Chol 336.0 mg; Potas 284.0 mg; Sod 807.0 mg.

North Carolina Corn Growers Association

ORIENTAL MUSHROOMS

1/4 cup chopped onion
1/4 cup butter
1 pound fresh mushrooms, sliced
2 teaspoons all-purpose flour
1/2 cup water
1 beef bouillon cube
2 tablespoons soy sauce
1/4 cup slivered almonds

Sauté onion in butter in skillet until tender. Stir in mushrooms. Sprinkle with flour; stir until mushrooms are coated. Add water, bouillon cube and soy sauce; mix until bouillon dissolves. Cook over medium heat for 3 minutes, stirring constantly. Spoon into serving dish. Sprinkle with almonds. Serve as vegetable side dish or as sauce over steak. Yield: 4 servings.

Approx Per Serving: Cal 194; Prot 5.0 g; Carbo 9.7 g; T Fat 16.5 g; Chol 31.1 mg; Potas 523.0 mg; Sod 833.0 mg.

North Carolina Soybean Growers Association

HERBED ONIONS

Leaves from 3 sprigs of fresh thyme or 1/2 teaspoon dried thyme
1/4 cup butter
2 large Vidalia onions, thinly sliced

Sauté thyme in butter in skillet for 5 minutes. Add onions. Cook, covered, for 15 minutes or until tender. Serve with meats. Yield: 4 servings.

Approx Per Serving: Cal 231; Prot 1.2 g; Carbo 6.0 g; T Fat 23.2 g; Chol 62.1 mg; Potas 133.0 mg; Sod 195.0 mg.

North Carolina Herb Association

VEGETABLES & SIDE DISHES

STUFFED PEPPERS

1 chicken bouillon cube
1 1/2 cups boiling water
1 cup bulgur
4 green bell peppers
1 small onion, chopped
1 clove of garlic, minced
1 tablespoon butter
1 tablespoon chopped fresh basil or 1 teaspoon dried basil
2 tomatoes, peeled, coarsely chopped

Dissolve bouillon cube in boiling water in saucepan. Pour over bulgur in bowl. Let stand until water is absorbed. Core and seed green peppers. Parboil in water to cover in saucepan for 5 to 10 minutes or just until tender; drain. Sauté onion and garlic in butter in skillet until onion is tender. Add basil and tomatoes. Cook until tomatoes are tender, stirring constantly. Add bulgur. Cook until heated through. Stuff into peppers. Place in baking dish. Spoon any remaining stuffing mixture around peppers. Bake at 350 degrees for 30 minutes. May sprinkle with Parmesan cheese before baking if desired. Yield: 4 servings.

Approx Per Serving: Cal 229; Prot 6.9 g; Carbo 43.9 g; T Fat 4.3 g; Chol 7.8 mg; Potas 547.0 mg; Sod 324.0 mg.

North Carolina Herb Association

GOURMET POTATOES

2 cups shredded Cheddar cheese
1/2 cup butter
1 1/2 cups sour cream at room temperature
1/2 cup chopped green onions
1 teaspoon salt
1/2 teaspoon pepper
8 medium potatoes, peeled, coarsely shredded
2 tablespoons butter

Heat cheese and 1/2 cup butter in saucepan over low heat until partially melted, stirring occasionally; remove from heat. Stir in sour cream, green onions, salt and pepper. Fold in potatoes. Spoon into greased 8-inch glass baking dish. Dot with 2 tablespoons butter. Bake at 350 degrees for 25 minutes or microwave, covered, on High for 12 minutes. Yield: 8 servings.

Approx Per Serving: Cal 480; Prot 11.7 g; Carbo 36.2 g; T Fat 33.0 g; Chol 87.7 mg; Potas 722.0 mg; Sod 594.0 mg.

North Carolina 3-N-1 Potatoes
MEMBER

VEGETABLES & SIDE DISHES 104

COUNTRY-STYLE POTATOES

1/4 cup melted butter
3 cups chopped cooked
   potatoes
3/4 teaspoon basil
1/2 teaspoon salt
1/8 teaspoon pepper
1 medium onion, chopped

Melt butter in skillet. Add potatoes, basil, salt and pepper. Sauté until potatoes are light brown. Add onion. Cook just until onion is tender-crisp. Yield: 6 servings.

Approx Per Serving: Cal 150; Prot 2.0 g; Carbo 18.9 g; T Fat 7.8 g; Chol 20.7 mg; Potas 356.0 mg; Sod 247.0 mg.

North Carolina 3-N-1 Potatoes
MEMBER

SUMMER SQUASH CASSEROLE

2 pounds fresh squash
1 medium onion, minced
1 carrot, grated
1/2 cup melted margarine
1 can cream of chicken
   soup
1 cup sour cream
1/2 cup shredded Cheddar
   cheese
1 (8-ounce) package
   stuffing mix

Slice squash. Combine with onion, carrot, margarine, soup, sour cream, cheese and half the stuffing mix in bowl; mix well. Spoon into baking dish. Sprinkle with remaining stuffing mix. Bake at 350 degrees for 25 minutes or until bubbly. Yield: 6 servings.

Approx Per Serving: Cal 417; Prot 9.7 g; Carbo 29.0 g; T Fat 30.4 g; Chol 30.9 mg; Potas 514.0 mg; Sod 907.0 mg.

North Carolina Department of Agriculture

SUMMER SQUASH PARMESAN

3 cups thinly sliced
   squash
1 cup thinly sliced onion
3 tablespoons cottonseed
   oil
1/2 teaspoon salt
1/4 teaspoon pepper
1/4 cup Parmesan cheese

Combine squash, onion and oil in glass dish; cover tightly with plastic wrap. Microwave on High for 5 to 8 minutes or until tender. Stir in salt, pepper and cheese. Let stand for several minutes. May stir in 1 to 2 teaspoons dillweed, 1 teaspoon paprika and 2 tablespoons vinegar at serving time if desired. Yield: 4 servings.

Approx Per Serving: Cal 147; Prot 3,7 g; Carbo 7.4 g; T Fat 12.1 g; Chol 3.9 mg; Potas 259.0 mg; Sod 364.0 mg.

North Carolina Cotton Promotion Association

VEGETABLES & SIDE DISHES

EXQUISITE SWEET POTATO CASSEROLE

3 cups mashed cooked sweet potatoes
1 cup sugar
2 eggs
1/2 cup margarine
1 cup raisins
1 teaspoon vanilla extract
1 cup packed brown sugar
1/3 cup all-purpose flour
1/2 cup margarine, softened
1 cup coconut
1 cup chopped pecans

Combine sweet potatoes, sugar, eggs, 1/2 cup margarine, raisins and vanilla in bowl; mix well. Spoon into baking dish. Mix brown sugar, flour, 1/2 cup margarine, coconut and pecans in bowl. Sprinkle over casserole. Bake at 350 degrees for 30 minutes. Yield: 6 servings.

Approx Per Serving: Cal 990; Prot 8.4 g; Carbo 135.0 g; T Fat 50.0 g; Chol 91.3 mg; Potas 763.0 mg; Sod 527.0 mg.

Carolina Nut Cracker
MEMBER

CANDIED SWEET POTATOES

1 cup sugar
1/4 cup orange juice
1/2 teaspoon cinnamon
1/2 teaspoon nutmeg
3 pounds sweet potatoes
1 teaspoon lemon juice
1/2 cup margarine

Combine sugar, orange juice, cinnamon and nutmeg in bowl; mix well. Peel sweet potatoes. Cut into halves lengthwise and then into 1/2-inch slices. Arrange 1 layer sweet potatoes in 10x15-inch baking dish. Sprinkle with a small amount of sugar mixture and lemon juice. Dot with margarine. Repeat layers until all ingredients are used. Bake at 350 degrees for 1 hour and 15 minutes, basting occasionally with pan juices. Yield: 8 servings.

Approx Per Serving: Cal 262; Prot 1.2 g; Carbo 39.9 g; T Fat 11.5 g; Chol 0.0 mg; Potas 223.0 mg; Sod 141.0 mg.

Wingfield Farms
MEMBER

MARINATED TOMATOES

1/2 cup soybean oil
1/4 cup vinegar
1 clove of garlic, minced
1 tablespoon sugar
1/2 teaspoon salt
1/4 teaspoon pepper
4 tomatoes, sliced or cut into quarters

Combine oil, vinegar, garlic, sugar, salt and pepper in jar with lid. Cover; shake to mix well. Pour over tomatoes in serving bowl. Marinate in refrigerator for 1 hour or longer. May store marinade, covered, in refrigerator for several days.
Yield: 4 servings.

Approx Per Serving: Cal 280; Prot 1.2 g; Carbo 9.7 g; T Fat 27.5 g; Chol 0.0 mg; Potas 275.0 mg; Sod 277.0 mg.

North Carolina Soybean Producers Association

TURNIPS IN CHEESE SAUCE

3 cups sliced peeled turnips
1/4 cup butter
1/4 cup all-purpose flour
1 1/2 cups light cream
1 tablespoon minced chives
1 cup shredded American cheese

Cook turnips in water to cover in saucepan for 8 to 10 minutes or until tender. Drain and cover to keep warm. Melt butter in skillet. Stir in flour. Add cream gradually. Cook until thickened, stirring constantly. Add turnips, chives and cheese. Heat to serving temperature. Spoon into serving bowl. Garnish with paprika and parsley.
Yield: 4 servings.

Approx Per Serving: Cal 525; Prot 10.1 g; Carbo 15.2 g; T Fat 48.2 g; Chol 157.0 mg; Potas 331.0 mg; Sod 599.0 mg.

North Carolina Department of Agriculture

STIR-FRIED VEGETABLES

3 tablespoons cottonseed oil
1 1/2 cups (1/4-inch thick) diagonally sliced carrots
1 cup broccoli flowerets
Sweet basil to taste

Heat oil in skillet or wok. Add carrots. Stir-fry for 2 minutes. Add broccoli. Stir-fry for 3 minutes. Crush basil over vegetables. May substitute salt to taste for sweet basil.
Yield: 4 servings.

Approx Per Serving: Cal 114; Prot 1.1 g; Carbo 5.3 g; T Fat 10.4 g; Chol 0.0 mg; Potas 205.0 mg; Sod 20.2 mg.

North Carolina Cotton Promotion Association

VEGGIES CASSEROLE

2 (17-ounce) cans small green peas, drained
1 (4-ounce) can sliced mushrooms, drained
1 (8-ounce) can sliced water chestnuts, drained
1 can cream of chicken soup
3/4 cup shredded Cheddar cheese
2 tablespoons minced onion
2 (15-ounce) cans asparagus spears, drained
1 cup soft bread crumbs
2 tablespoons melted butter

Combine peas, mushrooms, water chestnuts, soup, cheese and onion in bowl; mix lightly. Layer asparagus and soup mixture 1/2 at a time in lightly greased 8x12-inch baking dish. Toss bread crumbs with butter in bowl. Sprinkle over casserole. Bake at 350 degrees for 20 minutes or until heated through. Yield: 8 servings.

Approx Per Serving: Cal 239; Prot 12.3 g; Carbo 28.1 g; T Fat 9.9 g; Chol 22.0 mg; Potas 479.0 mg; Sod 1105.0 mg.

North Carolina Department of Agriculture

VEGETABLE PLATTER

1 pound fresh broccoli, cut into 1/2-inch pieces
Flowerets of 1/2 head cauliflower
1 medium zucchini, sliced 1/4 inch thick
1/4 cup butter
1/2 teaspoon garlic salt
2 medium tomatoes, cut into wedges
1/2 cup freshly grated Parmesan cheese

Arrange broccoli and cauliflower around edge of 12-inch plate. Place zucchini in center. Sprinkle vegetables with water. Cover tightly with heavy-duty plastic wrap, folding back 1 edge to vent. Microwave on High for 5 to 7 minutes or until tender-crisp, rotating plate once. Let stand, covered, for 2 minutes. Combine butter and garlic salt in 1-cup glass measure. Microwave on High for 55 seconds; mix well. Drain vegetable plate. Arrange tomato wedges on plate. Drizzle with garlic butter. Sprinkle with cheese. Yield: 8 servings.

Approx Per Serving: Cal 104; Prot 4.8 g; Carbo 6.3 g; T Fat 7.5 g; Chol 3.9 mg; Potas 386.0 mg; Sod 316.0 mg.

North Carolina Department of Agriculture

APPLE AND CHEESE CASSEROLE

1/2 cup all-purpose flour
1/2 cup sugar
1/4 teaspoon salt
1/4 cup butter
7 apples, peeled, sliced
6 tablespoons water
1 tablespoon lemon juice
1 cup shredded sharp Cheddar cheese

Mix flour, sugar and salt in small bowl. Cut in butter until crumbly. Toss apples with water and lemon juice in bowl. Spoon into greased 8-inch baking dish. Sprinkle with flour mixture. Bake at 350 degrees for 35 minutes. Sprinkle with cheese. Bake for 5 minutes longer. Yield: 8 servings.

Approx Per Serving: Cal 255; Prot 4.6 g; Carbo 37.1 g; T Fat 10.9 g; Chol 30.4 mg; Potas 165.0 mg; Sod 204.0 mg.

North Carolina Apple Growers Association

BAKED CINNAMON APPLES

4 baking apples
1/2 cup packed brown sugar
4 teaspoons butter
1/2 teaspoon cinnamon

Remove core from apples. Peel upper half of apple or 1-inch strip from middle to prevent splitting. Place upright in baking dish. Place 2 tablespoons brown sugar, 1 teaspoon butter and 1/8 teaspoon cinnamon in center of each apple. Pour water into baking dish to 1/4-inch depth. Bake at 375 degrees for 30 to 40 minutes or until tender when pierced with fork, basting several times. May omit water and microwave for 6 to 8 minutes. Rome Beauty, Golden Delicious and Greening are good baking apples to use. May substitute grenadine syrup for brown sugar or omit cinnamon and place 1 tablespoon granola, 2 teaspoons brown sugar and 1 teaspoon butter in each apple. Yield: 4 servings.

Approx Per Serving: Cal 220; Prot 0.4 g; Carbo 47.6 g; T Fat 4.4 g; Chol 11.1 mg; Potas 258.0 mg; Sod 15.0 mg.

North Carolina Apple Growers Association

LIVER PUDDING BRUNCH BAKE

1 pound Neese's liver pudding
1/2 cup chopped onion
1/2 cup finely chopped celery
1/2 cup chopped green bell pepper
2 tablespoons butter
12 slices white bread
1 cup shredded Cheddar cheese
3 eggs, beaten
1 teaspoon salt
Pepper to taste
1 1/2 cups milk

Slice liver pudding into 12 slices. Sauté onion, celery and green pepper in butter in skillet until tender. Trim crusts from bread slices. Arrange 6 slices in lightly greased 8x12-inch baking dish. Place 2 slices of liver pudding on each bread slice. Spoon onion mixture over top; sprinkle with cheese. Top with remaining bread slices. Combine eggs, salt, pepper and milk in bowl; mix well. Pour over bread. Bake at 350 degrees for 40 minutes or until set. Yield: 6 servings.

Approx Per Serving: Cal 593; Prot 25.4 g; Carbo 34.3 g; T Fat 38.8 g; Chol 293.0 mg; Potas 388.0 mg; Sod 1093.0 mg.

Neese's Country Sausage Company
MEMBER

OVERNIGHT CASSEROLE

1 pound bacon
8 slices whole wheat bread
6 eggs
1 1/2 cups milk
1 cup shredded Cheddar cheese
1/2 teaspoon dry mustard

Cut bacon slices into 1/2-inch pieces. Cook in skillet until crisp, stirring frequently; drain. Crumble onto paper towels. Trim crusts from bread; cut bread into cubes. Beat eggs in bowl until foamy. Stir in milk, cheese and mustard. Fold in bacon and bread cubes gently. Spoon into buttered 8-inch baking dish. Chill, covered, overnight. Let stand at room temperature for 15 minutes. Bake at 325 degrees for 45 minutes or until knife inserted near center comes out clean. Yield: 6 servings.

Approx Per Serving: Cal 740; Prot 40.5 g; Carbo 25.3 g; T Fat 53.1 g; Chol 366.0 mg; Potas 614.0 mg; Sod 1713.0 mg.

North Carolina Egg Association

EGG PIZZA OLÉ

2 eggs
1 tablespoon water
1/4 teaspoon salt
1/4 teaspoon chili powder
1 tablespoon butter
1   (10-inch) flour tortilla
1/3 cup drained chopped tomato
2 tablespoons sliced green onions with tops
2 tablespoons chopped green chilies
2 tablespoons sliced black olives
1/4 cup shredded Monterey Jack cheese
1/8 teaspoon oregano
1/4 avocado, sliced

Beat eggs, water, salt and chili powder in bowl until foamy. Pour into hot butter in 10-inch skillet. Cook for 3 to 4 minutes or until eggs are set, lifting edges and tilting pan to cook evenly. Place tortilla on greased 12-inch pizza pan. Top with cooked egg round. Sprinkle with tomato, onions, chilies, olives, cheese and oregano. Bake at 350 degrees for 8 to 10 minutes or until cheese is bubbly and edges of tortilla are crisp. Garnish with avocado. Serve with salsa. Yield: 1 serving.

Approx Per Serving: Cal 671; Prot 25.8 g; Carbo 42.1 g; T Fat 47.7 g; Chol 605.0 mg; Potas 752.0 mg; Sod 1295.0 mg.

North Carolina Egg Association

BREAKFAST PIZZA

1 teaspoon butter
2 eggs
1 slice bacon, crisp-fried, crumbled
1/2 teaspoon Parmesan cheese
1 teaspoon water
1 English muffin, split, toasted
2 tablespoons pizza sauce

Grease skillet with butter; pour off excess. Heat until hot enough to sizzle a drop of water. Break eggs gently into skillet. Sprinkle with bacon and cheese. Cook over low heat for about 1 minute or until edges turn white. Add water. Cook, tightly covered, to desired degree of doneness. Spread English muffin halves with pizza sauce. Top with fried eggs. Yield: 1 serving.

Approx Per Serving: Cal 381; Prot 19.4 g; Carbo 29.7 g; T Fat 19.5 g; Chol 564.0 mg; Potas 607.0 mg; Sod 850.0 mg.

North Carolina Egg Association

BRUNCH IN-A-DISH

1 pound bulk sausage
1 pound frozen hashed brown potatoes, thawed
6 eggs, beaten
1 1/2 cups milk
1 cup shredded Cheddar cheese

Brown sausage in skillet, stirring until crumbly; drain. Place potatoes in lightly greased 9x13-inch baking dish. Spread sausage over potatoes. Mix eggs, milk and salt and pepper to taste in bowl. Pour over sausage. Sprinkle with cheese. Bake, covered, at 350 degrees for 45 minutes. Bake, uncovered, for 15 minutes longer or until set and light brown. Yield: 8 servings.

Approx Per Serving: Cal 505; Prot 18.0 g; Carbo 19.3 g; T Fat 39.8 g; Chol 265.0 mg; Potas 486.0 mg; Sod 556.0 mg.

North Carolina Egg Association

EGG TACO

2 tablespoons Neese's hot sausage
1 egg
1/4 cup shredded Cheddar cheese
1 tablespoon Puro Fuego salsa
1 taco shell

Brown sausage in skillet, stirring until crumbly; drain. Beat egg in bowl until foamy. Add sausage, cheese and salsa; mix well. Pour into hot skillet. Cook until set but not dry, stirring frequently. Heat taco shell. Spoon scrambled egg mixture into taco shell. Yield: 1 serving.

Approx Per Serving: Cal 375; Prot 17.7 g; Carbo 11.0 g; T Fat 29.2 g; Chol 327.8 mg; Potas 196.3 mg; Sod 199.0 mg.

North Carolina Egg Association

BASIC QUICHE

3/4 cup crumbled crisp-fried bacon
1 cup shredded Cheddar cheese
1 unbaked deep-dish pie shell
5 eggs
1 cup half and half

Sprinkle bacon and cheese into pie shell. Beat eggs and half and half in bowl until foamy. Pour into pie shell. Bake at 375 degrees for 35 to 45 minutes or until set. Let stand for 10 minutes before slicing. Yield: 6 servings.

Approx Per Serving: Cal 507; Prot 21.4 g; Carbo 15.8 g; T Fat 39.5 g; Chol 287.0 mg; Potas 277.0 mg; Sod 826.0 mg.

North Carolina Egg Association

PASTA STUFFED WITH FIVE CHEESES

1 (8-ounce) package jumbo pasta shells
8 ounces cream cheese
1 cup low-fat cottage cheese
4 ounces mozzarella cheese, shredded
1/4 cup Parmesan and Romano cheese topping
1 egg, beaten
2 tablespoons chopped parsley
2 teaspoons basil
1/2 teaspoon oregano
1/2 teaspoon thyme
1/8 teaspoon lemon rind
Pinch of nutmeg
1 (14-ounce) can stewed tomatoes
1 cup tomato sauce
1 cup white wine
1 (8-ounce) can chopped mushrooms, drained
1 teaspoon oregano
1 teaspoon thyme
1 clove of garlic, minced

Cook pasta shells using package directions; drain. Combine softened cream cheese, cottage cheese, mozzarella cheese, Parmesan and Romano cheese topping, egg, parsley, basil, oregano, thyme, lemon rind and nutmeg in bowl; mix well. Stuff into pasta shells; place in 9x13-inch baking dish. Combine stewed tomatoes, tomato sauce, wine, mushrooms, oregano, thyme and garlic in saucepan. Bring to a boil. Pour over pasta shells. Sprinkle with additional cheese if desired. Bake at 350 degrees for 30 minutes or until hot and bubbly. Garnish with parsley sprigs. Yield: 8 servings.

Approx Per Serving: Cal 339; Prot 15.7 g; Carbo 30.2 g; T Fat 15.4 g; Chol 80.5 mg; Potas 443.0 mg; Sod 685.0 mg.

North Carolina Department of Agriculture

SPANISH RICE

1 pound ground beef
1/4 cup Carolina Treet barbecue sauce
4 ounces bacon
1 small onion
1 small green bell pepper
3/4 cup rice
3 cups tomato juice

Brown ground beef in skillet, stirring until crumbly; drain. Combine with barbecue sauce in bowl. Sauté chopped bacon, onion and green pepper in skillet; drain. Add to ground beef. Add rice, juice and salt and pepper to taste; mix well. Spoon into casserole. Bake at 350 degrees for 1 hour or until rice is tender. Yield: 6 servings.

Approx Per Serving: Cal 389; Prot 21.7 g; Carbo 27.7 g; T Fat 21.3 g; Chol 64.6 mg; Potas 632.0 mg; Sod 874.0 mg.

Carolina Treet, Inc.
MEMBER

Breads

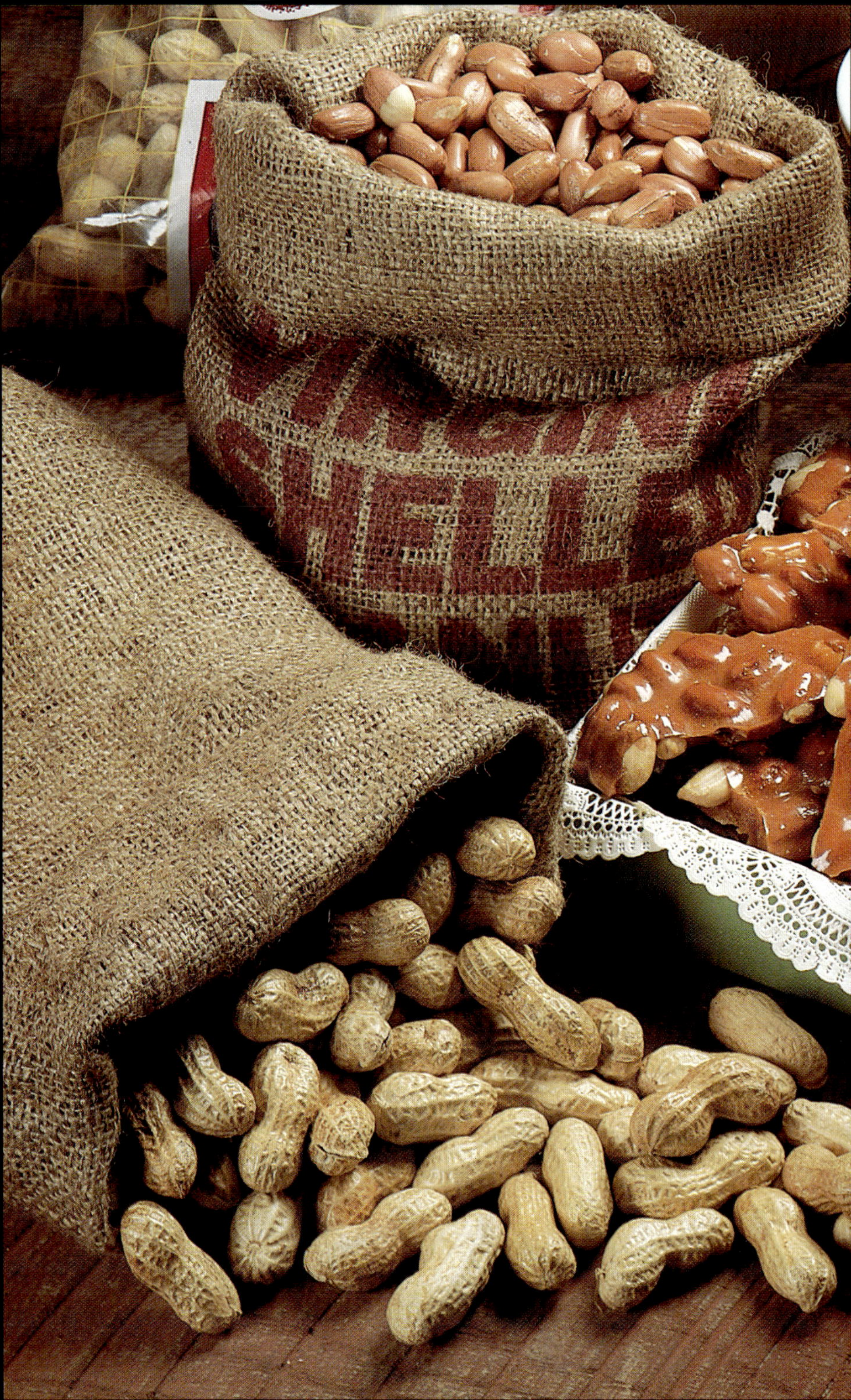

SWEET POTATO BISCUITS

1 1/4 cups all-purpose flour
1 tablespoon baking powder
1/2 teaspoon salt
3 tablespoons shortening
1 cup cold mashed sweet potatoes
1/4 cup (about) milk

Sift flour, baking powder and salt into bowl. Cut in shortening until crumbly. Add sweet potatoes; mix well. Stir in enough milk to make soft dough. Knead several times on floured surface. Roll 1/2 inch thick. Cut with biscuit cutter. Place on baking sheet. Bake at 450 degrees for 12 to 15 minutes or until brown. Yield: 18 biscuits.

Approx Per Biscuit: Cal 68; Prot 1.3 g; Carbo 10.2 g; T Fat 2.4 g; Chol 0.5 mg; Potas 43.4 mg; Sod 126.0 mg.

North Carolina Sweet Potato Commission

NEESE'S SAUSAGE COFFEE CAKE

1 cup raisins
1 pound Neese's mild country sausage, at room temperature
2 cups packed brown sugar
3 eggs
3 cups sifted all-purpose flour
1 teaspoon baking powder
1/2 teaspoon soda
1/2 teaspoon salt
1 teaspoon cinnamon
2 1/2 teaspoons pumpkin pie spice
1 cup orange juice
1 cup applesauce
1 cup chopped pecans

Soak raisins in hot water to cover in small bowl for 10 minutes; drain. Combine sausage and brown sugar in mixer bowl; mix well. Add eggs 1 at a time, beating well after each addition. Stir in sifted mixture of flour, baking powder, soda, salt, cinnamon and pumpkin pie spice alternately with orange juice. Add applesauce; mix well. Fold in raisins and pecans. Pour into greased and floured tube pan. Bake at 300 degrees for 1 1/2 hours. Let stand for 15 minutes; remove from pan. Store in refrigerator. Yield: 12 servings.

Approx Per Serving: Cal 554; Prot 10.4 g; Carbo 77.4 g; T Fat 23.8 g; Chol 94.4 mg; Potas 447.0 mg; Sod 439.0 mg.

Neese's Country Sausage Company
MEMBER

BROCCOLI CORN BREAD

1 large onion, chopped
1 (10-ounce) package frozen chopped broccoli, thawed
4 eggs, well beaten
1/2 cup melted margarine
6 ounces cottage cheese
1 teaspoon salt
1 (8-ounce) package Jiffy corn bread mix

Combine onion, broccoli and eggs in bowl; mix well. Add margarine, cottage cheese and salt; mix well. Stir in cornbread mix just until moistened. Pour into greased 9x13-inch baking dish. Bake at 400 degrees for 20 to 25 minutes or until brown. Yield: 12 servings.

Approx Per Serving: Cal 157; Prot 5.4 g; Carbo 9.6 g; T Fat 10.8 g; Chol 93.4 mg; Potas 145.0 mg; Sod 448.0 mg.

Albemarle Pride Broccoli
MEMBER

MICROWAVE CORN BREAD

1 tablespoon bacon drippings
1 cup cornmeal
1 egg
1/2 cup (about) milk
1 teaspoon melted margarine

Grease browning dish with bacon drippings. Microwave on High for 7 minutes according to browning dish instructions. Pour mixture of cornmeal, egg, milk and margarine into hot browning dish. Microwave on High for 2 minutes. Turn bread over in browning dish. Let stand until serving time. Bread will brown while standing. Yield: 6 servings.

Approx Per Serving: Cal 123; Prot 3.5 g; Carbo 16.1 g; T Fat 5.2 g; Chol 50.4 mg; Potas 96.1 mg; Sod 27.6 mg.

Davis Milling Company
MEMBER

SOUTHERN-STYLE SPOON BREAD

3 eggs
1 cup cornmeal
1/4 cup melted butter
1 teaspoon salt
1 tablespoon sugar
3 cups boiling water

Beat eggs in small bowl until very thick. Combine cornmeal, butter, salt and sugar in bowl; mix well. Add water gradually to make stiff dough. Mix in eggs. Spoon into baking dish. Bake at 375 degrees or until spoon bread tests done. Serve hot with butter. Yield: 6 servings.

Approx Per Serving: Cal 188; Prot 4.9 g; Carbo 17.4 g; T Fat 11.3 g; Chol 158.0 mg; Potas 92.8 mg; Sod 455.0 mg.

Buffaloe Milling Company
MEMBER

DESSERT CRÊPES

3 tablespoons butter
3 eggs, slightly beaten
1/2 cup milk
1/2 cup water
1 teaspoon vanilla extract
3/4 cup all-purpose flour
2 tablespoons sugar
1/2 teaspoon salt

Melt butter in 8-inch crêpe pan. Pour into bowl. Add eggs, milk, water and vanilla; beat with rotary beater until smooth. Blend in flour, sugar and salt until smooth. Pour scant 1/4 cup at a time into hot crêpe pan. Rotate pan to spread batter evenly. Bake until light brown on bottom. Stack between layers of waxed paper. Spoon 1/3 cup pie filling, custard, pudding, ice cream or fresh fruit on unbrowned side of each crêpe; roll to enclose filling. Serve warm or cold. Yield: 12 crêpes.

Approx Per Crêpe: Cal 88; Prot 2.7 g; Carbo 8.6 g; T Fat 4.7 g; Chol 77.6 mg; Potas 38.3 mg; Sod 135.0 mg.
Nutritional information does not include filling.

North Carolina Egg Association

HUSH PUPPIES

1 cup cornmeal
1/3 cup self-rising flour
1 teaspoon salt
1 teaspoon sugar
Water
1 onion, chopped
Oil for deep frying

Combine cornmeal, flour, salt and sugar in bowl; mix well. Add enough water to mixture to make sticky batter. Drop by spoonfuls into 350-degree oil. Deep-fry until golden brown. Drain on paper towels. Dip spoon in water occasionally to make batter slip from spoon easily. Yield: 6 servings.

Approx Per Serving: Cal 109; Prot 2.9 g; Carbo 22.9 g; T Fat 1.0 g; Chol 0.0 mg; Potas 106.0 mg; Sod 356.0 mg.
Nutritional information does not include oil for deep frying.

Atkinson Milling Company
MEMBER

APPLE BREAD

2 cups all-purpose flour, sifted
1 teaspoon baking powder
1 teaspoon soda
1/2 teaspoon cinnamon
1/2 teaspoon allspice
1/2 teaspoon salt
1/2 cup butter
1/2 cup sugar
1/2 cup honey
2 eggs, well beaten
1 cup shredded apple
1 teaspoon vanilla extract
1/2 cup chopped pecans

Sift flour, baking powder, soda, cinnamon, allspice and salt into bowl. Cream butter, sugar and honey in medium bowl until light and fluffy. Add eggs; mix well. Add apples and vanilla; mix well. Stir in flour mixture just until moistened. Fold in pecans. Pour into greased loaf pan. Bake at 325 degrees for 1 hour. Remove to wire rack to cool. Store bread in airtight container overnight before slicing. Yield: 8 servings.

Approx Per Serving: Cal 398; Prot 5.3 g; Carbo 55.6 g; T Fat 18.3 g; Chol 99.6 mg; Potas 106.0 mg; Sod 393.0 mg.

E. Lester Selph Bee Farm
MEMBER

CHEESE LOAF

3 cups self-rising flour
1/4 cup sugar
1 cup (4 ounces) shredded Cheddar cheese
1/2 teaspoon onion flakes
1 egg, slightly beaten
1 1/2 cups milk
1/4 cup oil

Mix flour, sugar, cheese and onion in bowl. Add egg, milk and oil; stir just until moistened. Pour into greased 5x9-inch loaf pan. Bake at 350 degrees for 1 hour or until golden brown. Cool in pan for 10 minutes. Remove to wire rack to cool completely. Yield: 12 servings.

Approx Per Serving: Cal 233; Prot 7.1 g; Carbo 29.6 g; T Fat 9.5 g; Chol 36.9 mg; Potas 86.3 mg; Sod 77.7 mg.

North Carolina Department of Agriculture

CRANBERRY PECAN BREAD

1/2 cup butter, softened
3/4 cup sugar
2 eggs, slightly beaten
1 teaspoon vanilla extract
3 cups all-purpose flour
1 tablespoon baking powder
1 teaspoon salt
1 teaspoon soda
1/2 teaspoon cinnamon
1/4 teaspoon nutmeg
1/3 cup orange juice
1 (10-ounce) package frozen cranberry-orange relish, thawed
1 teaspoon grated orange rind
1 cup chopped pecans

Cream butter and sugar in mixer bowl until light and fluffy. Beat in eggs and vanilla. Add mixture of flour, baking powder, salt, soda, cinnamon and nutmeg alternately with orange juice, mixing well after each addition. Fold in relish, orange rind and pecans. Pour into greased 5x9-inch loaf pan. Bake at 350 degrees for 70 to 75 minutes or until loaf tests done. Cool in pan for 15 minutes. Remove to wire rack to cool completely. Store, tightly wrapped in plastic wrap, for 24 hours before slicing. Yield: 12 servings.

Approx Per Serving: Cal 356; Prot 5.3 g; Carbo 50.1 g; T Fat 15.7 g; Chol 66.4 mg; Potas 107.0 mg; Sod 413.0 mg.

American Dairy Association of North Carolina

ORANGE NUT BREAD

2 3/4 cups all-purpose flour, sifted
2 1/2 teaspoons baking powder
1/2 teaspoon soda
1/2 teaspoon salt
2 tablespoons butter, softened
1 cup Master's Market Ministry honey
1 egg, slightly beaten
1 1/2 teaspoons grated orange rind
3/4 cup orange juice
3/4 cup chopped pecans

Sift flour, baking powder, soda and salt into bowl. Cream butter and honey in mixer bowl until light and fluffy. Add egg and orange rind; mix well. Add flour mixture alternately with orange juice, ending with flour mixture and mixing well after each addition. Fold in pecans. Pour into greased 5x9-inch loaf pan. Bake at 325 degrees for 1 to 1 1/4 hours or until loaf pulls slighly from sides of pan. Cool in pan for 10 minutes. Remove to wire rack to cool completely. Yield: 12 servings.

Approx Per Serving: Cal 263; Prot 4.1 g; Carbo 46.6 g; T Fat 7.7 g; Chol 28.0 mg; Potas 107.0 mg; Sod 216.0 mg.

Master's Market Ministry
MEMBER

MISS IDA'S SWEET PICKLE BREAD

1/2 cup butter, softened
1/2 cup sugar
1 cup packed dark brown sugar
2 eggs, well beaten
2 1/4 cups all-purpose flour
2 teaspoons allspice
1 teaspoon cinnamon
1/2 teaspoon cloves
4 teaspoons baking powder
1 teaspoon soda
2 cups (16-ounce jar) drained Cates sweet salad cubes
1/2 apple, peeled, chopped

Cream butter, sugar and brown sugar in mixer bowl until light and fluffy. Beat in eggs. Add mixture of flour, allspice, cinnamon, cloves, baking powder and soda alternately with pickles, mixing well after each addition. Fold in apple. Pour into greased and floured loaf pan. Bake at 350 degrees for 55 minutes or until loaf tests done. Garnish with confectioners' sugar or serve with butter, cream cheese or cold cuts. Yield: 12 servings.

Approx Per Serving: Cal 323; Prot 3.8 g; Carbo 59.3 g; T Fat 9.0 g; Chol 66.4 mg; Potas 188.0 mg; Sod 533.0 mg.

Cates Pickles, Inc.
MEMBER

PINEAPPLE AND APRICOT BREAD

1 tablespoon butter, softened
1/4 cup toasted sliced almonds
3/4 cup milk
1/2 cup melted butter, cooled
1 cup drained crushed pineapple
1 cup chopped dried apricots
1 egg, slightly beaten
3 cups all-purpose flour
3/4 cup sugar
1 tablespoon baking powder
1/4 teaspoon soda
3/4 teaspoon salt

Grease 5x9-inch loaf pan with 1 tablespoon butter. Sprinkle bottom and sides of pan with almonds. Combine milk, 1/2 cup melted butter, pineapple, apricots and egg in bowl. Add mixture of flour, sugar, baking powder, soda and salt, stirring just until moistened. Spoon batter gently into prepared pan. Bake at 350 degrees for 70 to 75 minutes or until toothpick inserted in center comes out clean. Cool in pan for 15 minutes. Remove to wire rack to cool completely. Store, tightly wrapped in plastic wrap, for 24 hours before slicing. Yield: 12 servings.

Approx Per Serving: Cal 304; Prot 5.2 g; Carbo 47.1 g; T Fat 11.0 g; Chol 48.2 mg; Potas 246.0 mg; Sod 320.0 mg.

American Dairy Association of North Carolina

PUMPKIN BREAD

3 1/2 cups all-purpose flour
1/2 teaspoon baking powder
2 teaspoons soda
1 1/2 teaspoons salt
1 teaspoon cinnamon
1 teaspoon ginger
1 teaspoon cloves
3 cups sugar
1 cup oil
4 eggs, slightly beaten
2 cups pumpkin purée

Combine flour, baking powder, soda, salt, cinnamon, ginger and cloves in bowl; mix well. Add sugar and oil; mix well. Stir in eggs and pumpkin until well blended. Pour into 2 greased and floured loaf pans. Bake at 350 degrees for 45 minutes to 1 hour or until loaves test done. Yield: 24 servings.

Approx Per Serving: Cal 264; Prot 3.2 g; Carbo 40.7 g; T Fat 10.3 g; Chol 45.7 mg; Potas 73.8 mg; Sod 222.0 mg.

North Carolina Department of Agriculture

PUMPKIN AND PECAN BREAD

1 3/4 cups all-purpose flour
1 teaspoon baking powder
1/2 teaspoon soda
1/4 teaspoon salt
1/2 cup sugar
3/4 teaspoon cinnamon
1/2 teaspoon nutmeg
3/4 cup pumpkin purée
1/3 cup skim milk
1/3 cup oil
1/2 cup egg substitute
1/2 cup chopped pecans

Mix flour, baking powder, soda, salt, sugar, cinnamon and nutmeg in large bowl. Make well in center. Combine pumpkin, milk, oil, egg substitute and pecans in medium bowl; mix well. Pour into well in flour mixture; stir just until moistened. Spoon into 4x8-inch loaf pan sprayed with nonstick cooking spray. Bake at 350 degrees for 55 minutes to 1 hour or until loaf tests done. Cool in pan for 10 minutes. Remove to wire rack to cool completely. Yield: 16 servings.

Approx Per Serving: Cal 143; Prot 2.8 g; Carbo 16.6 g; T Fat 7.5 g; Chol 0.2 mg; Potas 86.8 mg; Sod 97.0 mg.

North Carolina Department of Agriculture

STRAWBERRY BREAD

1 1/4 cups oil
3 eggs, slightly beaten
2 cups sugar
3 cups all-purpose flour
1 tablespoon cinnamon
1 teaspoon soda
1 teaspoon salt
2 (10-ounce) packages frozen strawberries, thawed, drained
1 cup chopped pecans

Combine oil, eggs and sugar in large bowl; mix well. Stir in mixture of flour, cinnamon, soda and salt just until moistened. Fold in strawberries and pecans. Spoon into 2 greased and floured loaf pans. Bake at 350 degrees for 1 hour or until loaves test done. Cool in pan for 10 minutes. Remove to wire rack to cool completely. Yield: 24 servings.

Approx Per Serving: Cal 273; Prot 2.9 g; Carbo 31.8 g; T Fat 15.6 g; Chol 34.2 mg; Potas 79.5 mg; Sod 133.0 mg.

North Carolina Strawberry Growers and Pick-Your-Own Association

SOUTHERN SWEET POTATO BREAD

1/4 cup butter, softened
1/2 cup packed brown sugar
2 eggs, slightly beaten
1 cup mashed cooked sweet potatoes
3 tablespoons milk
1 teaspoon grated orange rind
2 cups sifted self-rising flour
1/4 teaspoon nutmeg
1/4 teaspoon allspice
1/2 cup chopped pecans
3 ounces cream cheese, softened
1 tablespoon orange juice
1 teaspoon grated orange rind

Beat butter and brown sugar in mixer bowl until light and fluffy. Add eggs, sweet potatoes, milk and 1 teaspoon orange rind; mix until well blended. Stir in flour, nutmeg, allspice and pecans. Pour into greased 5x9-inch loaf pan. Bake at 350 degrees for 45 to 50 minutes or until loaf tests done. Cool in pan for 10 minutes. Remove to wire rack to cool completely. Serve with mixture of cream cheese, orange juice and remaining 1 teaspoon orange rind. Yield: 12 servings.

Approx Per Serving: Cal 234; Prot 4.5 g; Carbo 30.0 g; T Fat 11.0 g; Chol 64.3 mg; Potas 143.0 mg; Sod 86.7 mg.

North Carolina Sweet Potato Commission

ZUCCHINI BREAD

2 1/3 cups buttermilk baking mix
3/4 cup sugar
3 eggs
1/4 cup sour cream
1/4 cup oil
Grated rind of 1 orange
1 1/2 teaspoons cinnamon
1/2 teaspoon nutmeg
1 teaspoon vanilla extract
8 ounces zucchini, shredded
1/3 cup chopped pecans
8 ounces cream cheese, softened

Combine baking mix, sugar, eggs, sour cream, oil, orange rind, cinnamon, nutmeg and vanilla in bowl; mix well. Fold in zucchini and pecans. Pour into greased 5x9-inch loaf pan. Bake at 350 degrees for 1 hour or until loaf tests done. Cool in pan for 10 minutes. Remove to wire rack to cool completely. Slice loaf; serve with cream cheese. Yield: 12 servings.

Approx Per Serving: Cal 317; Prot 5.3 g; Carbo 31.5 g; T Fat 19.3 g; Chol 91.3 mg; Potas 147.0 mg; Sod 384.0 mg.

North Carolina Department of Agriculture

EVER-READY BRAN MUFFINS

1 (15-ounce) package bran flake cereal with raisins
5 cups all-purpose flour
3 cups sugar
5 teaspoons soda
2 teaspoons salt
4 eggs, well beaten
4 cups buttermilk
1 cup soybean oil

Combine cereal, flour, sugar, soda and salt in bowl. Make well in center. Pour mixture of eggs, buttermilk and oil into well; stir just until moistened. Fill greased muffin cups 2/3 full. Bake at 400 degrees for 12 to 15 minutes. May store in airtight container in refrigerator for up to 6 weeks. Yield: 60 muffins.

Approx Per Muffin: Cal 144; Prot 2.6 g; Carbo 24.5 g; T Fat 4.4 g; Chol 18.9 mg; Potas 83.7 mg; Sod 204.0 mg.

North Carolina Soybean Producers Association

CORNMEAL MUFFINS

1 cup oil
1/2 cup mayonnaise
4 eggs, slightly beaten
2 1/2 to 3 quarts buttermilk
5 pounds cornmeal mix

Mix oil, mayonnaise, eggs and buttermilk in large bowl. Add cornmeal mix; stir just until moistened. Fill greased muffin cups 3/4 full. Bake at 400 degrees for 25 minutes. Yield: 60 muffins.

Approx Per Muffin: Cal 205; Prot 5.5 g; Carbo 30.3 g; T Fat 7.4 g; Chol 21.1 mg; Potas 186.0 mg; Sod 66.7 mg.

North Carolina Corn Miller's Association

CRUSTY CHEESE CORN MUFFINS

1 recipe Cornmeal Muffin batter
2 cups shredded Cheddar cheese
1/2 cup chopped onion
2 cups shredded Cheddar cheese

Combine Cornmeal Muffin batter, 2 cups cheese and onion in bowl; mix well. Fill greased muffin cups 3/4 full. Bake at 400 degrees for 20 minutes. Sprinkle remaining cheese on muffins. Bake for 5 minutes longer. Yield: 60 muffins.

Approx Per Muffin: Cal 261; Prot 9.0 g; Carbo 30.6 g; T Fat 11.9 g; Chol 35.1 mg; Potas 198.2 mg; Sod 165.6 mg.

North Carolina Corn Miller's Association

SAUSAGE MUFFINS

1 pound Neese's sausage
Melted margarine
2 cups all-purpose flour
1 tablespoon baking powder
1/4 teaspoon salt
2 tablespoons sugar
1 egg, slightly beaten
1 cup milk
1/2 cup shredded Cheddar cheese

Brown sausage in skillet, stirring until crumbly. Drain, reserving drippings. Add enough margarine to drippings to measure 1/4 cup. Combine flour, baking powder, salt and sugar in bowl; mix well. Add mixture of egg, milk and reserved drippings, stirring just until moistened. Stir in sausage and cheese. Fill greased muffin cups 3/4 full. Bake at 350 degrees for 18 to 20 minutes. Yield: 12 muffins.

Approx Per Muffin: Cal 281; Prot 9.0 g; Carbo 19.6 g; T Fat 18.2 g; Chol 56.4 mg; Potas 135.0 mg; Sod 423.0 mg.
Nutritional information does not include margarine.

Neese's Country Sausage Company
MEMBER

NORTH CAROLINA SWEET POTATO MUFFINS

1 cup raisins
1 cup chopped pecans
1 cup mashed sweet potatoes
2 cups sugar
1 1/2 cups oil
4 eggs, slightly beaten
3 cups self-rising flour
1 teaspoon cinnamon

Rinse raisins and pecans in boiling water; drain. Combine sweet potatoes, sugar, oil and eggs in bowl; mix well. Add flour; mix just until moistened. Fold in raisins and pecans. Fill greased muffin cups 3/4 full. Bake at 350 degrees for 15 to 20 minutes. May store batter in airtight container in refrigerator. Yield: 36 muffins.

Approx Per Muffin: Cal 212; Prot 2.2 g; Carbo 24.8 g; T Fat 12.1 g; Chol 30.4 mg; Potas 79.8 mg; Sod 126.0 mg.

North Carolina Sweet Potato Commission

TROPIC ISLE MUFFINS

1 (8-ounce) can crushed pineapple
2 cups all-purpose flour
1/2 cup sugar
1 tablespoon baking powder
1 teaspoon salt
1 egg, well beaten
1/3 cup soybean oil
1/2 cup melted soybean oil margarine
1/4 cup sugar
1 teaspoon ginger

Drain pineapple, reserving juice. Add enough water to reserved juice to measure 3/4 cup. Combine flour, 1/2 cup sugar, baking powder and salt in bowl; mix well. Make well in center. Pour egg, oil and juice into well; stir just until moistened. Fold in pineapple. Fill greased muffin cups 2/3 full. Bake at 400 degrees for 18 to 20 minutes or until muffins test done. Dip each muffin in melted margarine; roll in mixture of 1/4 cup sugar and ginger. Serve warm with additional whipped soybean oil margarine. Yield: 18 muffins.

Approx Per Muffin: Cal 179; Prot 1.9 g; Carbo 21.8 g; T Fat 9.5 g; Chol 15.2 mg; Potas 35.4 mg; Sod 237.0 mg.

North Carolina Soybean Producers Association

HERB AND CHEESE PULL-APART ROLLS

8 ounces cream cheese, softened
1 teaspoon parsley flakes
1 teaspoon basil
1 teaspoon chopped chives
1/2 teaspoon dillseed
1/8 teaspoon garlic powder
1 (8-ounce) can refrigerator crescent rolls
1 egg, slightly beaten
1/2 teaspoon poppy seed

Beat cream cheese, parsley, basil, chives, dillseed and garlic powder in mixer bowl until well blended. Separate crescent roll dough into 2 rectangles. Place on baking sheet to form 1 long rectangle; seal ends and perforations. Spread cream cheese mixture over dough to within 1/2 inch of edge. Roll as for jelly roll; pinch edge to seal. Cut 1/2-inch thick slices with kitchen shears, alternating from right to left side of dough and taking care not to cut completely through the dough. Pull out slices, alternating sides, to expose rolled pattern. Brush with egg. Sprinkle with poppy seed. Bake at 375 degrees for 12 to 15 minutes or until golden brown. Yield: 8 servings.

Approx Per Serving: Cal 193; Prot 4.2 g; Carbo 10.1 g; T Fat 15.2 g; Chol 65.2 mg; Potas 105.0 mg; Sod 282.0 mg.

North Carolina Department of Agriculture

WHOLE WHEAT AND OATMEAL BREAD

2 cups water
1 cup oats
1/2 cup honey
2 teaspoons salt
1 tablespoon melted butter
1 package dry yeast
1/2 cup warm water
2 1/2 cups whole wheat flour
2 cups bread flour

Bring 2 cups water to a boil in saucepan. Pour over oats in large bowl. Let stand at room temperature for 1 hour. Add honey, salt and melted butter; mix well. Dissolve yeast in 1/2 cup warm (105 to 115-degree) water in small bowl. Let stand for 5 minutes or until bubbly. Stir into oats mixture until well blended. Add whole wheat flour and bread flour; mix well. Place dough in greased bowl, turning to grease surface. Cover with plastic wrap or clean towel. Let rise in warm (85 degrees), draft-free place for 1 hour or until doubled in bulk. Punch dough down. Turn out onto lightly floured surface. Knead for 8 to 10 minutes or until smooth and elastic. Divide dough into 2 equal portions. Shape each portion into loaf. Place in 2 well-greased 4x8-inch loaf pans. Cover with towel. Let rise in warm (85 degrees), draft-free place for 40 minutes or until doubled in bulk. Bake at 350 degrees for 50 minutes or until loaves sound hollow when tapped. Cover loosely with aluminum foil during last 10 to 15 minutes of baking time if necessary to prevent overbrowning. Loosen loaves from sides of pans with knife. Remove to wire racks to cool. Yield: 16 servings.

Approx Per Serving: Cal 198; Prot 6.0 g; Carbo 40.9 g; T Fat 1.9 g; Chol 1.9 mg; Potas 134.0 mg; Sod 274.0 mg.

North Carolina Small Grain Growers Association

WHOLE WHEAT-PEANUT BREAD

2½ cups warm water
⅓ cup honey
1 tablespoon sugar
⅓ cup shortening
2 packages Fleischmann's rapid-rise yeast
2 cups whole wheat flour
1½ teaspoons salt
1½ cups ground roasted peanuts
3 to 4 cups all-purpose flour
Melted margarine

Combine warm (105 to 115-degree) water, honey, sugar and shortening in large mixer bowl. Mix until sugar is dissolved and shortening is melted. Add yeast, whole wheat flour, and salt; beat until well blended. Stir in peanuts. Add enough all-purpose flour to make medium dough. Turn out onto lightly floured surface. Knead for 5 minutes or until smooth and elastic. Cover dough with mixer bowl. Let rest for 15 minutes. Divide dough into 2 equal portions. Shape each portion into loaf. Place in 2 well-greased 5x9-inch loaf pans. Place loaf pans in shallow baking dish half filled with hot tap water. Cover loosely with clean towel. Let rise in warm place for 30 to 45 minutes or until doubled in bulk. Remove loaf pans from dish of water. Bake at 350 degrees for 35 to 45 minutes or until loaves test done. Remove loaves from pans. Cool on wire racks. Brush warm loaves with melted margarine. This recipe won first place in the 1985 Cook-A-Peanut Contest.
Yield: 24 servings.

Approx Per Serving: Cal 204; Prot 6.2 g; Carbo 29.2 g; T Fat 7.7 g; Chol 0.0 mg; Potas 135.0 mg; Sod 174.0 mg.
Nutritional information does not include margarine.

North Carolina Peanut Growers Association

QUICK HONEY ROLLS

2 packages dry yeast
2 cups warm water
1/2 cup oil
1/2 cup honey
3 cups bread flour
2 cups whole wheat flour
2 teaspoons salt
Melted butter

Dissolve yeast in warm (90-degree) water in bowl. Stir in oil and honey. Reserve 1 cup bread flour for kneading. Sift whole wheat flour, remaining 2 cups bread flour and salt into large bowl. Add yeast mixture; mix well. Let dough stand for 15 minutes. Knead on floured surface until smooth and elastic. Roll 1/2 inch thick; cut with biscuit cutter. Place on greased baking sheets. Brush tops with melted butter. Let rise, covered, for 1 hour or until doubled in bulk. Bake at 400 degrees for 15 minutes. Yield: 48 rolls.

Approx Per Roll: Cal 74; Prot 1.6 g; Carbo 12.5 g; T Fat 2.1 g; Chol 0.0 mg; Potas 34.6 mg; Sod 112.0 mg.
Nutritional information does not include butter.

E. Lester Selph Bee Farm
MEMBER

NO-KNEAD REFRIGERATOR ROLLS

1/4 cup sugar
1/2 cup soybean oil shortening
1 teaspoon salt
1 cup hot water
1 package dry yeast
1/2 cup warm water
1 egg
3 cups all-purpose flour

Stir sugar, shortening and salt into hot water in large bowl. Cool. Dissolve yeast in warm (105 to 115-degree) water in small bowl. Let stand for 3 to 5 minutes. Beat in egg. Stir into sugar mixture. Add flour; beat for 2 minutes. Dough will be soft. Place in greased bowl, turning to grease surface. Chill, covered, in refrigerator until dough can be handled easily. Shape into rolls with greased hands. Place on greased baking sheet. Let rise, covered, for 1 hour or until doubled in bulk. Bake at 425 degrees for 15 minutes. Yield: 18 rolls.

Approx Per Roll: Cal 142; Prot 2.7 g; Carbo 18.8 g; T Fat 6.2 g; Chol 15.2 mg; Potas 31.3 mg; Sod 123.0 mg.

North Carolina Soybean Producers Association

SPEEDY PECAN ROLLS

1 cup all-purpose flour
1 package rapid-rise yeast
1/2 teaspoon salt
6 tablespoons water
1/4 cup milk
1 tablespoon honey
1 tablespoon butter
1 egg
1 cup all-purpose flour
1/2 cup packed brown sugar
1/4 cup butter
3 tablespoons honey
1/2 cup chopped pecans
3 tablespoons sugar
1 1/2 teaspoons cinnamon
1 tablespoon butter, softened

Combine 1 cup flour, yeast and salt in large mixer bowl; mix well. Combine water and milk in saucepan. Add 1 tablespoon honey and 1 tablespoon butter. Cook over low heat until mixture is very warm (120 to 130 degrees), stirring constantly. Do not boil. Add with egg to flour mixture, beating at low speed until dry ingredients are moistened. Beat at medium speed for 3 minutes longer. Add enough remaining 1 cup flour to make soft dough. Turn dough onto lightly floured surface. Knead for 5 minutes or until smooth and elastic. Place dough in greased bowl, turning to grease surface. Let rise, covered, in warm (85 degrees), draft-free place for 20 minutes or until doubled in bulk. Sprinkle brown sugar in bottom of greased 9x13-inch baking dish. Dot with 1/4 cup butter. Drizzle with remaining 3 tablespoons honey. Sprinkle with pecans. Combine 3 tablespoons sugar and cinnamon in small bowl; mix well. Roll dough into 8x12-inch rectangle on lightly floured surface. Spread remaining 1 tablespoon butter evenly over dough. Sprinkle with cinnamon-sugar. Roll as for jelly roll from long side. Cut into 1-inch slices. Arrange slices cut side down in prepared baking dish. Let rise, covered, in warm (85-degrees), draft-free place for 20 minutes or until doubled in bulk. Bake at 375 degrees for 20 minutes or until golden brown. Invert rolls onto serving platter immediately. Serve warm. Yield: 12 rolls.

Approx Per Roll: Cal 239; Prot 3.6 g; Carbo 35.2 g; T Fat 10.0 g; Chol 39.1 mg; Potas 102.0 mg; Sod 150.0 mg.

North Carolina Department of Agriculture

Desserts

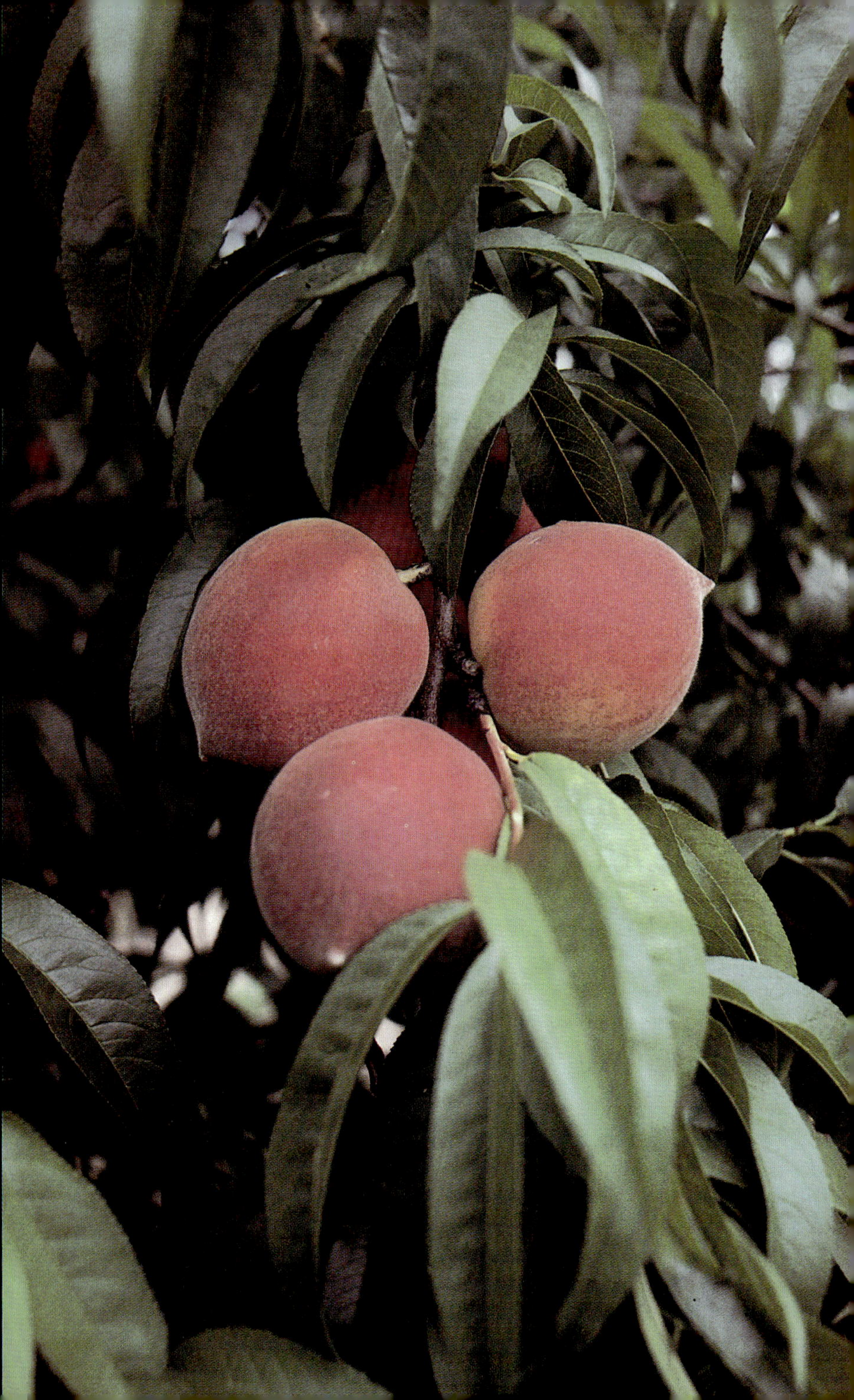

APPLE RUM BAKLAVA

3 cups chopped apples
2 1/2 cups chopped walnuts
3/4 cup sugar
1/2 cup raisins
2 tablespoons rum
2 teaspoons cinnamon
1 pound phyllo dough
1 pound butter, clarified, melted
1 cup honey

Combine first 6 ingredients in large bowl; mix well. Trim 8 sheets phyllo dough to fit 10x15-inch baking pan. Keep unused phyllo covered with damp cloth. Arrange in baking pan, brushing each sheet generously with melted butter. Spread half the apple mixture over phyllo dough. Arrange 6 buttered sheets phyllo dough over apple mixture. Spread with remaining apple mixture. Top with 8 buttered sheets phyllo dough. Cut into squares. Bake at 350 degrees for 40 minutes or until golden brown. Heat honey in small saucepan. Drizzle over hot baklava. May substitute 2 tablespoons lemon juice and 2 tablespoon lemon rind for rum. Yield: 12 servings.

Approx Per Serving: Cal 606; Prot 4.3 g; Carbo 49.6 g; T Fat 46.2 g; Chol 82.8 mg; Potas 277.0 mg; Sod 294.0 mg.
Nutritional information does not include phyllo dough.

E. Lester Selph Bee Farm
MEMBER

BAKED APPLE DUMPLINGS WITH LEMON SAUCE

1/2 cup packed brown sugar
1 1/2 teaspoons cinnamon
7 teaspoons butter, softened
7 medium apples, cored, peeled
2 cups buttermilk baking mix
1/3 cup ice water
1 tablespoon oil
2 cups water
1 cup sugar
1 tablespoon butter
1/2 teaspoon cornstarch
1 tablespoon lemon flavoring

Mix brown sugar and cinnamon in small bowl. Place 1 teaspoon butter and 2 teaspoons brown sugar mixture in each apple. Combine baking mix, 1/3 cup ice water and oil in bowl; mix well. Roll to 1/4-inch thickness on floured waxed paper. Cut into 7 squares. Place 1 apple on each square. Bring corners up to enclose apples; fasten with toothpicks. Place in greased 10x10-inch baking dish. Combine 2 cups water and sugar in saucepan. Bring to a boil, stirring until sugar dissolves. Add 1 tablespoon butter and cornstarch dissolved in a small amount of cold water. Cook until thickened, stirring constantly. Stir in lemon flavoring. Pour over dumplings. Bake at 350 degrees for 1 hour. Yield: 7 servings.

Approx Per Serving: Cal 471; Prot 2.9 g; Carbo 88.7 g; T Fat 13.1 g; Chol 14.8 mg; Potas 267.0 mg; Sod 525.0 mg.

North Carolina Apple Growers Association

GRANDMA'S BLACKBERRY COBBLER

1/2 cup sugar
1/2 cup water
2 cups fresh blackberries
3 tablespoons butter, softened
1/2 cup sugar
1 egg
1 cup self-rising flour
2/3 cup milk

Combine 1/2 cup sugar and water in saucepan. Bring to a boil. Boil for 5 minutes, stirring constantly. Add blackberries. Bring to a boil, stirring constantly; remove from heat. Cream butter, remaining 1/2 cup sugar and egg in mixer bowl until light and fluffy. Add flour and milk alternately, mixing well after each addition. Pour into buttered baking dish. Spoon blackberries over top. Bake at 375 degrees for 30 minutes or until golden brown. Yield: 4 servings.

Approx Per Serving: Cal 460; Prot 6.5 g; Carbo 84.2 g; T Fat 12.0 g; Chol 97.2 mg; Potas 244.0 mg; Sod 445.0 mg.

Killdeer Farm
MEMBER

BLACKBERRY CRUMBLE

1 quart fresh blackberries
3/4 cup sugar
1/2 cup quick-cooking oats
1/2 cup all-purpose flour
1/2 cup packed brown sugar
1 teaspoon cinnamon
1/4 cup margarine

Place blackberries in large bowl. Sprinkle with sugar; mix well. Let stand for several minutes. Combine oats, flour, brown sugar and cinnamon in bowl; mix well. Cut in margarine until crumbly. Spoon blackberries into buttered baking dish. Sprinkle oats mixture over top. Bake at 350 degrees for 30 to 35 minutes. One quart fresh blackberries equals 4 cups whole blackberries or 2 cups crushed blackberries. Yield: 6 servings.

Approx Per Serving: Cal 346; Prot 3.0 g; Carbo 67.3 g; T Fat 8.5 g; Chol 0.0 mg; Potas 290.0 mg; Sod 98.2 mg.

Killdeer Farm
MEMBER

BAKED FRUIT CRISP

4 layers Anne's frozen flat dumplings
1/4 cup melted margarine
1 (16-ounce) can blueberry pie filling
1/4 cup finely chopped walnuts
1 cup crushed cornflakes
1/2 cup packed light brown sugar

Partially thaw dumplings; cut strips in half. Drop dumplings into boiling water in large saucepan. Cook for 6 to 7 minutes; drain. Combine dumplings and margarine in bowl; toss to coat dumplings. Stir in pie filling. Spoon into 8x8-inch baking dish. Combine walnuts, cornflakes and brown sugar in small bowl; mix well. Sprinkle over top. Bake at 350 degrees for 30 to 40 minutes or until bubbly. May microwave on High for 8 minutes. May substitute apple or peach pie filling for blueberry.
Yield: 6 servings.

Approx Per Serving: Cal 353; Prot 1.7 g; Carbo 47.4 g; T Fat 18.6 g; Chol 0.0 mg; Potas 161.0 mg; Sod 349.0 mg.
Nutritional information does not include dumplings.

Anne's Old Fashioned Dumplings
MEMBER

CHOCOLATE SOUFFLÉ

2 ounces semisweet chocolate
1/2 cup milk
1/2 teaspoon vanilla extract
1 tablespoon sugar
1 1/2 tablespoons all-purpose flour
2 tablespoons melted butter
6 egg yolks
1/4 cup sugar
6 egg whites
1 tablespoon sugar

Combine chocolate, milk, vanilla and 1 tablespoon sugar in saucepan. Heat until chocolate melts, stirring constantly. Blend flour into melted butter in bowl gradually. Stir into hot mixture. Simmer for 5 minutes, stirring constantly. Cool slightly. Beat egg yolks and 1/4 cup sugar in mixer bowl until thick. Stir a small amount of hot mixture into egg yolks; fold egg yolks into hot mixture. Beat egg whites in mixer bowl until soft peaks form. Add remaining 1 tablespoon sugar gradually, beating until stiff peaks form. Fold into chocolate mixture gently. Butter 1 1/2-quart soufflé dish; sprinkle with additional sugar. Spoon chocolate mixture into prepared dish. Bake at 350 degrees for 35 to 45 minutes or until set. Yield: 8 servings.

Approx Per Serving: Cal 171; Prot 5.5 g; Carbo 15.7 g; T Fat 10.1 g; Chol 215.0 mg; Potas 96.6 mg; Sod 83.6 mg.

North Carolina Egg Association

DUPLIN FRUIT BOWL

1 fresh pineapple, cut into chunks
2 fresh peaches, sliced
1/2 cup grapes
1 banana, sliced
1/2 cup blueberries
1 orange, sliced
1 apple, chopped
1 cup Duplin Carolina red wine

Place pineapple, peaches, grapes, banana, blueberries, orange and apple in large glass bowl; toss well. Pour wine over fruit. Chill for 30 minutes before serving. Serve on cocktail picks as an appetizer or as a dessert. Yield: 10 servings.

Approx Per Serving: Cal 73.9; Prot 0.7 g; Carbo 14.9 g; T Fat 0.3 g; Chol 0.0 mg; Potas 201.0 mg; Sod 2.5 mg.

North Carolina Grape Growers Association

DESSERT OMELET

2 tablespoons water
1 teaspoon vanilla extract
1/2 teaspoon almond extract
2 tablespoons all-purpose flour
1 teaspoon sugar
2 eggs
2 teaspoons butter
1/2 cup cherry pie filling
1/4 cup sour cream
1/4 cup chopped pecans
3 tablespoons confectioners' sugar
1/4 cup Brandy

Combine water, vanilla and almond extract in bowl; mix well. Add flour and sugar, stirring until smooth. Add eggs; beat well with fork. Melt butter in skillet until foamy, tilting skillet to coat well. Pour in egg mixture. Cook until set, drawing cooked egg mixture to center of pan and allowing uncooked mixture to spread to outer edge. Fill with pie filling and sour cream. Fold omelet to enclose filling. Sprinkle with pecans and confectioners' sugar. Add Brandy; ignite. Serve hot. Yield: 2 servings.

Approx Per Serving: Cal 469; Prot 9.2 g; Carbo 46.5 g; T Fat 25.6 g; Chol 297.0 mg; Potas 220.0 mg; Sod 135.0 mg.

North Carolina Egg Association

GRAPE SHERBET

3 cups water
1½ cups sugar
2 cups grape juice
Juice of 1 lemon
1 egg white, stiffly beaten

Bring water and sugar to a boil in saucepan. Boil for 10 minutes, stirring constantly. Add grape juice and lemon juice; mix well. Cool. Pour into bowl. Freeze until partially frozen. Fold in egg whites gently. Freeze until firm. Yield: 6 servings.

Approx Per Serving: Cal 249; Prot 1.1 g; Carbo 63.1 g; T Fat 0.1 g; Chol 0.0 mg; Potas 130.0 mg; Sod 12.3 mg.

North Carolina Grape Growers Association

PEACHES AND CREAM DUMPLINGS

1 cup sugar
½ cup packed light brown sugar
½ cup butter
3½ cups half and half
1½ teaspoons vanilla extract
2 cups all-purpose flour
1 teaspoon salt
2½ teaspoons baking powder
6 tablespoons sugar
1 cup chopped peaches, drained
½ cup chopped pecans
6 tablespoons melted butter
2 cups minus 2 tablespoons whipping cream
1 teaspoon cinnamon

Combine 1 cup sugar, brown sugar, ½ cup butter and half and half in saucepan. Bring just to the boiling point over medium heat, stirring occasionally; remove from heat. Stir in vanilla. Pour into 3½-quart baking dish. Combine flour, salt, baking powder and 6 tablespoons sugar in medium bowl; mix well. Stir in peaches and pecans. Stir melted butter into whipping cream in small bowl. Pour into peach mixture; mix well. Drop by heaping tablespoons over warm sauce. Sprinkle with cinnamon. Bake at 375 degrees for 30 minutes. Serve immediately. Yield: 6 servings.

Approx Per Serving: Cal 1154; Prot 11.3 g; Carbo 109.0 g; T Fat 77.7 g; Chol 226.0 mg; Potas 449.0 mg; Sod 813.0 mg.

North Carolina Peach Growers Association

STRAWBERRY CHOCOLATE CHEESECAKE

12 ounces cream cheese, softened
1/2 cup sugar
1 teaspoon vanilla extract
3 eggs
1/2 cup strawberries
1 9-inch chocolate-flavored pie shell
1 teaspoon butter
1 ounce unsweetened chocolate
1/4 cup confectioners' sugar
1 teaspoon dark corn syrup
1 tablespoon cream
2 teaspoons boiling water
1/2 teaspoon vanilla extract

Beat cream cheese in mixer bowl until fluffy. Add sugar and 1 teaspoon vanilla gradually, beating constantly. Add eggs 1 at a time, beating well after each addition. Reserve several strawberries for garnish. Fold in remaining strawberries gently. Spoon strawberry mixture into pie shell. Place on baking sheet. Bake at 325 degrees for 35 minutes. Cool completely. Chill in refrigerator. Combine butter, chocolate, confectioners' sugar, corn syrup, cream and boiling water in saucepan. Cook over low heat until chocolate melts, stirring constantly; remove from heat. Stir in remaining 1/2 teaspoon vanilla. Pour over chilled cheesecake. Chill for 4 hours before serving. Garnish with reserved strawberries. May substitute drained frozen strawberries for fresh. Yield: 6 servings.

Approx Per Serving: Cal 513; Prot 9.8 g; Carbo 39.0 g; T Fat 36.6 g; Chol 204.0 mg; Potas 176.0 mg; Sod 394.0 mg.

North Carolina Egg Association

STRAWBERRY HEAVEN

8 ounces cream cheese, softened
12 ounces whipped topping
1 (16-ounce) package strawberry gelatin
2 cups sliced North Carolina strawberries
1 (8-ounce) can crushed pineapple

Combine cream cheese and whipped topping in mixer bowl. Beat until smooth. Sprinkle with gelatin; mix well. Fold in strawberries and pineapple gently. Spoon into parfait glasses. Chill until serving time. Garnish with whole strawberries. Yield: 8 servings.

Approx Per Serving: Cal 339; Prot 5.0 g; Carbo 35.7 g; T Fat 20.8 g; Chol 30.9 mg; Potas 134.0 mg; Sod 163.0 mg.

North Carolina Strawberry and Pick-Your-Own Association

CAROLINA SWEET RED STRAWBERRY PARFAIT

1 (12-ounce) package frozen strawberries, thawed
1 (3-ounce) package strawberry gelatin
1 tablespoon sugar
1/2 cup North Carolina red wine
1/2 cup whipped topping

Drain strawberries, reserving juice. Add enough water to juice to measure 1 cup. Bring juice to a boil in saucepan. Add gelatin and sugar; mix well. Add wine; mix well. Cool until mixture is foamy. Fold in whipped topping and strawberries gently. Spoon into parfait glasses. Chill until firm. Yield: 4 servings.

Approx Per Serving: Cal 172; Prot 2.5 g; Carbo 32.3 g; T Fat 2.5 g; Chol 0.0 mg; Potas 160.0 mg; Sod 73.3 mg.

North Carolina Grape Growers Association

STRAWBERRY PIZZA

1 1/2 cups all-purpose flour
1/2 cup chopped pecans
3/4 cup butter
2 cups confectioners' sugar
8 ounces cream cheese, softened
2 cups whipped topping
1 pint fresh strawberries, sliced
1 pint fresh strawberries, crushed
3/4 cup sugar
2 tablespoons cornstarch
2 drops of almond extract

Mix flour, pecans and butter in bowl until crumbly. Press into 9x13-inch baking dish. Bake at 350 degrees for 5 to 8 minutes or until light brown. Cool. Cream confectioners' sugar and cream cheese in mixer bowl until light and fluffy. Fold in whipped topping gently. Spread over baked layer. Top with sliced strawberries. Combine crushed strawberries, sugar, cornstarch and almond extract in saucepan. Cook until thickened, stirring constantly. Cool. Spread over sliced strawberries. Chill until serving time. Yield: 12 servings.

Approx Per Serving: Cal 429; Prot 4.0 g; Carbo 49.8 g; T Fat 25.0 g; Chol 51.7 mg; Potas 146.0 mg; Sod 158.0 mg.

North Carolina Strawberry and Pick-Your-Own Association

HOT MILK SHORTCAKE

3 eggs
2 cups sugar
2 cups sifted self-rising flour
1/2 cup butter
1 cup milk
2 cups sliced strawberries
1/4 cup sugar
1 cup sour cream
1 teaspoon confectioners' sugar

Combine eggs and 2 cups sugar in mixer bowl; mix well. Add flour; mix well. Combine butter and milk in small saucepan. Heat just until butter melts, stirring constantly; do not boil. Stir into batter gradually. Pour into 9x13-inch cake pan. Bake at 350 degrees until shortcake tests done. Cut into squares. Combine strawberries and 1/4 cup sugar in bowl. Let stand for several minutes. Pour over shortcake. Combine sour cream and confectioners' sugar in small bowl. Spoon dollops of sour cream mixture on each square. Yield: 8 servings.

Approx Per Serving: Cal 554; Prot 7.8 g; Carbo 85.5 g; T Fat 21.1 g; Chol 151.0 mg; Potas 204.0 mg; Sod 153.0 mg.

North Carolina Strawberry and Pick-Your-Own Association

SWEET POTATO PUDDING

3 cups shredded fresh sweet potatoes
1 cup milk
3/4 cup sugar
2 eggs, slightly beaten
2 tablespoons melted margarine
1 teaspoon cinnamon
1 teaspoon nutmeg
1/4 teaspoon salt

Stir sweet potatoes into milk in large bowl. Add sugar, eggs, margarine, cinnamon, nutmeg and salt, mixing well after each addition. Pour into well-greased 1 1/2-quart baking dish. Bake at 350 degrees for 1 hour. Serve warm. Shred sweet potatoes into milk to keep them from turning dark. Yield: 6 servings

Approx Per Serving: Cal 241; Prot 4.4 g; Carbo 40.9 g; T Fat 7.1 g; Chol 96.8 mg; Potas 278.0 mg; Sod 180.0 mg.

North Carolina Sweet Potato Commission

CAKES

APPLE DELUXE CAKE

2 eggs
1 cup oil
2 cups sugar
1 cup chopped dates
6 ounces butterscotch chips
3 cups all-purpose flour
1 teaspoon salt
1 teaspoon soda
1/2 teaspoon cinnamon
1 teaspoon vanilla extract
1 cup coconut
1 cup chopped pecans
3 1/2 cups shredded apples

Combine eggs, oil and sugar in large bowl; mix well. Coat dates and butterscotch chips with a small amount of flour. Stir into egg mixture. Add remaining flour, salt, soda, cinnamon, vanilla, coconut, pecans and apples, mixing well after each addition. Spoon into greased 9x13-inch cake pan. Bake at 350 degrees for 45 minutes. Garnish with whipped topping. Yield: 12 servings.

Approx Per Serving: Cal 642; Prot 6.2 g; Carbo 85.4 g; T Fat 33.4 g; Chol 45.7 mg; Potas 285.0 mg; Sod 263.0 mg.

North Carolina Apple Growers Association

FRESH APPLE CAKE

3 eggs
2 cups sugar
1 1/2 cups oil
3 cups all-purpose flour
1 teaspoon soda
1 teaspoon cinnamon
1 cup chopped dates
1 (8-ounce) can coconut
1 1/2 cups chopped pecans
1 cup sliced maraschino cherries
3 cups chopped apples
2 teaspoons vanilla extract
1/2 cup margarine
1 cup packed light brown sugar
1/4 cup milk

Beat eggs, sugar and oil in mixer bowl until light and lemon-colored. Sift flour, soda and cinnamon into bowl. Add to egg mixture; mix well. Stir in dates, coconut, pecans, maraschino cherries, apples and vanilla. Spoon into greased 9x13-inch cake pan. Bake at 325 degrees for 1 hour and 15 minutes or until cake pulls away from sides of pan. Combine margarine, brown sugar and milk in small saucepan. Bring to a boil, stirring constantly. Cook for 2 to 3 minutes, stirring constantly. Pour over hot cake. May substitute cream cheese frosting for brown sugar glaze. Yield: 12 servings.

Approx Per Serving: Cal 893; Prot 7.3 g; Carbo 104 g; T Fat 52.9 g; Chol 69.2 mg; Potas 396.0 mg; Sod 191.0 mg.
Nutritional information does not include maraschino cherries.

North Carolina Apple Growers Association

CHOCOLATE CHIP CAKE

1 (2-layer) package yellow cake mix
1 (3-ounce) package vanilla instant pudding mix
8 ounces sour cream, at room temperature
4 eggs, at room temperature
1/2 cup oil
1/2 cup water
1 (6-ounce) package German's sweet chocolate, grated
6 ounces semisweet chocolate chips

Combine cake mix, pudding mix, sour cream, eggs, oil and water in large bowl; mix well. Fold in chocolate and chocolate chips gently. Spoon into greased and floured bundt pan. Bake at 350 degrees for 50 to 60 minutes or until cake tests done. Cool in pan on wire rack. Invert onto cake plate. Yield: 16 servings.

Approx Per Serving: Cal 331; Prot 3.7 g; Carbo 35.7 g; T Fat 20.5 g; Chol 74.8 mg; Potas 106.0 mg; Sod 195.0 mg.

North Carolina Egg Association

LUSCIOUS DATE NUT CAKE

1 1/2 cups sugar
1 cup oil
3 eggs
2 cups sifted all-purpose flour
1 teaspoon soda
1 teaspoon salt
1 teaspoon nutmeg
1 teaspoon cinnamon
1 teaspoon allspice
1 cup buttermilk
1 cup chopped pecans
1 cup chopped dates
1 teaspoon vanilla extract

Beat sugar, oil and eggs in mixer bowl until smooth and creamy. Sift flour, soda, salt, nutmeg, cinnamon and allspice into bowl. Add flour mixture to egg mixture alternately with buttermilk, mixing well after each addition. Stir in pecans, dates and vanilla. Spoon into greased and floured 9x13-inch cake pan. Bake at 300 degrees for 55 to 60 minutes or until cake tests done. Cool in pan. Yield: 12 servings.

Approx Per Serving: Cal 462; Prot 5.3 g; Carbo 53.3 g; T Fat 26.7 g; Chol 69.2 mg; Potas 202.0 mg; Sod 286.0 mg.

Carolina Nut Cracker
MEMBER

HOLIDAY FRUITCAKES

2 pounds candied cherries
2 pounds candied pineapple
2 pounds white raisins
1 pound pecans, chopped
1 pound walnuts, chopped
4 cups all-purpose flour
2 cups butter, softened
12 egg yolks
2 cups sugar
1 teaspoon vanilla extract
1 teaspoon lemon juice
12 egg whites

Coat cherries, pineapple, raisins, pecans and walnuts with a small amount of flour in bowl. Combine remaining flour with butter in large bowl; mix well. Mix egg yolks and sugar in large mixer bowl. Add to flour mixture; mix well. Stir in vanilla and lemon juice. Fold fruit and nuts into cake batter gently. Beat egg whites in mixer bowl until stiff peaks form. Fold into cake batter gently. Spoon into 2 greased and floured 5x9-inch loaf pans. Bake at 325 degrees for 2 hours or until cake tests done. Remove to wire rack to cool. May bake in tube pan. Yield: 20 servings.

Nutritional information for this recipe is not available.

Carolina Nut Cracker
MEMBER

YUMMY FRUIT COCKTAIL CAKE

1½ cups sugar
2 cups self-rising flour
2 teaspoons soda
2 eggs
1 (16-ounce) can fruit cocktail
1½ cups sugar
1 cup evaporated milk
½ cup margarine
1 cup coconut
1 cup coarsely chopped pecans
1 teaspoon vanilla extract

Mix 1½ cups sugar, flour, soda, eggs and fruit cocktail in bowl. Spoon into 3 greased and floured 9-inch cake pans. Bake at 350 degrees for 15 to 20 minutes or until cake tests done. Remove to wire rack to cool. Combine remaining 1½ cups sugar, milk and margarine in saucepan. Bring to a boil, stirring constantly. Boil for 5 minutes. Let stand in pan of cold water until cool. Stir in coconut, pecans and vanilla. Spread between layers and over top of cake.
Yield: 12 servings.

Approx Per Serving: Cal 497; Prot 5.6 g; Carbo 79.1 g; T Fat 19.1 g; Chol 51.8 mg; Potas 192.0 mg; Sod 489.0 mg.

Carolina Nut Cracker
MEMBER

CAROLINA NUT FEUD CAKE

8 eggs
1 cup self-rising flour
2 cups sugar
1 (6-ounce) package vanilla instant pudding mix
1 tablespoon vanilla extract
5 cups pecan meal
Pecan Frosting
1/4 cup chopped pecans

Beat eggs in large mixer bowl for 5 minutes. Add flour, sugar, pudding mix and vanilla. Beat for 5 minutes. Add pecan meal gradually. Beat at low speed for 1 minute longer. Spoon into 2 greased and floured 9-inch round cake pans. Bake at 350 degrees for 15 to 20 minutes or until cake tests done. Do not overbake. Remove to wire rack to cool. Spread Pecan Frosting between layers and over top of cake. Sprinkle with chopped pecans. Make pecan meal at home by feeezing pecans and chopping in food processor to the consistency of fine meal. Yield: 12 servings.

Approx Per Serving: Cal 1257; Prot 15.2 g; Carbo 104.0 g; T Fat 93.6 g; Chol 224 mg; Potas 518.0 mg; Sod 376.0 mg.

PECAN FROSTING

1/2 cup butter, softened
8 ounces cream cheese, softened
1 teaspoon vanilla extract
1 pound confectioners' sugar
1/2 cup pecan meal

Cream butter and cream cheese in mixer bowl until light and fluffy. Add vanilla and confectioners' sugar. Beat until creamy. Add pecan meal; mix well.

Nutritional information is included in recipe above.

Carolina Nut Cracker
MEMBER

PEACHY DELIGHT

1 (2-layer) package
  yellow cake mix
3/4 cup melted butter
1 pound peaches, sliced,
  sweetened
2 cups sour cream
1/4 cup sugar
3 egg yolks
Cinnamon to taste

Combine cake mix and butter in bowl; mix well. Spread in bottom of lightly greased 9x12-inch cake pan. Layer peaches over top. Blend sour cream, sugar and egg yolks in bowl. Spoon over peaches. Sprinkle with cinnamon. Bake at 350 degrees for 30 to 35 minutes or until set. Yield: 12 servings.

Approx Per Serving: Cal 358; Prot 3.4 g; Carbo 35.1 g; T Fat 23.3 g; Chol 116.0 mg; Potas 99.5 mg; Sod 296.0 mg.

North Carolina Peach Growers Association

PEANUT PUDDING CAKE

2/3 cup chopped roasted
  peanuts
1 cup all-purpose flour
1/2 cup butter, softened
1/3 cup creamy peanut
  butter
8 ounces cream cheese,
  softened
1 cup confectioners' sugar
4 ounces whipped topping
1 (3-ounce) package
  vanilla instant pudding
  mix
1 (3-ounce) package
  chocolate instant
  pudding mix
2 3/4 cups milk
9 ounces whipped topping
1 ounce sweet chocolate,
  grated
1/3 cup chopped roasted
  peanuts

Mix 2/3 cup peanuts, flour and butter in small bowl until crumbly. Press into bottom of 8x12-inch cake pan. Bake at 350 degrees for 20 minutes. Cool completely. Cream peanut butter and cream cheese in mixer bowl until light and fluffy. Add confectioners' sugar; mix well. Fold in 4 ounces whipped topping gently. Spread over cooled cake. Combine pudding mixes and milk in bowl. Beat until thickened. Spread over peanut butter layer. Spread 9 ounces whipped topping over top. Sprinkle with chocolate and remaining 1/3 cup peanuts. Chill for 2 to 3 hours. Yield: 12 servings.

Approx Per Serving: Cal 516; Prot 10.2 g; Carbo 44.7 g; T Fat 34.8 g; Chol 48.9 mg; Potas 259.0 mg; Sod 328.0 mg.

North Carolina Peanut Growers Association

PINEAPPLE CAKE

1 (2-layer) package pineapple cake mix
3 eggs
1 (3-ounce) package vanilla instant pudding mix
1 cup club soda
2 (16-ounce) cans crushed pineapple
1 1/2 cups sugar
1/4 cup cornmeal
3/4 cup water

Combine cake mix, eggs, pudding mix and club soda in bowl; mix well. Spoon into 2 greased and floured 9-inch cake pans. Bake at 350 degrees for 30 to 35 minutes or until cake tests done. Remove to wire rack to cool. Split cake layers horizontally. Combine pineapple and sugar in saucepan. Cook until sugar is dissolved, stirring constantly. Bring to a boil. Mix cornmeal and water in small bowl until smooth. Stir into pineapple mixture gradually. Cook until thickened, stirring constantly. Cool slightly. Spread pineapple mixture between layers and over top of cake. Chill until serving time. Yield: 10 servings.

Approx Per Serving: Cal 400; Prot 3.9 g; Carbo 87.7 g; T Fat 4.7 g; Chol 82.2 mg; Potas 120.0 mg; Sod 294.0 mg.

Atkinson Milling
MEMBER

GOOD PLUM CAKE

2 cups self-rising flour
2 cups sugar
1 teaspoon cloves
1 teaspoon cinnamon
3 eggs, beaten
1 cup oil
2 (4-ounce) jars baby food plums
1 cup chopped pecans

Mix flour, sugar, cloves and cinnamon in medium bowl. Combine eggs, oil and plums in bowl; mix well. Add to flour mixture; mix well. Stir in pecans. Pour into greased and floured 9x13-inch cake pan. Bake at 325 degrees for 1 hour. Serve warm. Yield: 15 servings.

Approx Per Serving: Cal 369; Prot 3.5 g; Carbo 43.2 g; T Fat 21.2 g; Chol 54.8 mg; Potas 88.1 mg; Sod 195.0 mg.

North Carolina Department of Agriculture

CHERRY-PECAN POUND CAKE

1 cup butter, softened
1 cup sugar
4 eggs
1 teaspoon vanilla extract
1/2 teaspoon salt
1/2 teaspoon almond extract
1/8 teaspoon ground mace
1 1/2 cups all-purpose flour
1 (6-ounce) jar maraschino cherries, drained, chopped
1/4 cup chopped pecans

Beat butter and sugar in mixer bowl at medium speed until light and fluffy. Add eggs, vanilla, salt, almond extract and mace; beat well. Add flour 1/2 at a time, beating at low speed just until blended. Stir in maraschino cherries and pecans. Spoon into greased and floured 5x9-inch loaf pan. Bake at 325 degrees for 60 to 70 minutes or until cake tests done. Cool in pan on wire rack for 10 minutes. Remove from pan; cool completely. Yield: 8 servings.

Approx Per Serving: Cal 449; Prot 6.0 g; Carbo 43.7 g; T Fat 28.5 g; Chol 199.0 mg; Potas 77.6 mg; Sod 362.0 mg.
Nutritional information does not include maraschino cherries.

North Carolina Egg Association

SWEET POTATO POUND CAKE

1/2 cup shortening
1/2 cup butter, softened
2 cups sugar
6 eggs
3 cups all-purpose flour
1/2 teaspoon salt
1/4 teaspoon soda
1 teaspoon baking powder
1 cup buttermilk
1 cup puréed cooked sweet potato
1/2 teaspoon almond extract
1/4 teaspoon coconut extract
1/4 cup slivered almonds, toasted, finely chopped
1/4 cup flaked coconut

Cream shortening and butter in mixer bowl until light. Add sugar gradually, beating until fluffy. Add eggs 1 at a time, beating well after each addition. Combine flour, salt, soda and baking powder in bowl; mix well. Add to creamed mixture alternately with buttermilk, mixing well after each addition. Stir in sweet potato and flavorings. Sprinkle almonds and coconut into bottom of greased and floured 12-cup bundt pan. Pour batter into prepared pan. Bake at 350 degrees for 1 hour. Cool in pan for 10 minutes; remove to wire rack to cool completely. Yield: 16 servings.

Approx Per Serving: Cal 350; Prot 5.9 g; Carbo 46.4 g; T Fat 16.1 g; Chol 119.0 mg; Potas 117.0 mg; Sod 193.0 mg.

North Carolina Sweet Potato Commission

OLD-FASHIONED POUND CAKE

1 cup butter, softened
1/2 cup shortening
3 cups sugar
5 eggs
3 cups all-purpose flour
1/2 teaspoon baking powder
1 cup milk
1 teaspoon vanilla extract
1 teaspoon almond extract

Cream butter, shortening and sugar in mixer bowl until light and fluffy. Add eggs 1 at a time, beating well after each addition. Sift flour and baking powder together 3 times. Add to creamed mixture alternately with milk, mixing well after each addition. Stir in vanilla and almond extract. Spoon into well-greased and floured tube pan. Bake at 350 degrees for 1 hour and 15 minutes. Remove to wire rack to cool. Yield: 12 servings.

Approx Per Serving: Cal 563; Prot 6.6 g; Carbo 74.8 g; T Fat 27.2 g; Chol 158.0 mg; Potas 91.0 mg; Sod 182.0 mg.

North Carolina Egg Association

DELIGHTFUL STRAWBERRY NUT CAKE

1 cup oil
4 eggs
1/2 cup milk
1 (3-ounce) package strawberry gelatin
1 cup frozen strawberries, thawed
1 (2-layer) package yellow cake mix
1 cup chopped pecans
1 cup coconut
1 pound confectioners' sugar
1/2 cup margarine, softened
1/2 cup chopped strawberries
1/2 cup chopped pecans
1/2 cup coconut

Combine oil, eggs and milk in mixer bowl; mix well. Add gelatin, 1 cup strawberries and cake mix. Beat until smooth. Fold in 1 cup pecans and 1 cup coconut gently. Spoon into 2 greased and floured 9-inch cake pans. Bake at 350 degrees for 20 minutes. Remove to wire rack to cool. Combine confectioners' sugar, margarine, remaining 1/2 cup strawberries, 1/2 cup pecans and 1/2 cup coconut in bowl; mix well. Spread between layers and over top and side of cake. Yield: 12 servings.

Approx Per Serving: Cal 668; Prot 5.9 g; Carbo 67.6 g; T Fat 43.3 g; Chol 92.7 mg; Potas 157.0 mg; Sod 338.0 mg.

Carolina Nut Cracker
MEMBER

FESTIVE WATERMELON CAKE

1 tablespoon all-purpose flour
1 (2-layer) package white cake mix
1 (3-ounce) package mixed fruit gelatin
3/4 cup oil
1 cup chopped watermelon
4 eggs
1/2 cup margarine, softened
1 pound confectioners' sugar
1/2 to 1 cup chopped watermelon

Sprinkle flour over cake mix in mixer bowl. Add gelatin, oil and 1 cup watermelon; beat well. Add eggs 1 at a time, beating well after each addition. Spoon batter into 2 greased and floured 8-inch cake pans. Bake at 325 degrees for 30 minutes. Remove to wire rack to cool. Cream margarine and confectioners' sugar in small bowl until light and fluffy. Add enough remaining watermelon gradually to make of spreading consistency. Spread between layers and over top of cake. May tint frosting with red food coloring if desired. Yield: 10 servings.

Approx Per Serving: Cal 582; Prot 5.1 g; Carbo 73.6 g; T Fat 30.6 g; Chol 110.0 mg; Potas 79.7 mg; Sod 373.0 mg.

North Carolina Watermelon Association

VANILLA WAFER CAKE

1 cup butter, softened
2 cups sugar
6 eggs
1 teaspoon vanilla extract
1 (12-ounce) package vanilla wafers, crushed
1/2 cup milk
1 cup chopped pecans
2 cups coconut

Cream butter and sugar in mixer bowl until light and fluffy. Add eggs 1 at a time, mixing well after each addition. Stir in vanilla. Add vanilla wafers alternately with milk 1/4 at a time, mixing well after each addition. Stir in pecans and coconut. Spoon into well-greased tube pan. Bake at 350 degrees for 1 hour or until cake is brown and tests done. Cool in pan on wire rack for 10 minutes. Invert onto cake plate to cool completely. Yield: 16 servings.

Approx Per Serving: Cal 424; Prot 4.6 g; Carbo 46.6 g; T Fat 25.6 g; Chol 148.0 mg; Potas 124.0 mg; Sod 230.0 mg.

North Carolina Egg Association

SCUPPERNONG WINE CAKE

½ cup chopped pecans
1 (2-layer) package butter-recipe golden cake mix
1 (3½-ounce) package vanilla instant pudding mix
½ cup oil
4 eggs
1 cup Southland Scuppernong wine
½ cup confectioners' sugar
2 tablespoons Scuppernong wine

Sprinkle pecans in bottom of greased and floured tube pan. Combine cake mix, pudding mix, oil, eggs and 1 cup wine in mixer bowl. Beat for 2 minutes. Pour into prepared pan. Bake at 325 degrees for 50 to 60 minutes or until cake tests done. Remove to wire rack to cool. Combine confectioners' sugar and remaining 2 tablespoons wine in small bowl. Mix until of desired spreading consistency. Drizzle over cake. Yield: 16 servings.

Approx Per Serving: Cal 243; Prot 2.8 g; Carbo 27.9 g; T Fat 12.5 g; Chol 68.5 mg; Potas 51.6 mg; Sod 169.0 mg.

Southland Estate Winery
MEMBER

CHOCOLATE TRUFFLES

2 cups semisweet chocolate chips
6 tablespoons butter
6 tablespoons confectioners' sugar
6 egg yolks
1 teaspoon almond extract
½ cup cocoa

Melt chocolate chips in top of double boiler over 1-inch simmering water. Remove from heat. Stir in butter and confectioners' sugar until mixture is well blended. Add egg yolks 1 at a time, mixing well after each addition. Add almond extract; mix well. Pour mixture into medium bowl. Let stand, covered with plastic wrap, in a cool, dark place for 18 hours. Do not store in refrigerator. Shape into 1-inch balls. Chill truffles for 3 hours. Roll in cocoa. Store in airtight container in refrigerator. Serve at room temperature. May use chopped pecans, coconut or melted dipping chocolate to coat truffles. Yield: 50 truffles.

Approx Per Truffle: Cal 57.1; Prot .629 g; Carbo 4.6 g; T Fat 4.5 g; Chol 36.4 mg; Potas 26.0 mg; Sod 13.5 mg.

North Carolina Egg Association

EASIEST YET PEANUT BUTTER FUDGE

2 cups milk chocolate chips
1 (12-ounce) jar crunchy peanut butter
1 (14-ounce) can sweetened condensed milk

Melt chocolate chips and peanut butter in top of double boiler. Remove from heat. Stir in condense milk until well blended. Pour into waxed paper-lined 8x8-inch dish. Chill until firm. Cut into squares.
Yield: 24 squares.

Approx Per Square: Cal 209; Prot 5.9 g; Carbo 19.3 g; T Fat 13.8 g; Chol 5.6 mg; Potas 208.0 mg; Sod 80.2 mg.

North Carolina Peanut Growers Association

JIFFY GOOBER HAYSTACKS

1 cup butterscotch chips
1/3 cup creamy peanut butter
1 cup roasted peanuts
1 (3-ounce) can chow mein noodles

Melt butterscotch chips and peanut butter in top of double boiler over hot not boiling water, stirring until well blended. Add peanuts and chow mein noodles; stir until well coated. Drop by spoonfuls onto waxed paper. Let stand until firm.
Yield: 36 haystacks.

Approx Per Haystack: Cal 72.8; Prot 2.3 g; Carbo 5.2 g; T Fat 5.5 g; Chol 0.3 mg; Potas 62.7 mg; Sod 51.2 mg.

North Carolina Peanut Growers Association

CHOCOLATE-COATED PEANUTS

1 cup semisweet chocolate
2 1/2 cups roasted shelled peanuts, skins on

Melt chocolate chips in top of double boiler over hot water. Add peanuts; stir to coat. Pour onto waxed paper; separate with fork. Let stand until firm. Yield: 3 cups.

Approx Per Cup: Cal 988; Prot 34.7 g; Carbo 54.7 g; T Fat 79.8 g; Chol 0.0 mg; Potas 1048.0 mg; Sod 26.3 mg.

North Carolina Peanut Growers Association

SUGAR-COATED PEANUTS

1 cup sugar
1/2 cup water
2 cups raw shelled peanuts, skins on

Dissolve sugar in water in saucepan over medium heat. Add peanuts. Cook over medium heat until peanuts are coated with sugar, stirring frequently. Pour onto ungreased baking sheet. Separate peanuts with fork. Bake at 300 degrees for 30 minutes, stirring every 10 minutes. Yield: 16 ounces.

Approx Per Ounce: Cal 61; Prot 1.9 g; Carbo 6.3 g; T Fat 3.5 g; Chol 0.0 mg; Potas 52.1 mg; Sod 0.7 mg.

North Carolina Peanut Growers Association

DIXIE PEANUT BRITTLE

2 cups sugar
1 cup light corn syrup
1/2 cup water
1/2 teaspoon salt
3 cups raw shelled peanuts, skins on
2 tablespoons butter
2 teaspoons soda

Combine first 4 ingredients in heavy saucepan. Bring to a boil over medium-high heat. Add peanuts; mix well to coat. Reduce heat to medium. Cook, uncovered, to 293 degrees on candy thermometer, hard-crack stage, stirring constantly. Remove from heat. Stir in butter and soda. Spread into 1/4-inch layer on buttered baking sheet. Cool. Break into pieces. Store in airtight container. Yield: 32 ounces.

Approx Per Ounce: Cal 161; Prot 3.5 g; Carbo 22.7 g; T Fat 7.4 g; Chol 2.0 mg; Potas 99.6 mg; Sod 96.7 mg.

North Carolina Peanut Growers Association

MICROWAVE PEANUT BRITTLE

1 1/2 cups raw shelled peanuts, skins on
1 cup sugar
1/2 cup light corn syrup
1/8 teaspoon salt
1 teaspoon butter
1 teaspoon vanilla extract
1 teaspoon soda

Place peanuts, sugar, corn syrup and salt in 1 1/2-quart glass dish; mix well. Microwave on High for 8 minutes, stirring once. Add butter and vanilla, mixing until well blended. Microwave on High for 2 minutes longer. Add soda, stirring until light and foamy. Spread into 1/4-inch layer on buttered baking sheet. Cool. Break into pieces. Store in airtight container. Yield: 16 ounces.

Approx Per Ounce: Cal 158; Prot 3.5 g; Carbo 22.6 g; T Fat 7.0 g; Chol 0.6 mg; Potas 99.5 mg; Sod 76.0 mg.

North Carolina Peanut Growers Association

CANDY

BAKED CARAMEL CORN

1 cup margarine
2 cups packed light brown sugar
1/2 cup light corn syrup
1 teaspoon salt
1/2 teaspoon soda
1 teaspoon vanilla extract
6 quarts air-popped popcorn

Combine margarine, brown sugar, corn syrup and salt in heavy saucepan. Bring to a boil, stirring constantly. Cook for 5 minutes; do not stir. Remove from heat. Stir in soda and vanilla. Pour over popcorn into large bowl; mix well. Spread in two 9x13-inch baking pans. Bake at 250 degrees for 1 hour, stirring every 15 minutes. Cool completely. Break into pieces. Yield: 10 servings.

Approx Per Serving: Cal 445; Prot 2.6 g; Carbo 69.3 g; T Fat 19.2 g; Chol 0.0 mg; Potas 212.0 mg; Sod 496.0 mg.

Carolina's Best Popcorn
MEMBER

BLAIR'S SQUARES

1 cup butter
2 cups packed brown sugar
2 eggs, slightly beaten
1 cup cornmeal
1/2 cup self-rising flour
1 cup chopped pecans
1 teaspoon vanilla extract

Melt butter in 10x15-inch baking dish. Pour butter into bowl. Add brown sugar; mix well. Stir in eggs until well blended. Add sifted mixture of cornmeal and flour; mix well. Stir in pecans and vanilla. Pour into prepared baking dish. Bake at 375 degrees for 20 to 25 minutes or until brown. Cool in pan for 10 minutes. Cut into squares. Yield: 20 squares.

Approx Per Square: Cal 247; Prot 2.0 g; Carbo 30.1 g; T Fat 13.9 g; Chol 52.2 mg; Potas 120.0 mg; Sod 128.0 mg.

Atkinson Milling Company
MEMBER

CHOCOLATE TOFFEE SQUARES

1/2 cup self-rising cornmeal
1/2 cup sifted self-rising flour
1 cup oats
1/3 cup melted butter
1/2 cup packed brown sugar
1/4 cup dark corn syrup
1 egg, beaten
1 1/2 teaspoons vanilla extract
1 cup semisweet chocolate chips
1/2 cup chopped pecans

Combine cornmeal, flour and oats in bowl; mix well. Add butter; toss to mix. Add brown sugar, corn syrup, egg and vanilla; mix well. Spread in greased and waxed paper-lined 7x11-inch baking pan. Bake at 450 degrees for 12 minutes or until golden brown. Remove to wire rack immediately; peel off waxed paper. Cool. Melt chocolate chips in double boiler over hot water. Spread over cooled layer; sprinkle with pecans. Cut into squares. Yield: 24 squares.

Approx Per Square: Cal 138; Prot 1.8 g; Carbo 17.9 g; T Fat 7.3 g; Chol 18.3 mg; Potas 71.5 mg; Sod 57.7 mg.

North Carolina Corn Miller's Association

CORNMEAL COOKIES

1 cup butter, softened
1 1/2 cups sugar
2 eggs
1 teaspoon lemon extract
3 cups sifted all-purpose flour
1 teaspoon baking powder
1/2 teaspoon salt
1 teaspoon cinnamon
1 cup cornmeal
1/2 cup raisins

Cream butter and sugar in bowl until light and fluffy. Add eggs and lemon extract; mix well. Sift in flour, baking powder, salt, cinnamon and cornmeal; mix well. Stir in raisins. Roll dough to 1/8-inch thickness on lightly floured surface. Cut with floured cookie cutter. Place on greased cookie sheet. Bake at 400 degrees for 10 to 15 minutes or until light brown. Remove to wire rack to cool. Yield: 60 cookies.

Approx Per Cookie: Cal 82; Prot 1.1 g; Carbo 12.3 g; T Fat 3.3 g; Chol 17.4 mg; Potas 22.0 mg; Sod 51.8 mg.

North Carolina Corn Miller's Association

HONEY AND NUT CORNMEAL COOKIES

1 cup butter, softened
1 1/2 cups sugar
2 tablespoons honey
2 eggs
2 cups all-purpose flour
2 cups cornmeal
1/8 teaspoon soda
1 teaspoon salt
1 teaspoon nutmeg (optional)
1 tablespoon baking powder
1 cup chopped pecans
1/4 cup buttermilk
1 cup semisweet chocolate chips

Cream butter and sugar in mixer bowl until light and fluffy. Add honey; mix well. Add eggs; mix well. Sift flour, cornmeal, soda, salt, nutmeg and baking powder into medium bowl. Stir in pecans. Add to creamed mixture alternately with buttermilk, mixing well after each addition. Stir in chocolate chips. Drop by teaspoonfuls onto greased cookie sheet; flatten with floured fork. Bake at 375 degrees for 10 minutes or until light brown. Remove to wire rack to cool. May omit pecans, chocolate chips and nutmeg and add the grated rind of 1 lemon and 3 tablespoons lemon juice. Yield: 78 cookies.

Approx Per Cookie: Cal 85; Prot 1.0 g; Carbo 11.1 g; T Fat 4.4 g; Chol 13.5 mg; Potas 25.0 mg; Sod 63.8 mg.

Atkinson Milling Company
MEMBER

GRAPE CRUNCH SQUARES

1 cup packed brown sugar
1 1/2 cups all-purpose flour
3/4 cup butter, softened
1 1/2 cups oats
3/4 cup grape jam, jelly or preserves

Combine brown sugar and flour in bowl; mix well. Cut in butter until crumbly. Stir in oats. Press half the mixture into 9x11-inch baking dish. Spread grape jam over top. Top with remaining mixture. Bake at 325 degrees for 40 to 45 minutes or until golden brown. Cool. Cut into squares.
Yield: 16 servings.

Approx Per Serving: Cal 236; Prot 2.6 g; Carbo 36.8 g; T Fat 9.2 g; Chol 23.3 mg; Potas 99.9 mg; Sod 82.0 mg.

North Carolina Grape Growers Association

HONEY AND PECAN BALLS

1 cup butter, softened
1/4 cup Master's Market Ministry honey
2 teaspoons vanilla extract
2 cups sifted all-purpose flour
1/2 teaspoon salt
2 cups chopped pecans
1 cup confectioners' sugar

Cream butter, honey and vanilla in mixer bowl until light and fluffy. Sift in flour and salt; mix well. Stir in pecans. Shape by teaspoonfuls into balls. Place on cookie sheets. Bake at 350 degrees for 20 minutes or until light brown. Roll in confectioners' sugar. Yield: 100 cookies.

Approx Per Cookie: Cal 47; Prot 0.5g; Carbo 4.0 g; T Fat 3.5 g; Chol 5.0 mg; Potas 12.8 mg; Sod 26.3 mg.

Master's Market Ministry
MEMBER

OLD-FASHIONED LEMON DROPS

1/2 cup butter, softened
3/4 cup sugar
1 egg
1 cup self-rising cornmeal
1/2 cup self-rising flour
1/2 cup milk
1/2 teaspoon grated lemon rind
1 teaspoon lemon flavoring
1/2 cup confectioners' sugar
3 or 4 tablespoons milk
1 teaspoon grated lemon rind

Cream butter and sugar in mixer bowl until light and fluffy. Add egg; mix well. Add cornmeal and flour; mix well. Stir in 1/2 cup milk, 1/2 teaspoon lemon rind and 1 teaspoon flavoring. Drop by teaspoonfuls onto greased cookie sheet. Bake at 375 degrees for 8 minutes or until light brown. Place confectioners' sugar in bowl. Add enough remaining milk to make of spreading consistency. Stir in remaining 1 teaspoon lemon rind. Spread over warm cookies. Let stand on wire rack until glaze is set. Yield: 42 cookies.

Approx Per Cookie: Cal 59; Prot 0.7 g; Carbo 8.6 g; T Fat 2.5 g; Chol 13.0 mg; Potas 13.7 mg; Sod 38.1 mg.

Atkinson's Milling Company
MEMBER

PEANUTTY CHOCOLATE SNACK SQUARES

5 graham crackers, broken into squares
1/2 cup sugar
1 cup light corn syrup
1 cup semisweet chocolate chips
1 cup peanut butter
1 cup dry roasted peanuts

Line bottom of 8x8-inch baking dish with graham crackers squares, cutting to fit as necessary. Combine sugar and corn syrup in 2-quart glass bowl. Microwave on High until mixture boils, stirring every 2 minutes. Microwave for 3 minutes longer. Stir in chocolate chips, peanut butter and peanuts. Pour over graham crackers, spreading to cover. Chill, covered, until firm. Cut into 2-inch squares.
Yield: 16 squares.

Approx Per Square: Cal 291; Prot 7.5 g; Carbo 33.4 g; T Fat 16.8 g; Chol 0.0 mg; Potas 222.0 mg; Sod 90.8 mg.

North Carolina Department of Agriculture

SWEETHEART COOKIES

1 cup butter, softened
1 1/3 cups sugar
1 1/3 cups packed brown sugar
2 eggs
1 teaspoon vanilla extract
1 1/2 cups all-purpose flour
1 teaspoon soda
3 cups oats
1 1/2 cups chopped roasted peanuts
1 cup semisweet chocolate chips

Cream butter, sugar and brown sugar in mixer bowl until light and fluffy. Add eggs and vanilla; mix well. Combine flour and soda in medium bowl; mix well. Add oats; mix well. Add to creamed mixture 1 cup at a time, beating well after each addition. Stir in peanuts and chocolate chips. Drop by teaspoonfuls onto cookie sheet. Bake at 375 degrees for 10 to 12 minutes or until light brown. Remove to wire rack to cool.
Yield: 72 cookies.

Approx Per Cookie: Cal 98; Prot 1.6 g; Carbo 12.5 g; T Fat 5.2 g; Chol 14.5 mg; Potas 54.2 mg; Sod 66.0 mg.

North Carolina Peanut Growers Association

SHOWCASE SHORTBREAD

2 cups all-purpose flour
1/2 cup confectioners' sugar
1 cup butter, softened
5 egg yolks
1 teaspoon vanilla extract
1/2 cup semisweet chocolate chips

Sift flour and confectioners' sugar into bowl. Cut in butter until crumbly. Add egg yolks and vanilla; mix well. Stir in chocolate chips. Spread in 9x9-inch baking dish. Bake at 300 degrees for 40 to 45 minutes or until light brown. Remove to wire rack to cool. Cut into bars. Yield: 27 bars.

Approx Per Bar: Cal 129; Prot 1.7 g; Carbo 10.7 g; T Fat 9.1 g; Chol 68.8 mg; Potas 24.8 mg; Sod 59.5 mg.

North Carolina Egg Association

SWEET POTATO AND APPLE BARS

1/4 cup margarine, softened
1/2 cup packed brown sugar
3 eggs
1/2 teaspoon cinnamon
1/4 teaspoon nutmeg
2 cups biscuit mix
1 cup chopped peeled tart apple
1/3 cup raisins
1/4 cup chopped pecans
3 cups chopped, cooked sweet potatoes
3/4 cup confectioners' sugar
2 tablespoons orange juice

Combine margarine, brown sugar, eggs, cinnamon and nutmeg in large mixer bowl. Beat at high speed until well mixed. Add biscuit mix; mix well. Fold in apple, raisins, pecans and sweet potatoes. Spread in greased 9x13-inch baking dish. Bake at 350 degrees for 30 to 35 minutes or until mixture tests done. Cool. Drizzle with mixture of confectioners' sugar and orange juice. Cut into 2x3-inch bars. Yield: 15 bars.

Approx Per Bar: Cal 381; Prot 15.9 g; Carbo 35.8 g; T Fat 19.2 g; Chol 603.0 mg; Potas 345.0 mg; Sod 441.0 mg.

North Carolina Sweet Potato Commission

CRISP APPLE CREAM PIE

1/4 cup melted butter
1 1/2 cups graham cracker crumbs
1 (14-ounce) can sweetened condensed milk
1 cup sour cream
1/4 cup lemon juice
1 (16-ounce) can apple pie filling
1/4 cup chopped walnuts
1/2 teaspoon cinnamon

Combine butter and graham cracker crumbs in 1 1/2-quart baking dish; mix well. Press evenly over bottom of dish. Mix condensed milk, sour cream and lemon juice in medium bowl. Spread over crumb layer. Spoon pie filling over top. Bake at 350 degrees for 25 to 30 minutes or until set. Cool slightly. Mix walnuts and cinnamon in small bowl. Sprinkle over pie. Serve warm or cold. May substitute other flavors of pie filling for apple. Yield: 6 servings.

Approx Per Serving: Cal 476; Prot 6.8 g; Carbo 60.9 g; T Fat 24.4 g; Chol 47.3 mg; Potas 338.0 mg; Sod 328.0 mg.

North Carolina Apple Growers Association

GRAND CHAMPION PIE

4 eggs
1 1/2 cups applesauce
3/4 cup packed brown sugar
3 tablespoons all-purpose flour
1 teaspoon grated lemon rind
3 tablespoons lemon juice
1/2 teaspoon salt
1/2 teaspoon cinnamon
1/4 teaspoon nutmeg
1 unbaked 9-inch deep-dish pie shell
1 apple, peeled, thinly sliced
1 tablespoon lemon juice
1/4 cup apricot jam

Mix eggs, applesauce, brown sugar, flour, lemon rind, 3 tablespoons lemon juice, salt, cinnamon and nutmeg in large mixer bowl. Pour into pie shell. Bake at 450 degrees for 15 minutes. Reduce oven temperature to 300 degrees. Bake for 45 minutes longer or until knife inserted near center comes out clean. Cool slightly on wire rack. Combine apple slices and 1 tablespoon lemon juice in bowl; mix well. Arrange apple slices pinwheel-fashion over top of baked pie. Melt jam in small saucepan over low heat, stirring constantly. Brush apple slices with melted jam. Place pie on rack in broiler pan. Broil 6 inches from heat source for 3 minutes or until apples are tender and jam is bubbly. Yield: 8 servings.

Approx Per Serving: Cal 305; Prot 4.9 g; Carbo 49.5 g; T Fat 10.4 g; Chol 137.0 mg; Potas 166.0 mg; Sod 317.0 mg.

North Carolina Egg Association

BERRY NUTTY PIE

1 cup whipping cream
2 tablespoons confectioners' sugar
1/2 teaspoon vanilla extract
1 pint strawberries, sliced
Meringue Pie Shell
2 tablespoons semisweet chocolate chips
2 tablespoons finely chopped pecans

Whip cream, confectioners' sugar and vanilla in small mixer bowl until soft peaks form. Reserve 3/4 cup strawberries. Fold remaining strawberries gently into whipped cream mixture. Spread over Meringue Pie Shell. Top with reserved strawberries, chocolate chips and pecans.
Yield: 8 servings.

Approx Per Serving: Cal 381; Prot 4.1 g; Carbo 41.8 g; T Fat 25.3 g; Chol 40.7 mg; Potas 201.0 mg; Sod 159.0 mg.

MERINGUE PIE SHELL

3 egg whites
3/4 cup sugar
1/2 teaspoon baking powder
1/2 cup plus 2 tablespoons semisweet chocolate chips, coarsely chopped
6 tablespoons chopped pecans, ground
1 cup crushed butter-flavor crackers
1 teaspoon almond extract

Beat egg whites in small mixer bowl until soft peaks form. Combine sugar and baking powder in bowl; mix well. Add to egg whites gradually, beating until stiff peaks form. Fold chocolate chips and pecans in gently. Fold in cracker crumbs and almond extract gently. Spread in greased 9-inch pie plate to form shell. Bake at 350 degrees for 25 minutes. Cool completely.

Nutritional information is included in recipe above.

North Carolina Strawberry and Pick-Your-Own Association

ROYAL BANANA SPLIT PIES

1 (12-ounce) package
  vanilla wafers, crumbled
3/4 cup melted butter
2 cups confectioners'
  sugar
1/2 cup melted butter
2 eggs
5 bananas, sliced
1 (20-ounce) can crushed
  pineapple, drained
13 ounces whipped
  topping
1 cup chopped pecans

Combine vanilla wafers and 3/4 cup melted butter in bowl; mix well. Press into two 9-inch pie plates. Cream confectioners' sugar, butter and eggs in mixer bowl until light and fluffy. Spoon over crust. Arrange bananas over creamed layer; spoon pineapple over bananas. Spread with whipped topping, sealing to edge. Sprinkle with pecans. Garnish with maraschino cherries. Chill until serving time. Yield: 12 servings.

Approx Per Serving: Cal 688; Prot 5.7 g; Carbo 72.0 g; T Fat 44.5 g; Chol 115.0 mg; Potas 401.3 mg; Sod 318.0 mg.

Carolina Nut Cracker
MEMBER

BLACK BOTTOM EGGNOG CHIFFON PIE

3 tablespoons water
2 tablespoons rum
2 tablespoons Brandy
1 1/2 envelopes unflavored
  gelatin
1 1/4 cups eggnog
1/4 cup sugar
1/4 teaspoon salt
1 1/4 cups eggnog
2 ounces semisweet
  chocolate
1 baked 9-inch pie shell
1 cup whipping cream

Mix water, rum and Brandy in small bowl. Sprinkle with gelatin. Combine 1 1/4 cups eggnog, sugar and salt in saucepan. Heat just to the boiling point, stirring constantly. Add gelatin mixture. Cook until gelatin is dissolved, stirring constantly. Remove from heat. Add remaining eggnog; mix well. Pour into bowl, reserving 1 cup. Chill, covered, for 50 minutes or until partially set. Combine reserved 1 cup eggnog mixture and chocolate in saucepan. Heat until chocolate melts, stirring constantly. Pour into bowl. Chill for 40 minutes or until partially set. Beat until smooth. Spread in bottom of pie shell. Chill until set. Whip cream until soft peaks form. Fold gently into chilled eggnog mixture. Spoon over chocolate layer. Chill, covered, for 4 hours to overnight. Garnish with whipped cream and chocolate curls. Yield: 8 servings.

Approx Per Serving: Cal 403; Prot 6.4 g; Carbo 33.0 g; T Fat 27.0 g; Chol 87.3 mg; Potas 190.0 mg; Sod 261.0 mg.

American Dairy Association of North Carolina

FRUITED RAINBOW PIE

1 1/3 cups gingersnap crumbs
1/4 cup melted butter
3 tablespoons sugar
1 quart vanilla ice cream, softened
1 pint orange sherbet, softened
1/2 cup juice-pack pineapple chunks, drained
1/2 cup sliced fresh strawberries
1/2 cup seeded green grape halves
1/4 cup orange juice

Combine gingersnap crumbs, butter and sugar in bowl; mix well. Press over bottom and up side of 9-inch pie plate. Bake at 350 degrees for 5 minutes. Cool. Chill in freezer. Spoon ice cream and sherbet alternately into chilled crust to give swirled appearance. Freeze until firm. Combine pineapple, strawberries and grapes in small bowl. Add orange juice; toss to mix. Chill for 1 hour. Spoon over pie just before serving. Yield: 8 servings.

Approx Per Serving: Cal 339; Prot 3.7 g; Carbo 47.8 g; T Fat 15.7 g; Chol 54.8 mg; Potas 258.0 mg; Sod 167.0 mg.

American Dairy Association of North Carolina

SCUPPERNONG PIE

4 cups (2 pounds) Scuppernongs
1 cup sugar
1/4 cup all-purpose flour
1/8 teaspoon salt
1 tablespoon lemon juice
1 1/2 tablespoons melted butter
1 unbaked 9-inch pie shell
1/2 cup all-purpose flour
1/4 cup sugar
1/3 cup butter

Rinse scuppernongs; drain well. Remove and reserve skins. Place peeled grapes in heavy saucepan. Bring to a boil, stirring constantly. Reduce heat. Simmer, uncovered, for 5 minutes. Press through sieve to remove seeds. Combine pulp, reserved skins, 1 cup sugar, 1/4 cup flour, salt, lemon juice and melted butter in bowl; mix well. Pour into pie shell. Mix remaining 1/2 cup flour and 1/4 cup sugar in bowl. Cut in remaining 1/3 cup butter with pastry blender until crumbly. Sprinkle over pie. Bake at 400 degrees for 40 minutes. Yield: 8 servings.

Approx Per Serving: Cal 419; Prot 3.2 g; Carbo 64.3 g; T Fat 17.8 g; Chol 26.3 mg; Potas 177.0 mg; Sod 255.0 mg.

North Carolina Grape Growers Association

GRAPE TARTS

1/2 cup grape juice
1 cup sugar
1/2 cup water
1 teaspoon cornstarch
1 cup seeded grape halves
6 baked tart shells
1 cup whipped cream
6 grapes

Combine juice, sugar and water in saucepan. Bring to a boil, stirring constantly. Stir in cornstarch dissolved in a small amount of cold water. Add grapes; mix well. Simmer until grapes are soft, stirring constantly. Spoon into tart shells. Top with whipped cream. Garnish with whole grapes. Yield: 6 tarts.

Approx Per Tart: Cal 352; Prot 2.3 g; Carbo 57.5 g; T Fat 13.3 g; Chol 0.0 mg; Potas 95.7 mg; Sod 188.0 mg.

North Carolina Grape Growers Association

PATRIOT PEACH PIE

1 1/4 cups chopped fresh peaches, well drained
1 unbaked 9-inch pie shell
1/3 cup sugar
1/2 teaspoon cinnamon
1/4 teaspoon nutmeg
1/4 cup coconut
4 eggs, slightly beaten
1 1/2 cups milk, scalded
1 teaspoon vanilla extract
1/4 teaspoon salt

Arrange peaches in bottom of pie shell. Combine 1 tablespoon sugar, cinnamon and nutmeg in bowl; mix well. Sprinkle sugar mixture and coconut over peaches. Combine eggs, remaining sugar, milk, vanilla and salt in mixer bowl; mix well. Pour over peaches. Bake at 400 degrees for 30 to 35 minutes or until knife inserted halfway between center and outside edge comes out clean. Chill until serving time. Yield: 6 servings.

Approx Per Serving: Cal 312; Prot 8.2 g; Carbo 32.8 g; T Fat 16.8 g; Chol 191.0 mg; Potas 220.0 mg; Sod 352.0 mg.

North Carolina Peach Growers Association

LEMON PIE

1 3/4 cups sugar
2 tablespoons cornmeal
2 tablespoons all-purpose flour
4 eggs
1/4 cup melted butter
1/4 cup milk
1/4 cup lemon juice
5 teaspoons grated lemon rind
1 teaspoon vinegar
1 unbaked Cornmeal Pie Shell

Combine sugar, cornmeal and flour in mixer bowl; mix well. Add eggs 1 at a time, beating well after each addition. Stir in butter, milk, lemon juice, lemon rind and vinegar. Pour into Cornmeal Pie Shell. Place on lower oven rack. Bake at 350 degrees for 45 minutes. Yield: 6 servings.

Approx Per Serving: Cal 592; Prot 7.9 g; Carbo 89.5 g; T Fat 23.5 g; Chol 205.0 mg; Potas 119.0 mg; Sod 285.0 mg.

CORNMEAL PIE SHELL

3/4 cup cornmeal
3/4 cup sifted self-rising flour
1/3 cup shortening
5 to 8 tablespoons cold water

Mix cornmeal and flour in bowl. Cut in shortening until crumbly. Add enough water to make soft dough. Roll 1/8 inch thick on lightly floured surface. Press into 9-inch pie plate.

Nutritional information for pie shell is included in recipe above.

North Carolina Corn Miller's Association

FRESH PEACH TARTS

4 cups sliced fresh peaches
3/4 cup sugar
2 teaspoons fresh lemon juice
1 tablespoon cornstarch
4 baked 5-inch tart shells

Combine peaches, sugar and lemon juice in bowl; mix well. Let stand for 20 minutes. Drain, reserving juice. Add enough water to reserved juice to measure 1 cup. Pour juice into saucepan. Stir in cornstarch gradually. Cook until transparent, stirring constantly. Cool. Spoon peaches into tart shells. Pour juice syrup over peaches. Chill until glaze is set. Garnish with clusters of dark grapes. Yield: 4 tarts.

Approx Per Tart: Cal 450; Prot 4.0 g; Carbo 78.0 g; T Fat 15.2 g; Chol 0.0 mg; Potas 362.0 mg; Sod 276.0 mg.

North Carolina Peach Growers Association

FLUFFY FROZEN PEANUT BUTTER PIE

3 ounces cream cheese, softened
1 cup confectioners' sugar
1/3 cup creamy peanut butter
1/2 cup milk
9 ounces whipped topping
1 baked 9-inch pie shell
1/4 cup chopped roasted peanuts

Beat cream cheese in mixer bowl until light and fluffy. Add confectioners' sugar and peanut butter; mix well. Add milk gradually, mixing well after each addition. Fold in whipped topping gently. Pour into pie shell. Sprinkle with peanuts. Freeze until serving time. Store, tightly covered, in freezer. Yield: 6 servings.

Approx Per Serving: Cal 531; Prot 9.8 g; Carbo 44.2 g; T Fat 36.6 g; Chol 18.2 mg; Potas 208.0 mg; Sod 328.0 mg.

North Carolina Peanut Growers Association

PEANUT BUTTER CUSTARD PIE

1 cup confectioners' sugar
1/2 cup creamy peanut butter
1 baked 9-inch pie shell
1/4 cup cornstarch
2/3 cup sugar
1/4 teaspoon salt
2 cups milk, scalded
3 egg yolks, beaten
2 tablespoons butter, softened
1/4 teaspoon vanilla extract
3 egg whites
1/2 cup sugar

Mix confectioners' sugar and peanut butter in bowl until crumbly. Reserve 1/4 of the peanut butter mixture. Spread remaining mixture in bottom of pie shell. Mix cornstarch, 2/3 cup sugar and salt in bowl. Add hot milk; mix well. Stir a small amount of hot mixture into egg yolks; stir egg yolks into hot mixture. Pour into top of double boiler. Cook over medium heat until thickened, stirring constantly. Remove from heat. Stir in butter and vanilla. Pour over peanut butter layer. Beat egg whites in mixer bowl until foamy. Add 1/2 cup sugar gradually, beating until stiff peaks form. Spread meringue over top of pie, sealing to edge. Sprinkle with reserved peanut butter mixture. Bake at 350 degrees until lightly browned. Yield: 8 servings.

Approx Per Serving: Cal 475; Prot 10.3 g; Carbo 60.2 g; T Fat 22.8 g; Chol 118.0 mg; Potas 228.0 mg; Sod 342.0 mg.

North Carolina Peanut Growers Association

SOUTHERN PEANUT PIE

3 eggs
1/2 cup sugar
1 1/2 cups dark corn syrup
1/4 cup melted butter
1/4 teaspoon salt
1/2 teaspoon vanilla extract
1 1/2 cups chopped roasted peanuts
1 unbaked 9-inch deep-dish pie shell

Beat eggs in mixer bowl until foamy. Add sugar, corn syrup, butter, salt and vanilla; mix well. Stir in peanuts. Pour into pie shell. Bake at 375 degrees for 50 to 55 minutes or until set. Serve warm or cold. Garnish with whipped cream or ice cream. Yield: 6 servings.

Approx Per Serving: Cal 760; Prot 14.6 g; Carbo 98.3 g; T Fat 38.3 g; Chol 158.0 mg; Potas 319.0 mg; Sod 565.0 mg.

North Carolina Peanut Growers Association

PECAN CHESS TARTS

½ cup packed dark brown sugar
¼ cup sugar
1 tablespoon cornmeal
1 egg
1 tablespoon evaporated milk
¼ cup melted butter
1 teaspoon vanilla extract
2 tablespoons dark corn syrup
½ cup chopped pecans
12 Tiny Tart Shells

Combine brown sugar, sugar and cornmeal in bowl; mix well. Beat egg in mixer bowl until foamy. Add milk, butter, vanilla and corn syrup; mix well. Combine with dry ingredients; mix well. Stir in pecans. Spoon into greased shallow baking dish. Place in baking pan half filled with water. Bake at 375 degrees for 35 minutes or until knife inserted in center comes out clean. Spoon into Tiny Tart Shells. Yield: 12 tarts.

Approx Per Tart: Cal 179; Prot 1.6 g; Carbo 22.5 g; T Fat 9.8 g; Chol 38.8 mg; Potas 69.4 mg; Sod 62.1 mg.

North Carolina Corn Miller's Association

TINY TART SHELLS

½ cup self-rising cornmeal
½ cup all-purpose flour
2 tablespoons sugar
½ teaspoon grated lemon rind
¼ cup butter
2 tablespoons ice cold water

Mix cornmeal, flour, sugar and lemon rind in bowl. Cut in butter until crumbly. Add water; mix lightly. Roll dough on floured board. Cut into 2-inch squares. Press on back of small muffin pans. Pierce with floured fork. Bake at 400 degrees for 5 minutes. Remove to wire rack to cool. Yield: 24 tart shells.

Approx Per Tart Shell: Cal 41; Prot 0.5 g; Carbo 5.3 g; T Fat 2.0 g; Chol 5.2 mg; Potas 6.7 mg; Sod 16.2 mg.

North Carolina Corn Miller's Association

FRENCH STRAWBERRY TART

16 ounces cream cheese, softened
1/4 cup sugar
2 teaspoons grated lemon rind
2 tablespoons lemon juice
Special Tart Shell
1 quart fresh strawberries, sliced
2 tablespoons cornstarch
1/4 cup cold water
1 (12-ounce) jar strawberry preserves
2 tablespoons lemon juice

Combine cream cheese, sugar, lemon rind and 2 tablespoons lemon juice in bowl; mix well. Spread in bottom of Special Tart Shell. Arrange strawberries over top. Combine cornstarch and water in saucepan. Add preserves; mix well. Bring to a boil, stirring constantly. Cook until thickened, stirring constantly. Remove from heat. Add remaining 2 tablespoons lemon juice; mix well. Cool to room temperature. Pour over strawberries. Chill until serving time. Garnish with whipped cream. Yield: 12 servings.

Approx Per Serving: Cal 464; Prot 6.4 g; Carbo 52.1 g; T Fat 26.6 g; Chol 64.1 mg; Potas 172.0 mg; Sod 347.0 mg.

SPECIAL TART SHELL

1/2 cup margarine, softened
1/4 cup sugar
1/4 teaspoon salt
1 egg
1 1/2 cups sifted all-purpose flour

Stir margarine in bowl to soften. Add sugar and salt; mix well. Add egg; mix well. Stir in flour. Chill for several minutes. Roll dough into 12-inch circle on floured surface. Pastry should be of uniform thickness. Press over bottom of 9-inch round cake pan. Trim edge; prick with fork. Place pan, crust side up, on baking sheet. Bake at 450 degrees for 8 to 10 minutes or until light brown. Cool for several minutes. Invert onto serving plate while still warm.

Nutritional information is included in recipe above.

North Carolina Strawberry and Pick-Your-Own Association

STRAWBERRY CHIFFON PIE

1/2 cup sugar
1 pint fresh strawberries, crushed
1 envelope unflavored gelatin
1/4 cup cold water
1/2 cup hot water
1 tablespoon lemon juice
Salt to taste
1/2 cup heavy cream, whipped
2 egg whites
1/4 cup sugar
Graham Cracker Pie Shell

Sprinkle 1/2 cup sugar over strawberries in large bowl. Let stand for 30 minutes. Soften gelatin in cold water in bowl. Add hot water; stir until dissolved. Cool. Add strawberries, lemon juice and salt to taste; mix well. Chill until partially set. Fold in whipped cream gently. Beat egg whites in mixer bowl until soft peaks form. Add 1/4 cup sugar gradually, beating until stiff peaks form. Fold into strawberry mixture gently. Pour into Graham Cracker Pie Shell. Chill until firm. Garnish with additional whipped cream and whole berries.
Yield: 6 servings.

Approx Per Serving: Cal 759; Prot 7.6 g; Carbo 95.1 g; T Fat 40.3 g; Chol 27.2 mg; Potas 286.0 mg; Sod 708.0 mg.

GRAHAM CRACKER PIE SHELL

1 1/2 cups graham cracker crumbs
1/4 cup sugar
1/2 cup melted margarine

Combine graham cracker crumbs, sugar and margarine in bowl; mix until crumbly. Press into 9-inch pie plate. Bake at 375 degrees for 8 minutes or until lightly browned. Cool. Chill unbaked crust for 45 minutes or until set before filling.

Nutritional information is included in recipe above.

North Carolina Strawberry and Pick-Your-Own Association

PECAN PIE SUPREME

3 eggs
1 cup sugar
2 tablespoons butter, softened
1 cup dark corn syrup
1 teaspoon vanilla extract
1 cup chopped pecans
1 unbaked 9-inch pie shell

Beat eggs in mixer bowl until foamy. Add sugar, butter, corn syrup, vanilla and pecans; mix well. Spoon into pie shell. Bake at 350 degrees for 15 minutes. Bake, covered with foil, for 30 minutes longer. If you have recipes calling for black walnuts, you may use 2 teaspoons black walnut flavoring per 1 cup of pecans for a perfect black walnut taste. Yield: 6 servings.

Approx Per Serving: Cal 486; Prot 4.6 g; Carbo 78.1 g; T Fat 20.0 g; Chol 147.0 mg; Potas 122.0 mg; Sod 92.4 mg.

Carolina Nut Cracker
MEMBER

SOUTHERN SWEET POTATO PIE

1/3 cup butter, softened
3/4 cup sugar
2 eggs, beaten
2 cups mashed sweet potatoes
3/4 cup evaporated milk
1 teaspoon vanilla extract
1/4 teaspoon salt
1 unbaked 9-inch deep-dish pie shell

Cream butter and sugar in mixer bowl until light and fluffy. Add eggs; mix well. Add sweet potatoes; mix well. Stir in evaporated milk, vanilla and salt. Pour into pie shell. Bake at 375 degrees for 40 minutes. May add 1/2 teaspoon each cinnamon and nutmeg or 1 tablespoon grated lemon rind and 2 tablespoons lemon juice for extra flavor. Yield: 6 servings.

Approx Per Serving: Cal 491; Prot 7.8 g; Carbo 61.1 g; T Fat 24.6 g; Chol 128.0 mg; Potas 315.0 mg; Sod 478.0 mg.

North Carolina Sweet Potato Commission

SWEET POTATO PIES

2 (Number 10) cans sweet potatoes
3/4 cup butter, softened
5 cups milk
3 cups honey
12 eggs
3/4 teaspoon salt
2 1/2 tablespoons pumpkin pie spice
1/4 cup lemon juice
Pastry for two 18x26-inch baking pans

Mash sweet potatoes in mixer bowl. Add butter, milk, honey, eggs, salt, pumpkin pie spice and lemon juice. Beat at medium speed for 5 minutes. Spoon into 2 pastry-lined 18x26-inch baking pans. Bake at 350 degrees for 40 to 45 minutes or until set. Yield: 100 servings.

Approx Per Serving: Cal 199; Prot 3.4 g; Carbo 30.8 g; T Fat 7.4 g; Chol 38.3 mg; Potas 177.0 mg; Sod 179.0 mg.

E. Lester Selph Bee Farm
MEMBER

SWEET POTATO SURPRISE PIES

8 ounces cream cheese, softened
2 eggs, beaten
3/4 cup sugar
2 graham cracker pie shells
2 (4-ounce) packages vanilla instant pudding mix
3/4 cup milk
2 cups mashed cooked sweet potatoes
Dash of cinnamon
12 ounces whipped topping
1/2 cup chopped pecans

Beat cream cheese and eggs in mixer bowl until smooth. Add sugar; beat until fluffy. Spread in pie shells. Bake at 350 degrees for 20 minutes. Cool. Prepare pudding mix according to package directions using 3/4 cup milk. Add sweet potatoes and cinnamon; mix well. Fold in 1 cup whipped topping gently. Spoon over cream cheese layer. Spread with remaining whipped topping, sealing to edge. Sprinkle with chopped pecans. Chill until serving time.
Yield: 12 servings.

Approx Per Serving: Cal 628; Prot 6.9 g; Carbo 78.6 g; T Fat 33.2 g; Chol 68.4 mg; Potas 253.0 mg; Sod 526.0 mg.

Wingfield Farms
MEMBER

QUICK AND EASY WATERMELON PIE

1 (14-ounce) can sweetened condensed milk
4 ounces whipped topping
1/4 cup lime juice
2 cups watermelon balls
1 9-inch graham cracker pie shell

Combine condensed milk and whipped topping in bowl; mix well. Stir in lime juice. Reserve 5 watermelon balls. Fold in remaining watermelon balls gently. Spoon into graham cracker crust. Arrange reserved watermelon balls over top. Chill for 2 hours or longer. Yield: 6 servings.

Approx Per Serving: Cal 473; Prot 5.9 g; Carbo 63.7 g; T Fat 22.8 g; Chol 12.8 mg; Potas 302.0 mg; Sod 372.0 mg.

North Carolina Watermelon Association

SURPRISE WATERMELON PIE

1 cup buttermilk baking mix
3 tablespoons boiling water
1/4 cup margarine
1/2 cup sugar
1 (3-ounce) package mixed fruit gelatin
3 tablespoons cornstarch
1 1/2 cups water
3 cups watermelon ball halves

Mix baking mix, boiling water and margarine in pie plate until crumbly. Press over bottom and side of pie plate. Bake at 450 degrees for 10 minutes. Cool. Combine sugar, gelatin, cornstarch and water in saucepan. Cook until thickened, stirring constantly. Cool. Add watermelon. Spoon into cooled pie shell. Chill until serving time. Garnish with whipped topping. Yield: 6 servings.

Approx Per Serving: Cal 315; Prot 3.4 g; Carbo 52.4 g; T Fat 11.0 g; Chol 0.0 mg; Potas 128.0 mg; Sod 401.0 mg.

Murfreesboro Farms, Inc.
MEMBER

CRUNCHY PIE CRUST

3/4 cup finely chopped roasted peanuts
1 cup graham cracker crumbs
1/3 cup melted butter

Combine peanuts, graham cracker crumbs and butter in small bowl; mix until crumbly. Press into 9-inch pie plate. Fill with favorite pie filling. Yield: 1 pie shell.

Approx Per Pie Shell: Cal 1681; Prot 38.6 g; Carbo 113.0 g; T Fat 127.0 g; Chol 164.0 mg; Potas 1093.0 mg; Sod 1717.0 mg.

North Carolina Peanut Growers Association

North Carolina Celebrity Selections

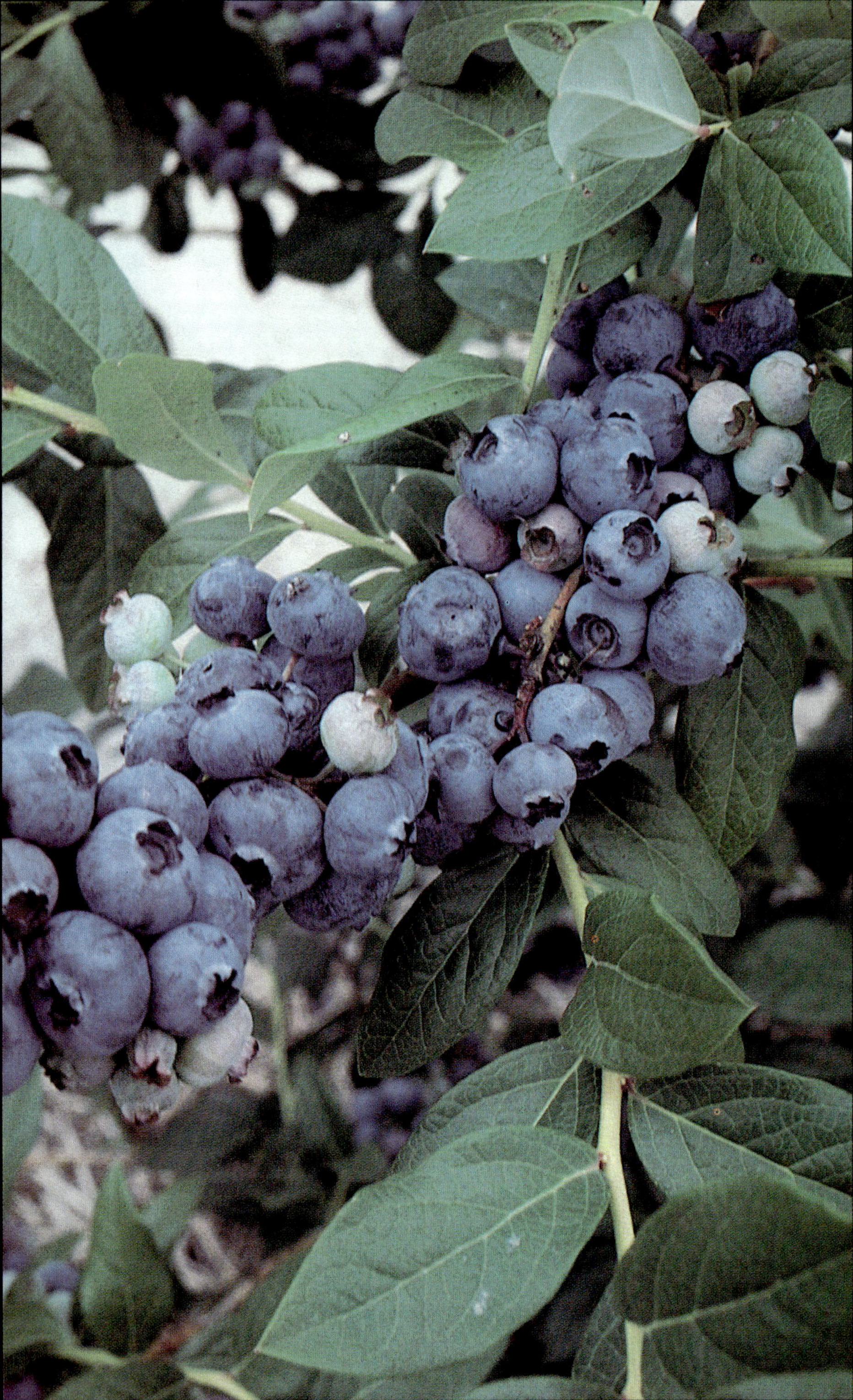

NEW ORLEANS-STYLE FETTUCINI SAUCE (Shotgun)

This is great with chicken, duck and shellfish.

1 1/3 pounds unsalted butter
3/4 pound yellow onions, chopped
1 ounce whole cloves of garlic
1 ounce minced garlic
Seasoning Mix
5 cups chicken stock
1/4 cup Worcestershire sauce
1 1/4 ounces Tabasco sauce
8 cups tomato sauce
1/3 cup sugar
8 ounces green onions, chopped

Melt butter in large saucepan. Add yellow onions and whole garlic cloves. Sauté until onions are translucent. Add minced garlic and Seasoning Mix. Simmer for 15 minutes. Stir in chicken stock, Worcestershire sauce and Tabasco sauce. Simmer for 15 minutes. Add tomato sauce. Simmer for 20 minutes. Stir in sugar and green onions. Simmer for 1 hour or longer. Serve over hot cooked fettucini. Yield: 12 servings.

Approx Per Serving: Cal 482; Prot 6.3 g; Carbo 25.4 g; T Fat 41.8 g; Chol 110.0 mg; Potas 894.0 mg; Sod 1381.0 mg.

SEASONING MIX

1 tablespoon white pepper
1 tablespoon garlic powder
2 teaspoons cayenne pepper
1/2 teaspoon cumin
1/2 teaspoon basil

Combine white pepper, garlic powder, cayenne pepper, cumin and basil in small bowl. Yield: 3 tablespoons.

Nutritional information is included in recipe above.

Dwight Clark
San Francisco 49ers

ALASKAN LOW BUSH CRANBERRY-APPLE PIE

1¾ cups all-purpose flour
10 tablespoons butter, softened
2 to 3 tablespoons cold water
1 teaspoon salt
½ cup packed brown sugar
½ cup all-purpose flour
½ cup butter, chilled
Cranberry-Apple Filling
Cinnamon to taste

Sift 1¾ cups flour onto large board; make wide well in center. Place 10 tablespoons butter in well; cover with flour. Mix with fingers until crumbly. Make well in center. Add cold water and salt. Mix lightly with fingers; do not knead. Chill, tightly wrapped, for 30 minutes. Roll pastry into circle on floured surface. Fit into 9-inch deep dish-pie plate. Trim and flute edges. Mix brown sugar and ½ cup flour in small bowl. Cut in ½ cup butter until crumbly. Spoon Cranberry-Apple Filling into pie shell. Sprinkle crumb mixture over filling. Sprinkle with cinnamon. Place inside double thickness brown bag; staple tightly. Do not use a bag made of recyled material as this can be toxic when heated. Bake at 425 degrees for 40 to 45 minutes or until apples are tender. Remove from bag. Bake for 10 minutes longer or until topping is golden brown. Yield: 8 servings.

Approx Per Serving: Cal 593; Prot 4.7 g; Carbo 87.6 g; T Fat 26.8 g; Chol 69.9 mg; Potas 286.0 mg; Sod 492.0 mg.

CRANBERRY-APPLE FILLING

8 large Granny Smith apples
1½ cups low bush cranberries
¾ cup sugar
¼ cup all-purpose flour
Grated zest of 1 lemon
½ teaspoon freshly grated nutmeg
½ teaspoon cinnamon

Peel and slice apples. Combine with cranberries in bowl. Add sugar, flour, lemon zest and spices; mix well.
Yield: Enough filling for 1 pie.

Nutritional information for Filling is included in recipe above.

Steve Cowper
Governor of Alaska and native North Carolinian

PORK BRAINS 'N EGGS (A Southern Delight)

My mother used to prepare Brains 'n Eggs for breakfast and I've enjoyed them ever since. The name of the dish is not the most appetizing, but try 'em, you might like 'em!

2½ tablespoons bacon drippings
1 (5-ounce) can pork brains packed in gravy
¼ teaspoon salt
¼ teaspoon freshly ground pepper
4 eggs
⅓ cup milk

Melt bacon drippings in iron skillet over low heat. Add pork brains; mix well with fork. Add salt and pepper; mix well. Combine eggs and milk in bowl. Beat with wire whisk until blended. Add to pork brains. Cook until eggs are of desired consistency, stirring frequently. Serve immediately over toast with grits and apple butter for a truly southern dish. Yield: 2 servings.

Nutritional information for this recipe is not available.

Howard Coble
U.S. Congressman

CHICKEN AND WILD RICE CASSEROLE

1 (6-ounce) package long grain and wild rice mix
½ cup chopped onion
½ cup margarine
¼ cup all-purpose flour
1 (6-ounce) can mushrooms
1 cup chicken broth
¼ cup cream
3 cups chopped cooked chicken
¾ teaspoon salt
¼ teaspoon pepper
1 (4-ounce) jar pimento
½ cup slivered almonds

Prepare rice mix using package directions. Sauté onion in margarine in saucepan until tender. Stir in flour. Drain mushrooms, reserving liquid. Add enough chicken broth to reserved liquid to measure 1½ cups. Stir into onion mixture. Add cream. Cook until thickened, stirring constantly. Add chicken, seasonings, mushrooms and chopped pimento. Pour into 2 to 4-quart casserole. Sprinkle with almonds. Bake at 350 degrees for 20 to 30 minutes until bubbly. This freezes well. Yield: 10 servings.

Approx Per Serving: Cal 308; Prot 16.2 g; Carbo 19.9 g; T Fat 18.3 g; Chol 45.7 mg; Potas 235.0 mg; Sod 457.0 mg.

Elizabeth Dole, Secretary
U.S. Department of Labor

CELEBRITY SELECTIONS 178

BANANA NUT BREAD

Good served with cream cheese as sandwiches.

2 cups all-purpose flour
2 teaspoons baking powder
1/4 teaspoon soda
1 teaspoon salt
1/3 cup shortening
2/3 cup sugar
2 eggs
3 ripe bananas, mashed
1 teaspoon vanilla extract
1/2 cup chopped pecans

Sift flour, baking powder, soda and salt into bowl. Cream shortening and sugar in mixer bowl until light and fluffy. Beat in eggs. Add bananas, vanilla and pecans. Add dry ingredients; mix well. Spoon into greased 4x8-inch loaf pan. Bake at 350 degrees for 45 to 50 minutes or until bread tests done. Remove to wire rack to cool. May add a small amount of milk if batter is too dry. Yield: 12 servings.

Approx Per Serving: Cal 238; Prot 3.8 g; Carbo 33.8 g; T Fat 10.2 g; Chol 45.7 mg; Potas 150.0 mg; Sod 262.0 mg.

Ava Gardner
Actress and North Carolina farmer's daughter

PARTY CASSEROLE POTATOES

8 ounces cream cheese, softened
1 cup sour cream
10 potatoes, cooked, mashed
Chives, parsley flakes and garlic salt to taste
1/4 cup melted butter
Paprika to taste

Beat cream cheese and sour cream in mixer bowl until smooth. Add to mashed potatoes gradually, beating until light and fluffy. Add chives, parsley flakes and garlic salt; mix well. Spoon into buttered baking dish. Brush top with melted butter. Sprinkle with paprika. Bake at 350 degrees for 30 minutes. May top with shredded cheese if desired. May be stored in refrigerator or freezer for up to 10 days before baking. Yield: 12 servings.

Approx Per Serving: Cal 324; Prot 5.9 g; Carbo 43.8 g; T Fat 14.6 g; Chol 39.5 mg; Potas 755.0 mg; Sod 112.0 mg.

Billy Graham
Evangelist

TAR HEEL BRUNSWICK STEW

1 large stewing chicken
1 pound veal
2 large potatoes, chopped
1 large onion, chopped
4 cups corn
4 cups lima beans
2   (8-ounce) cans tomatoes
Texas Pete hot sauce to taste
1 teaspoon Worcestershire sauce
2 tablespoons butter
Salt and pepper to taste

Cook chicken and veal in water to cover in large saucepan until very tender. Remove and cool chicken and veal. Shred meat with fingers, discarding skin and bones. Skim broth. Return meat to broth. Simmer for 30 minutes. Combine potatoes, onion, corn, lima beans and tomatoes in saucepan. Cook until potatoes are tender. Add to broth. Season with hot pepper sauce, Worcestershire sauce, butter and salt and pepper. Simmer for several hours or until thickened to desired consistency. May substitute beef, goat or squirrel for veal. Yield: 12 servings.

Approx Per Serving: Cal 285; Prot 24.4 g; Carbo 35.8 g; T Fat 5.7 g; Chol 72.6 mg; Potas 912.0 mg; Sod 433.0 mg.

Jim Graham, Commissioner
North Carolina Department of Agriculture

CAROLINA STIR-FRY

1 pound lean pork
2 tablespoons soy sauce
2 tablespoons vinegar
1/2 teaspoon ginger
1 clove of garlic, minced
1 stalk celery
2 green, red or yellow bell peppers
1/4 cup soy oil
1 cup thinly sliced green onions

Slice pork across the grain into thin strips. Combine with soy sauce, vinegar, ginger and garlic in bowl. Marinate for several minutes. Slice celery and peppers into thin strips. Heat oil in large skillet or wok. Add pork and marinade. Stir-fry until brown. Reduce heat. Simmer, covered, until pork is tender. Increase heat. Add vegetables. Stir-fry for 10 minutes or until vegetables are tender. May substitute beef or chicken for pork. Yield: 4 servings.

Approx Per Serving: Cal 370; Prot 28.3 g; Carbo 5.9 g; T Fat 25.8 g; Chol 86.1 mg; Potas 559.0 mg; Sod 587.0 mg.

Dix Harper, Director, Agricultural Productions
WRAL/WRAL-TV/TRN Farm News Networks

FRUIT COBBLER

Fresh blueberries are also delicious in this cobbler.

2 cups sliced fresh peaches
1/2 cup sugar
2/3 cup all-purpose flour
2 teaspoons baking powder
1/2 teaspoon salt
2/3 cup sugar
2/3 cup milk
1/4 cup butter

Mix peaches with 1/2 cup sugar in bowl. Sift flour, baking powder and salt into bowl. Add 2/3 cup sugar. Add milk, mixing just until moistened. Melt butter in glass baking dish. Spoon batter into dish. Spoon peaches into center of batter; do not stir. Bake at 350 degrees until light brown. May substitute blueberries or other fruit for peaches. Yield: 8 servings.

Approx Per Serving: Cal 233; Prot 2.1 g; Carbo 42.9 g; T Fat 6.6 g; Chol 18.3 mg; Potas 99.8 mg; Sod 274.0 mg.

Jesse Helms
U.S. Senator

B. E. L. T. (Bacon, Egg, Lettuce and Tomato Sandwich)

This is my all-time favorite food, served to me on my birthday or whenever somebody wants something.

1 tablespoon mayonnaise
2 slices bread
1 crisp lettuce leaf
2 slices North Carolina tomato
Salt and pepper to taste
1 egg, fried, over well
2 slices bacon, crisp-fried

Spread mayonnaise on bread. Layer lettuce and tomato on 1 slice of bread. Sprinkle with salt and pepper. Top with fried egg, bacon and remaining bread. Bread can be toasted before assembling sandwich. Yield: 1 serving.

Approx Per Serving: Cal 409; Prot 15.2 g; Carbo 30.2 g; T Fat 25.1 g; Chol 293.0 mg; Potas 289.0 mg; Sod 641.0 mg.

Johnnie Hood, Farm Director
WPTF Radio

SQUASH CASSEROLE

3 yellow squash, chopped
1 medium onion, chopped
3 tablespoons butter
2 tablespoons all-purpose flour
1 cup milk
5 slices American cheese
1 (3-ounce) can mushrooms, drained
2 tablespoons melted butter
1/2 cup butter cracker crumbs
1/2 cup chopped pecans

Cook squash and onion in just enough salted water to cover in saucepan for 5 minutes; drain. Melt 3 tablespoons butter in heavy saucepan over low heat. Add flour. Cook for 1 minute, stirring constantly. Add milk gradually. Cook over medium heat until thickened, stirring constantly. Add chopped cheese; stir until melted. Add squash mixture and mushrooms. Spoon into 1 1/2-quart baking dish. Mix 2 tablespoons butter with cracker crumbs and pecans in small bowl. Sprinkle over casserole. Bake at 350 degrees for 30 minutes or until heated through. Yield: 6 servings.

Approx Per Serving: Cal 286; Prot 6.5 g; Carbo 17.4 g; T Fat 23.3 g; Chol 40.4 mg; Potas 356.0 mg; Sod 365.0 mg.

Walter B. Jones
U.S. Congressman

DORIS GURLEY'S BLUEBERRY-PINEAPPLE CRUNCH

2 cups blueberries
1/4 cup cornstarch
1 cup sugar
Juice of 1/2 lemon
Dash of cinnamon
1 (20-ounce) can crushed pineapple
1/2 (2-layer) package yellow cake mix
1 cup chopped pecans
3/4 cup melted butter

Combine blueberries, cornstarch, sugar, lemon juice, cinnamon and salt to taste in saucepan. Cook until thickened, stirring constantly. Spoon into greased 9x13-inch baking pan. Drain pineapple, reserving juice. Layer pineapple over blueberry mixture. Sprinkle with cake mix and pecans. Pour reserved pineapple juice over layers. Drizzle with butter. Bake at 325 degrees for 25 to 30 minutes or until light brown. Serve with vanilla ice cream. Yield: 12 servings.

Approx Per Serving: Cal 374; Prot 2.1 g; Carbo 49.9 g; T Fat 19.9 g; Chol 31.1 mg; Potas 118.0 mg; Sod 216.0 mg.

Martin Lancaster
U.S. Congressman

BETTY GOOD RICE

1½ cups Uncle Ben's rice
4 packets MBT chicken broth mix
1 pound ground round
1 green bell pepper
2 frying peppers
2 medium onions
¼ cup margarine
1 (8-ounce) can small green peas, drained
4 slices bacon, crisp-fried
1 teaspoon Soul Seasoning
½ teaspoon oregano
¼ teaspoon thyme

Cook rice in 3½ cups water and chicken broth mix in saucepan until tender. Brown ground round in skillet, stirring until crumbly; drain. Add to rice. Chop peppers and onions. Sauté peppers and onion in margarine in skillet. Add to rice. Add peas, crumbled bacon and seasonings; mix well. Simmer until heated through.
Yield: 6 servings.

Approx Per Serving: Cal 365; Prot 19.7 g; Carbo 30.4 g; T Fat 18.1 g; Chol 46.5 mg; Potas 474.0 mg; Sod 275.0 mg.
Nutritional information does not include broth mix or Seasoning.

Ben E. King
Singer

TURKEY OMELET

2 eggs
2 teaspoons water
1 tablespoon chopped onion
1 tablespoon butter
½ cup chopped cooked turkey
2 tablespoons Parmesan cheese
2 tablespoons alfalfa sprouts
3 mushrooms, sliced

Combine eggs, water and onion in bowl; mix well with fork. Season with salt and pepper to taste. Heat butter in skillet until drop of water sizzles. Pour in eggs gently. Cook until soft-set, stirring cooked portion to center. Sprinkle turkey, cheese, alfalfa sprouts and mushrooms on 1 side of omelet. Fold omelet over. Remove to warm plate. Garnish with sour cream. Yield: 1 serving.

Approx Per Serving: Cal 494; Prot 38.4 g; Carbo 4.4 g; T Fat 35.3 g; Chol 653.0 mg; Potas 475.0 mg; Sod 489.0 mg.

Edie Low, Food Editor
The Charlotte Leader

CAROLINA APPLE CAKE

1 1/2 cups oil
2 cups sugar
4 eggs, beaten
3 cups all-purpose flour
1 teaspoon soda
1 teaspoon salt
2 teaspoons vanilla extract
3 cups chopped peeled apples
1 cup chopped pecans
Brown Sugar Glaze

Beat oil, sugar and eggs in mixer bowl until thick and lemon-colored. Sift flour, soda and salt together. Add to egg mixture; mix well. Add vanilla, apples and pecans; mix well. Spoon into greased and floured tube pan. Bake at 350 degrees for 1 hour or until cake tests done. Remove to serving plate to cool. Drizzle Brown Sugar Glaze over cake. Yield: 16 servings.

Approx Per Serving: Cal 504; Prot 4.7 g; Carbo 60.7 g; T Fat 28.0 g; Chol 71.0 mg; Potas 145.0 mg; Sod 186.0 mg.

BROWN SUGAR GLAZE

1 cup packed brown sugar
1/4 cup milk
1 tablespoon butter
Vanilla extract to taste

Combine brown sugar, milk and butter in saucepan. Bring to a boil over low heat. Cook for 10 minutes. Stir in vanilla. Cool.

Nutritional information is included in recipe above.

Jim Martin
Governor of North Carolina

FAVORITE CARAMEL CAKE

1 cup butter, softened
1/2 cup shortening
3 cups sugar
6 eggs, at room temperature
3 cups cake flour, sifted
1 cup evaporated milk
1/2 teaspoon baking powder
1 teaspoon vanilla extract
Caramel Frosting

Cream butter and shortening in mixer bowl until light. Add sugar 1 cup at a time, beating until fluffy. Add eggs 1 at a time, beating constantly at low speed. Add flour alternately with evaporated milk, mixing well after each addition and beginning and ending with flour. Mix in baking powder and vanilla. Pour into 3 greased and floured 9-inch cake pans. Bake at 325 degrees for 30 to 35 minutes or until layers test done. Remove to wire rack to cool. Spread Caramel Frosting between layers and over top and side of cake. Yield: 16 servings.

Approx Per Serving: Cal 730; Prot 5.4 g; Carbo 105.0 g; T Fat 33.5 g; Chol 172.0 mg; Potas 218.0 mg; Sod 269.0 mg.

CARAMEL FROSTING

1 cup butter
2 cups packed light brown sugar
1/2 cup evaporated milk
1 1/2 teaspoons vanilla extract
4 cups confectioners' sugar, sifted

Melt butter in saucepan. Stir in brown sugar and evaporated milk. Cook over medium-high heat for 2 minutes, stirring constantly. Remove from heat. Add vanilla. Pour over confectioners' sugar in bowl; beat until smooth. Cool completely.

Nutritional information is included in recipe above.

Steve Neal
U.S. Congressman

CHICKEN TETRAZZINI

8 chicken breast fillets
1 (16-ounce) package rotini noodles
1/4 cup butter
1/2 cup Parmesan cheese
1/2 cup margarine
2/3 cup all-purpose flour
4 cups half and half
1/4 cup Sauterne
2 teaspoons salt
2 tablespoons Parmesan cheese

Cook chicken in water to cover in saucepan until tender. Drain, reserving 2 cups broth. Cut chicken into strips. Cook noodles using package directions. Add 1/4 cup butter and 1/2 cup cheese; toss until noodles are coated. Spoon into large baking dish. Top with chicken. Melt 1/2 cup margarine in large saucepan. Stir in flour gradually. Add reserved chicken broth and half and half gradually. Cook over medium heat until thickened, stirring constantly. Stir in wine and salt. Simmer for several minutes. Pour over noodles and chicken. Top with 2 tablespoons cheese. Bake at 350 degrees for 20 to 30 minutes or until bubbly. Yield: 8 servings.

Approx Per Serving: Cal 681; Prot 28.1 g; Carbo 56.4 g; T Fat 37.2 g; Chol 87.6 mg; Potas 468.0 mg; Sod 1133.0 mg.

Sue Myrick
Mayor of Charlotte

DEEP-DISH PEACH PIE

1/2 cup packed brown sugar
3 tablespoons cornstarch
1/4 teaspoon salt
1/2 cup light corn syrup
5 cups sliced peeled peaches
2 tablespoons margarine
1 recipe 1-crust pie pastry

Combine brown sugar, cornstarch and salt in bowl. Stir in corn syrup. Add peaches; toss to coat well. Spoon into 6x10-inch or 1 1/2-quart baking dish. Dot with margarine. Top with pastry. Seal to edge of dish; cut steam vents. Bake at 425 degrees for 40 minutes or until brown. Yield: 8 servings.

Approx Per Serving: Cal 303; Prot 2.2 g; Carbo 53.0 g; T Fat 10.5 g; Chol 0.0 mg; Potas 273.0 mg; Sod 253.0 mg.

Richard Petty
NASCAR Driver

APPLE CAKE

This is one of our favorite desserts. It reminds my wife Lisa of the wonderful cakes that her grandmother used to make. It can be made with apples, peaches or plums. Sometimes we mix peaches and blueberries together.

1 cup sifted all-purpose flour
1 teaspoon baking powder
1/4 teaspoon salt
2 tablespoons sugar
1 1/2 to 3 tablespoons butter
1 egg
1/2 teaspoon vanilla extract
1/4 cup (about) milk
4 cups sliced peeled apples
Cinnamon Topping

Sift flour with baking powder, salt and sugar in bowl. Add 1 1/2 to 3 tablespoons butter. Work lightly with fingers until of consistency of coarse crumbs. Beat egg with vanilla in measuring cup. Add enough milk to egg mixture to measure 1/2 cup. Add to crumb mixture; mix to form a stiff dough. Pat into greased baking pan with floured palm of hand or spread with spoon. Arrange apples in overlapping rows on dough, pushing dough with apple slices to even surface. Sprinkle Cinnamon Topping over apples. Bake for 25 minutes. Serve with vanilla ice cream or whipped cream. Yield: 8 servings.

Approx Per Serving: Cal 241; Prot 2.8 g; Carbo 36.0 g; T Fat 9.9 g; Chol 58.6 mg; Potas 99.2 mg; Sod 193.0 mg.

CINNAMON TOPPING

1/2 cup sugar
2 teaspoons cinnamon
3 tablespoons melted butter

Mix sugar and cinnamon in bowl. Add butter, mixing until crumbly. Use as topping for Apple Cake or fruit crisps.

Nutritional information is included in recipe above.

David Price
U.S. Congressman

MAKE-AHEAD LETTUCE AND CAULIFLOWER SALAD

1 head lettuce, shredded
1/2 cup chopped celery
1/4 cup chopped green bell pepper
1/2 cup chopped red onion
Flowerets of 1 small head cauliflower
1 (10-ounce) package frozen tiny peas, thawed
2 cups mayonnaise
1 tablespoon sugar
1 cup Parmesan cheese
1 cup shredded sharp Cheddar cheese
1 cup crumbled crisp-fried bacon

Layer lettuce, celery, green pepper, onion, cauliflower and peas in order listed in large glass bowl. Spread mayonnaise over top, sealing to edge of bowl. Sprinkle with sugar, Parmesan cheese, Cheddar cheese and bacon. Chill, covered, in refrigerator overnight. Spoon through all layers to serve. Yield: 16 servings.

Approx Per Serving: Cal 294; Prot 6.8 g; Carbo 6.5 g; T Fat 27.4 g; Chol 30.3 mg; Potas 200.0 mg; Sod 369.0 mg.

Charlie Rose
U.S. Congressman

CHEESE GRITS

1 cup quick-cooking grits
4 cups boiling water
2 tablespoons butter
2 cups shredded sharp Cheddar cheese
2 eggs
3/4 cup (about) milk

Stir grits gradually into boiling water in saucepan. Cook for 3 to 5 minutes or until thickened, stirring constantly. Remove from heat. Stir in butter and cheese until melted. Beat eggs in measuring cup. Add enough milk to measure 1 cup; mix well. Stir into grits mixture. Spoon into greased baking dish. Bake at 375 degrees for 40 to 45 minutes or until set. Yield: 8 servings.

Approx Per Serving: Cal 362; Prot 14.8 g; Carbo 22.8 g; T Fat 23.4 g; Chol 156.0 mg; Potas 138.0 mg; Sod 335.0 mg.

Terry Sanford
U. S. Senator

SPICED GROUND MEAT

This can be shaped around a spit or into patties or a meat loaf and broiled over a charcoal fire or under a broiler.

1 pound lean lamb, ground
1 pound beef round steak, ground
2 slices firm white bread, crusts trimmed
1 large clove of garlic, chopped
1 egg, slightly beaten
2 tablespoons chopped parsley
1/2 teaspoon ground cumin seed
1 teaspoon chili powder
2 tablespoons paprika
1/4 teaspoon finely ground fenugreek seed
1 1/2 teaspoons salt
Cayenne pepper to taste

Grind lamb, beef and bread together, using the finest blade of meat grinder. Combine with garlic, egg, parsley, cumin, chili powder, paprika, fenugreek seed, salt and cayenne pepper in bowl; mix well. Shape around spit or skewer. Cook over charcoal fire until well browned on outside and barely pink in center. Yield: 6 servings.

Approx Per Serving: Cal 315; Prot 30.8 g; Carbo 4.8 g; T Fat 17.8 g; Chol 145.0 mg; Potas 387.0 mg; Sod 683.0 mg.

Dean Smith, Head Basketball Coach
University of North Carolina

GIN FIZZ - EGG PIE

6 slices bacon
1 onion, chopped
1 (28-ounce) can peeled tomatoes
1 (2½-ounce) can sliced mushrooms
2 (5-ounce) cans Vienna sausage, sliced ¼ inch thick
6 slices American or Monterey Jack cheese
12 eggs
½ cup milk
Parmesan cheese to taste
Shaker of Gin Fizzes

Cut bacon into 1-inch pieces. Fry in cast-iron skillet until crisp. Remove to paper towel to drain. Drain all but a small amount of drippings from skillet. Add onion. Sauté in bacon drippings. Add tomatoes, mushrooms and sausage. Simmer for 15 minutes. Stir in cheese slices until melted. Beat eggs with milk in bowl. Add to skillet; mix gently. Bake at 350 degrees for 30 minutes or until top is golden brown. Sprinkle with Parmesan cheese after 25 minutes. Mix a shaker of Gin Fizzes as skillet goes into oven and enjoy, enjoy until eggs are done. Cut pie into wedges. Garnish with thin strips of pimento. Serve with sour cream. May increase ingredients by ⅓ to serve 12. Yield: 8 servings.

Approx Per Serving: Cal 362; Prot 20.7 g; Carbo 8.9 g; T Fat 27.1 g; Chol 455.0 mg; Potas 472.0 mg; Sod 1026.0 mg.
Nutritional information does not include gin fizzes.

GIN FIZZES

8 jiggers sloe gin
Juice of 4 lemons
3 tablespoons confectioners' sugar
Soda, chilled

Combine sloe gin, lemon juice and confectioners' sugar in shaker with ice. Shake until well mixed. Strain into highball glasses. Fill with soda. Yield: 4 servings.

Nutritional information is not available.

Theodore Taylor
Author

BAKED TOMATOES WITH ROSEMARY AND GARLIC

4 plum tomatoes
2 cloves of garlic, cut into slivers
2 tablespoons olive oil
1 tablespoon chopped fresh rosemary
Salt and freshly ground pepper to taste
2 tablespoons chopped parsley

Cut tomatoes into halves lengthwise. Place cut side down in baking dish. Cut 2 small slits in each tomato half. Insert a sliver of garlic in each slit. Brush tomatoes with olive oil. Sprinkle with rosemary and salt and freshly ground pepper to taste. Bake at 450 degrees for 5 to 6 minutes. Remove garlic if desired. Sprinkle with parsley.
Yield: 4 servings.

Approx Per Serving: Cal 86; Prot 1.2 g; Carbo 5.8 g; T Fat 7.0 g; Chol 0.0 mg; Potas 261.0 mg; Sod 10.3 mg.

Dave Spatola
WNCT Radio

ITALIAN SAUSAGE BREAD

This recipe is from my mother, Angelina Valvano, of Seaford, New York.

2 pounds Italian sausage
2 cups shredded mozzarella cheese
1/4 cup grated Romano cheese
1 egg
1 pound pizza dough
1 egg yolk, beaten

Remove casing from sausage. Crumble into skillet. Cook until brown; drain. Combine with cheeses and 1 egg in bowl; mix well. Roll pizza dough into circle on floured surface. Spread sausage mixture on dough. Roll up to enclose filling. Place seam side down on baking sheet, sealing edges. Brush top with egg yolk. Bake at 350 degrees for 35 minutes. Yield: 8 servings.

Approx Per Serving: Cal 767; Prot 24.8 g; Carbo 29.5 g; T Fat 59.7 g; Chol 174.0 mg; Potas 50.1 mg; Sod 1613.0 mg.

Jim Valvano, Head Basketball Coach
North Carolina State University

Charts and Tables

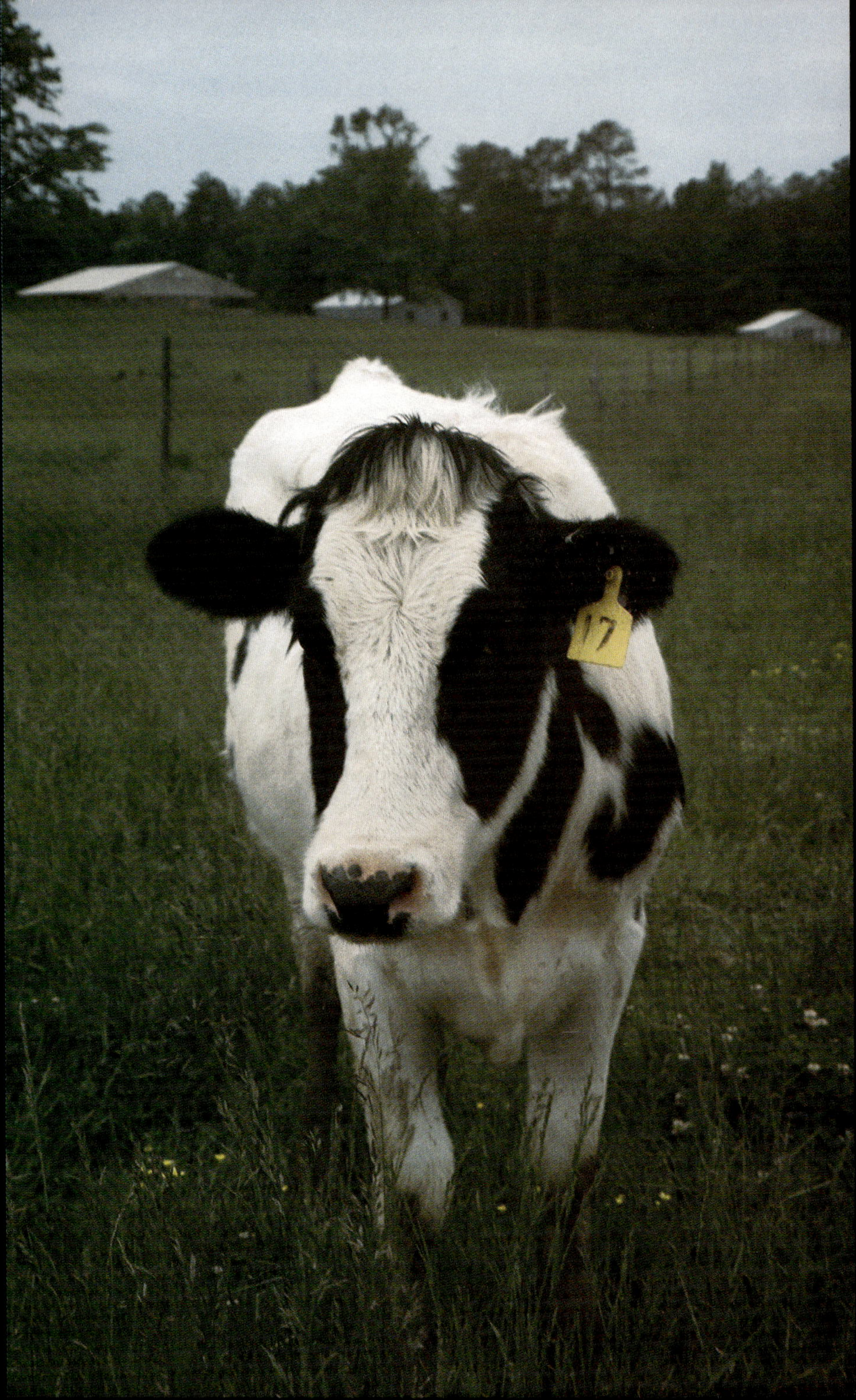

Wine Selections

Semidry White Wine

These wines have a fresh fruity taste and are best served young and slightly chilled.

- Johannisberg Riesling – *(Yo-hann-is-burg Rees-ling)*
- Frascati – *(Fras-cah-tee)*
- Gewurztraminer – *(Ge-vert-tram-me-ner)*
- Bernkasteler – *(Barn-kahst-ler)*
- Sylvaner Riesling – *(Sil-vah-nur Rees-ling)*
- Est! Est! Est!
- Fendant – *(Fahn-dawn)*
- Dienheimer – *(Deen-heim-er)*
- Krauznacher – *(Kroytz-nock)*

North Carolina Varietals

- Carlos – A soft-dry white wine with a delectable flavor. Serve with seafood, fish, pork and poultry.
- Chenin Blanc – A sweet white wine with a fruity bouquet and rich taste. An ideal dessert wine.
- Riesling – A crisp white wine with a spicy taste and floral aroma. Ita has a slightly sweet aftertaste that goes well with fresh fruit. Serve also with seafood or poultry.

Dry White Wines

These wines have a crisp, refreshing taste and are best served young and slightly chilled.

- Vouvray – *(Voo-vray)*
- Chablis – *(Shab-lee)*
- Chardonnay – *(Shar-doh-nay)*
- Pinot Blanc – *(Pee-no Blawn)*
- Chenin Blanc – *(Shay-nan Blawn)*
- Pouilly Fuisse – *(Pwee-yee-Fwee-say)*
- Orvieto Secco – *(Orv-yay-toe Sek-o)*
- Piesporter Trocken – *(Peez-porter)*
- Meursault – *(Mere-so)*
- Hermitage Blanc – *(Air-me-tahz Blawn)*
- Pinot Grigio – *(Pee-no Gree-jo)*
- Verdicchio – *(Ver-deek-ee-o)*
- Sancerre – *(Sahn-sehr)*
- Soave – *(So-ah-veh)*

North Carolina Varietals

- Savignon Blanc – A complex white wine with a taste of plum and apricots as well as a lingering dry finish. Serve with seafood, poultry, pork or veal.
- Chardonnay – Dry with a trace of fruitiness. Serve with seafood, poultry, pork, veal or pasta with white sauce.

WINE TABLE

White Dessert Wines

These wines are delicious dessert wines. Serve well chilled.

North Carolina Varietals
- Magnolia – A soft-dry white wine that captures the fruity bouquet of the magnolia grape. Excellent served as a dessert wine or with fresh fruit.
- Scuppernong – A fruity, sweet white wine with the distinctive flavor of the native scuppernong grape. Serve as an aperitif, with desserts or over fresh sliced strawberries.

Light Red Wines

These wines have a light taste and are best served young at cool room temperature.

- Beaujolais – *(Bo-sho-lay)*
- Bardolino – *(Bar-do-leen-o)*
- Valpolicella – *(Val-po-lee-chel-la)*
- Moulin-A-Vent Beaujolais – *(Moo-lon-ah-vahn)*
- Barbera – *(Bar-bear-ah)*
- Lambrusco – *(Lom-bruce-co)*
- Lirac – *(Lee-rack)*
- Nuits-Saint Georges "Villages" – *(Nwee San Zhorzh)*
- Gamay Beaujolais – *(Ga-mai Bo-sho-lay)*
- Santa Maddalena – *(Santa Mad-lay-nah)*
- Merlo di Ticino – *(Mair-lo dee Tee-chee-no)*

Hearty Red Wines

These wines have a heavier taste, improve with age, and are best opened thirty minutes before serving.

- Barbaresco – *(Bar-bah-rez-coe)*
- Barolo – *(Bah-ro-lo)*
- Zinfandel – *(Zin-fan-dell)*
- Chianti Riserva – *(Key-ahn-tee Ree-sairv-ah)*
- Cote Rotie – *(Coat Ro-tee)*
- Hermitage – *(Air-me-tahz)*
- Taurasi – *(Tah-rah-see)*
- Merlot – *(Mair-lo)*
- Syrah – *(Sir-rah)*
- Chateauneuf-Du-Pape – *(Shot-toe-nuff dew Pop)*
- Petite Sirah – *(Puh-teet Seer-rah)*
- Cote de Beaune – *(Coat duh Bone)*
- Cabernet Sauvignon – *(Cab-air-nay So-vin-yawn)*

North Carolina Varietals
- Cabernet Savignon – A full-bodied dry red wine with a fine delicate bouquet. Serve at room temperture with beef, lamb, veal, pork or turkey.

Blush Wines

- North Carolina Varietals include a broad category of blended wines normally salmon pink in color. They are semi-dry wines that complement a variety of dishes.

Wine and Cheese Complements

	Wine List	Cheeses
RED	Beaujolais Bordeaux Burgundy Cabernet Sauvignon Chianti Claret Rosé Zinfandel	Bel Paese Cheddar Edam Monterey Jack Piquant Bleu Roquefort Swiss Tilsit
WHITE	Chablis Chardonnay Chenin Blanc Moselle Pouilly Fuisse Riesling Sauterne Sauvignon Blanc Soave	Boursin Brie Camembert Creamy Bleu Gouda Gruyère Montrachet Port Salut Roquefort
SPARKLING	Champagne Sparkling Burgundy Sparkling Rosé	Any of the cheeses listed above would be appropriate complements to any of the sparkling wines.

Presentation

- Allow a total of 8 ounces or more wine for each person.
- Allow a total of 4 ounces or more cheese for each person. Cut cheeses into bite-sized pieces or place large pieces on cheese boards with cheese servers or knives for slicing as desired.
- Peel fruit if necessary and cut or slice into bite-sized pieces. Cut grapes into small clusters. Select fruit for visual and taste variety.
- Arrange groupings of wine with appropriate cheeses and an assortment of fruit and crackers. Provide an ample supply of small plates, napkins and silverware. Glasses should be small for sampling but in ample supply.

Herb Chart

Plant	Description	Meats
Basil	Strong Aromatic Herb Good Salt Replacer Main Ingredient In Pesto Sauce	Use With Meat Loaf, Meat Balls, Spaghetti, Pizza, Chili & Hamburgers
Chives	Mild Onion Flavor Use Fresh Or Frozen	Use On Any Meat That Needs A Mild Onion Flavor
Parsley	Most Popular Herb Carrot-like Flavor	Delicious In Lasagna & In Stews Add To Roast Lamb
Marjoram/Oregano	Milder Flavor Than Oregano; Salt Replacer For All Dishes Pizza Herb	All Italian Dishes, Meat Loaf, Pork & Lamb; Add To Hamburger, Casseroles, Chili & Fried Chicken
Sage	Strongly Aromatic With A Slight Taste Of Nutmeg	Roast Pork, Ham Loaf, Goose & Duck Try On Veal, Baked Ham, Pork, & Sausage
Savory	(Summer & Winter) Strong With Pepper-like Taste The "Bean Herb"	Roast Duck & Game Use In Stews
Thyme	One Of The Most Versatile Herbs Very Fragrant	Lamb, Beef, Pork, Game & Barbeque Sauces Add To Meat Loaf

Fish/Poultry	Vegetables/Soups/Salads	Eggs/Cheese/Sauces, Etc
All Fish Dishes & Poultry Dishes	Use With All Vegetables Good On Tomato Dishes Especially Good On Squash; Add To Salad Dressings; Sprinkle Over Tomato Soup	Omelets Scrambled Eggs Cheese Soufflé Good In Quiche
Use In Sauce For Fish Sauté With Chicken Try In Tuna Salad Or Tuna Casserole	Sprinkle On Baked Potatoes & Salads Cook With Rice & New Potatoes; Use In Soups & Mashed Potatoes	Sprinkle Over Eggs & Cream Cheese Sandwich Add To Biscuit Dough Or Corn Muffins
Sprinkle Over Chicken & Fish Dishes Use In Chicken Salad	Toss With New Potatoes Cut For Fresh Salads & Soups Add To Potato Salad	Good In Omelets & Sandwiches Add To Gravies, Sauces & Quiche
All Baked Fish & Crab Dishes; Good In Chicken Cacciatore Add To Poultry Casseroles	Blend In Butter To Season All Vegetables Add To Salad Dressings Use in Potatoes	Sprinkle Over Cheese In Grilled Cheese Sandwich Try In White Sauce, Omelets & Marinades
Add To Bread Stuffing For Poultry & For Fish	Add To Baked Onions Sprinkle Over Beans	Add To Cheese Sauce Try In Gravies All Cheese Dishes
Use Sparingly With Fish Mix With Other Herbs In Tuna Salad	Any Green Vegetable & Salads; Good In Soups	Blend With Other Herbs In Eggs
Baked or Broiled Fish, Shrimp, Chicken, & Turkey Add To Tuna Casseroles	Sauté With Butter & Pour Over Vegetables Use In Clam Chowder Good On Peas, Carrots & Onions; Sprinkle Over Baked Potatoes	Use On Spanish Omelet Add To Salad Dressing, Soufflé & Quiche

Equivalent Chart

	When the recipe calls for	Use
Baking	½ cup butter 2 cups butter 4 cups all-purpose flour 4½ to 5 cups sifted cake flour 1 square chocolate 1 cup semisweet chocolate chips 4 cups marshmallows 2¼ cups packed brown sugar 4 cups confectioners' sugar 2 cups granulated sugar	4 ounces 1 pound 1 pound 1 pound 1 ounce 6 ounces 1 pound 1 pound 1 pound 1 pound
Cereal – Bread	1 cup fine dry bread crumbs 1 cup soft bread crumbs 1 cup small bread cubes 1 cup fine cracker crumbs 1 cup fine graham cracker crumbs 1 cup vanilla wafer crumbs 1 cup crushed cornflakes 4 cups cooked macaroni 3½ cups cooked rice	4 to 5 slices 2 slices 2 slices 28 saltines 15 crackers 22 wafers 3 cups uncrushed 8 ounces uncooked 1 cup uncooked
Dairy	1 cup shredded cheese 1 cup cottage cheese 1 cup sour cream 1 cup whipped cream ⅔ cup evaporated milk 1⅔ cups evaporated milk	4 ounces 8 ounces 8 ounces ½ cup heavy cream 1 small can 1 13-ounce can

Fruit	4 cups sliced or chopped apples
	1 cup mashed banana
	2 cups pitted cherries
	3 cups shredded coconut
	4 cups cranberries
	1 cup pitted dates
	1 cup candied fruit
	3 to 4 tablespoons lemon juice plus
	    1 tablespoon grated lemon rind
	⅓ cup orange juice plus 2 teaspoons
	    grated orange rind
	4 cups sliced peaches
	2 cups pitted prunes
	3 cups raisins
		4 medium
		3 medium
		4 cups unpitted
		8 ounces
		1 pound
		1 8-ounce package
		1 8-ounce package
		
		1 lemon
		
		1 orange
		8 medium
		1 12-ounce package
		1 15-ounce package

Equivalent Chart

	When the recipe calls for	Use
Meats	4 cups chopped cooked chicken 3 cups chopped cooked meat 2 cups cooked ground meat	1 5-pound chicken 1 pound, cooked 1 pound, cooked
Nuts	1 cup chopped nuts	4 ounces shelled 1 pound unshelled
Vegetables	2 cups cooked green beans 2½ cups lima beans or red beans 4 cups shredded cabbage 1 cup grated carrot 8 ounces fresh mushrooms 1 cup chopped onion 4 cups sliced or chopped potatoes 2 cups canned tomatoes	½ pound fresh or 1 16-ounce can 1 cup dried, cooked 1 pound 1 large 1 4-ounce can 1 large 4 medium 1 16-ounce can

Measurement Equivalents

1 tablespoon = 3 teaspoons
2 tablespoons = 1 ounce
4 tablespoons = ¼ cup
5⅓ tablespoons = ⅓ cup
8 tablespoons = ½ cup
12 tablespoons = ¾ cup
16 tablespoons = 1 cup
1 cup = 8 ounces or ½ pint
4 cups = 1 quart
4 quarts = 1 gallon

1 6½ to 8-ounce can = 1 cup
1 10½ to 12-ounce can = 1¼ cups
1 14 to 16-ounce can = 1¾ cups
1 16 to 17-ounce can = 2 cups
1 18 to 20-ounce can = 2½ cups
1 20-ounce can = 3½ cups
1 46 to 51-ounce can = 5¾ cups
1 6½ to 7½- pound can or Number 10 = 12 to 13 cups

Measurement Equivalents

Liquid

1 teaspoon = 5 milliliters
1 tablespoon = 15 milliliters
1 fluid ounce = 30 milliliters
1 cup = 250 milliliter
1 pint = 500 milliliters

Dry

1 quart = 1 liter
1 ounce = 30 grams
1 pound = 450 grams
2.2 pounds = 1 kilogram

NOTE: *The metric measures are approximate benchmarks for puposes of home food preparation.*

Substitution Chart

	Instead of	Use
Baking	1 teaspoon baking powder 1 tablespoon cornstarch (for thickening) 1 cup sifted all-purpose flour 1 cup sifted cake flour	1/4 teaspoon soda plus 1/2 teaspoon cream of tartar 2 tablespoons flour or 1 tablespoon tapioca 1 cup plus 2 tablespoons sifted cake flour 1 cup minus 2 tablespoons sifted all-purpose flour
	1 cup dry bread crumbs	3/4 cup cracker crumbs
Dairy	1 cup buttermilk 1 cup heavy cream 1 cup light cream 1 cup sour cream 1 cup sour milk	1 cup sour milk or 1 cup yogurt 3/4 cup skim milk plus 1/3 cup butter 7/8 cup skim milk plus 3 tablespoons butter 7/8 cup sour milk plus 3 tablespoons butter 1 cup milk plus 1 tablespoon vinegar or lemon juice or 1 cup buttermilk
Seasoning	1 teaspoon allspice 1 cup catsup 1 clove of garlic 1 teaspoon Italian spice 1 teaspoon lemon juice 1 tablespoon mustard 1 medium onion	1/2 teaspoon cinnamon plus 1/8 teaspoon cloves 1 cup tomato sauce plus 1/2 cup sugar plus 2 tablespoons vinegar 1/8 teaspoon garlic powder or 1/8 teaspoon instant minced garlic or 3/4 teaspoon garlic salt or 5 drops of liquid garlic 1/4 teaspoon each oregano, basil, thyme, rosemary plus dash of cayenne 1/2 teaspoon vinegar 1 teaspoon dry mustard 1 tablespoon dried minced onion or 1 teaspoon onion powder
Sweet	1-ounce square chocolate 1 2/3 ounces semisweet chocolate 1 cup honey 1 cup granulated sugar	1/4 cup cocoa plus 1 teaspoon shortening 1 ounce unsweetened chocolate plus 4 teaspoons granulated sugar 1 to 1 1/4 cups sugar plus 1/4 cup liquid or 1 cup corn syrup or molasses 1 cup packed brown sugar or 1 cup corn syrup, molasses or honey minus 1/4 cup liquid

Quantities to Serve 100

Baked beans	5 gallons
Beef	40 pounds
Beets	30 pounds
Bread	10 loaves
Butter	3 pounds
Cabbage for slaw	20 pounds
Cakes	8 cakes
Carrots	33 pounds
Cauliflower	18 pounds
Cheese	18 pounds
Chicken for chicken pie	40 pounds
Coffee	3 pounds
Cream	3 quarts
Fruit cocktail	1 gallon
Fruit juice	4 (No. 10) cans
Fruit salad	20 quarts
Ground beef	30 to 36 pounds
Ham	40 pounds
Ice Cream	4 gallons
Lettuce	20 heads
Meat loaf	24 pounds
Milk	6 gallons
Nuts	3 pounds
Olives	1¾ pounds
Oysters	18 quarts
Pickles	2 quarts
Pies	18 pies
Potatoes	35 pounds
Roast pork	40 pounds
Rolls	200 rolls
Salad dressing	3 quarts
Scalloped potatoes	5 gallons
Soup	5 gallons
Sugar cubes	3 pounds
Tomato juice	4 (No. 10) cans
Vegetables	4 (No. 20) cans
Vegetable salad	20 quarts
Whipping cream	4 pints
Wieners	25 pounds

INDEX

APPETIZERS
Angels on Horseback, 11
Bacon Pizza Snacks, 11
Cha-Chos, 12
Cheese
  Ball
    Liver, 12
    Quick and Zesty, 12
  Crisps, Mildred Garner's, 13
  Dip, Chili Cheese, 16
  Picklewiches, 21-22
  Popcorn, Fan-Tastic, 19
  Ring, Our Favorite, 13
Chicken
  Mousse Phyllo Triangles, 15
  Wings
    Capsicana, 14
    Buffalo-Style, 14
Dip
  Bacon-Horseradish, 15
  Bean and Bacon, Mexican, 16
  Chili Cheese, 16
  Curry, 17
  East Indian, 17
  Egg, Incredible, 17
  Shrimp Chip, 18
Meatballs, Turkey, 18
Melon Cup, 18
Mix
  Dix, 19
  Tex Mex, 20
Pecans, Scuppernong Spiced, 20
Pizza Squares, 20
Popcorn, Fan-Tastic Cheese, 19
Sandwiches
  B.E.L.T., 180
  Cucumber Open-Faced, Tiny, 21
  Picklewiches, 21–22
Sausage
  Balls, 22
  Poppy Rolls, 23
Spare Ribs, Zingy, 22

BEEF
and Broccoli with Chive Gravy, 47
Chinese, 48
and Green Peppers, 49
Kabobs
  Beef and Bacon, Marinated, 50
  Sweet and Spicy, 50

Malaya, 47
Ribs, Honey-Glazed, 49
Steak
  Barbecue, Special, 49
  Green Pepper, (Duplin Style), 51
  Teriyaki, Marinated, 51
Stew
  Easy Baked, 52
  Rosé
  Vineyard, 53
Stroganoff, 53
Tenderloin, Marinated, 54
and Wine Casserole, 48
Winemaker's, 54

BEVERAGES
Champagne Float, Duplin, 23
Coffee Cooler, 24
Gin Fizzies, 189
Grape Punch, Party, 24
Orange Dream Shake, 24
Punch
  Grape, Party, 24
  Melon, 25
  Minted, 25
Strawberry Rosé, 26
Syllabub, Country, 26
Tea, Russian, 26

BREAD
Biscuits, Sweet Potato, 115
Coffee Cake, Neese's Sausage, 115
Corn
  Broccoli, 116
  Hush Puppies, 118
  Microwave, 116
  Muffins, 124
  Spoon, Southern-Style, 117
Crêpes, Dessert, 117
Hush Puppies, 118
Loaves
  Apple, 118
  Banana Nut, 178
  Cheese, 119
  Cranberry Pecan, 119
  Oatmeal, Whole Wheat and, 127
  Orange Nut, 120
  Peanut, Whole Wheat, 128
  Pickle, Miss Ida's Sweet, 120
  Pineapple and Apricot, 121

INDEX

Pumpkin, 121
   and Pecan, 122
Sausage, Italian 190
Strawberry, 122
Sweet Potato, Southern, 123
Zucchini, 123
Muffins
   Bran, Ever-Ready, 124
   Cornmeal, 124
      Crusty Cheese, 124
   Sausage, 125
   Sweet Potato, North Carolina, 125
   Tropic Isle, 126
Rolls
   Herb and Cheese Pull-Apart, 126
   Honey, Quick, 129
   No-Knead Refrigerator, 129
   Pecan, Speedy, 130

CHICKEN
Brunswick Stew, Tar Heel, 179
Casserole, 67
   and Vegetable, 68
   and Wild Rice, 177
Cheese, Microwave, 71
and Dumplings, Old-Fashioned, 68
Duplin, 69
Family, with Brown Sugar Glaze, 69
Gourmet Stuffed, Breasts, 70
Honey
   Mustard Drumstick Wrap-Ups, 71
   and Sweet Potatoes, 70
Jambalaya, and Sausage, 72
with Lime Butter, 72
Mexican Super Supper, 73
North Carolina, 73
Nuggets, Sesame, 71
Pie
   Cheese, Super, 74
   with Sweet Potato Crust, 74
Plum Good, 75
Salad
   Avocado, Stuffed, 76
   Carolina Coast, Miss Ida's, 75
   Fruit, 76
   Hot, 77
   Tortelini, 77
Skewered, with Sour Cream Dip, 78
Stir-Fry, and Broccoli, 79
Succulent, 78
Super-Fast, 79
Tacos, 80
Tetrazzini, 185
Wine, 80

CAKES
Apple, 186
   Carolina, 183
   Deluxe, 141
   Fresh, 141
Caramel, Favorite, 184
Chocolate Chip, 142
Date Nut, Luscious, 142
Fruit
   Holiday, 143
   Cocktail, Yummy, 143
Nut Feud, Carolina, 144
Peachy Delight, 145
Peanut Pudding, 145
Pineapple, 146
Plum, Good, 146
Pound
   Cherry-Pecan, 147
   Old-Fashioned, 148
   Sweet Potato, 147
Strawberry Nut, Delightful, 148
Watermelon, Festive, 149
Vanilla Wafer, 149
Wine, Scuppernong, 150

CANDY
Caramel Corn, Baked, 153
Chocolate
   Coated Peanuts, 151
   Truffles, 150
Peanut
   Brittle
      Dixie, 152
      Microwave, 152
   Butter Fudge, Easiest Yet, 151
   Chocolate-Coated, 151
   Haystacks, Jiffy Goober, 151
   Sugar-Coated, 152

COOKIES
Blair's Squares, 153
Chocolate
   Snack Squares, Peanutty, 157
   Toffee Squares, 154
Cornmeal, 154
   Honey and Nut, 155
Grape Crunch Squares, 155
Honey
   and Nut Cornmeal, 155
   and Pecan Balls, 156
Lemon Drops, Old-Fashioned, 156
Peanutty Chocolate Snack
      Squares, 157
Shortbread, Showcase, 158

Sweetheart, 157
Sweet Potato and Apple Bars, 158

DESSERTS
Apple
  Baklava, Rum, 133
  Dumplings with Lemon Sauce,
    Baked, 133
Baklava, Apple Rum, 133
Blackberry
  Cobbler, Grandma's, 134
  Crumble, 134
Blueberry-Pineapple Crunch,
    Doris Gurley's, 181
Chocolate
  Cheesecake, Strawberry, 138
  Soufflé, 135
Cobbler
  Blackberry, Grandma's, 134
  Fruit, 180
Crêpes, 117
Dumplings
  Apple with Lemon Sauce,
    Baked, 133
  Peaches and Cream, 137
Fruit
  Bowl, Dublin, 136
  Cobbler, 180
  Crisp, Baked, 135

Grape Sherbet, 137
Parfait, Carolina Sweet Red
    Strawberry, 139
Pudding, Sweet Potato, 140
Omelet, 136
Peach
  Cobbler, Fruit, 180
  and Cream Dumplings, 137
Sherbet, Grape, 137
Shortcake, Hot Milk, 140
Soufflé, Chocolate, 135
Strawberry
  Cheesecake, Chocolate, 138
  Heaven, 138
  Parfait, Carolina Sweet Red, 139
  Pizza, 139
  Shortcake, Hot Milk, 140
Sweet Potato Pudding, 140

DUCKLING
Mexitalian, Dinner, 82
with Mushroom and Wine Sauce, 81
Roast, Milano, 81

Frankfurters, Apple and Sweet Potato, 60

FROSTING
Brown Sugar Glaze, 183
Caramel, 184
Pecan, 144

GROUND BEEF
Barbecue and Cheese Corn Bread
    Casserole, 55
Burgers, Skillet Barbecued, 55
and Biscuit Casserole, 56
Burritos, Chili, 56
Chinese, and Tofu, 56
Chili
  Burritos, 56
  Pizza, 59
  Stuffed Peppers, 59
Lasagna, Cheesy, 57
Meat Loaf, 58
  Herbed, 58
Peppers, Chili-Stuffed, 59
Pizza, Chili, 59

HAM
Casserole with Biscuits, 61
Dixie Style, and Yams, 60

PIES
Apple
  Cranberry, Alaskan Low Bush, 176
  Cream, Crisp, 159
Banana Split, Royal, 161
Berry Nutty, 160
Black Bottom Eggnog Chiffon, 161
Fruited Rainbow, 162
Gin Fizz-Egg, 189
Grand Champion, 159
Grape
  Scuppernong, 162
  Tarts, 163
Lemon, 164
Peach
  Deep-Dish, 185
  Patriot, 163
  Tarts, Fresh, 165
Peanut, Southern, 166
Peanut Butter
  Custard, 166
  Fluffy Frozen, 165
Pecan
  Chess Tarts, 167
  Supreme, 170

Strawberry
  Berry Nutty, 160
  Chiffon Pie, 169
  Tart, French, 168
Sweet Potato, 171
  Southern, 170
  Surprise, 171
Tarts
  Grape, 163
  Peach, Fresh, 165
  Pecan Chess, 167
  Strawberry, French, 168
Watermelon
  Quick and Easy, 172
  Surprise, 172

PIE SHELLS
Cornmeal, 164
Crunchy, 172
Graham Cracker, 169
Meringue, 160
Tart
  Special, 168
  Tiny, 167

PORK
Bacon, Egg, Lettuce and Tomato
    Sandwich, 180
Brains 'n Eggs, 177
Chops
  Baked Dill, Miss Ida's, 62
  Herbed, 61
  Mushroom and Beer, 63
  North Carolina, 62
  Southern, Bake, 63
  Special, 62
Ham. *See* Ham
Ribs
  Marmalade and Ginger, 64
  Zingy, 22
Roast, Cajun, 64
Sausage
  Balls, 22
  Bread, Italian, 190
    Coffee Cake, 115
  Jambalaya, 72
  and Macaroni Bake, 67
  Muffins, 125
  Rolls, Poppy, 23
Stir-Fry
  Carolina, 179
  and Sweet Potato, 65
Tacos Deliciosos, 65
Tenderloin
  Medallions, 66
  au Vin, 66

SEAFOOD
en Casserole, 93
Catfish
  Blackened, 88
  Broiled, 87
  Charcoal Grilled, 88
  Diane, 89
  Fried, Spicy, 89
  Roll-Ups, 90
Crab Meat
  Pie, Hot, 92
  St. Jacques, 92
Fillets with Herbs, Rolled, 90
Flounder
  Kiev, 91
  Supreme, 91
Oysters and Macaroni au Gratin, 93
Shrimp
  Dinner Casserole, 94
  Dip, Chip, 18
  and Pepper Combo, 94

SIDE DISHES
Apple
  and Cheese Casserole, 108
  Cinnamon, Baked, 108
Egg
  Brunch in-a-Dish, 111
  Liver Pudding Brunch Bake, 109
  Overnight Casserole, 109
  Pizza
    Breakfast, 110
    Olé, 110
  Snacks, Bacon, 11
  Squares, 20
  Quiche, Basic, 111
  Taco, 111
Grits, Cheese, 187
Pasta
  Fettucini Sauce, New
      Orleans-Style, 175
  Stuffed with Five Cheeses, 112
Rice
  Betty Good, 182
  Spanish, 112

SALADS
Chicken. *See* Chicken
Fruit
  Ambrosia, Fresh, 33
  Blueberry Dessert, 33

INDEX

Melon, Frosty, 35
On-the-Go, 34
Peach, Queen, 35
Six-Cup, 35
Strawberry Pretzel, 36
Tower, 34
Waldorf, Californian, 36
Tuna, Herb Garden, 44
Turkey, Oriental, 86
Vegetable
   Black-eyed Pea, 37
   Broccoli, Fresh, 37
      and Bacon, 38
   Cauliflower, 38
      Lettuce and, Make-Ahead, 187
   Coleslaw, Overnight, 38
   Green, Tossed Hydroponic, 39
   Lettuce
      and Cauliflower,
         Make-Ahead, 187
      Hydroponic Wilted, 39
   Marinated Fresh, 41
   Potato
      Championship, 40
      Dilled, Miss Ida's, 40
   Spinach, 41
   Summer Garden, with Bacon, 42
   Sweet Potato, 43
   Tofu Mix, Savory, 43

SALAD DRESSINGS
French, Sweet, 39
Honey
   Herbed, 44
   Vinaigrette, 43
Italian, Zesty, 44
Vinaigrette, 42
   Honey, 43

SOUP
Broccoli, Cream of, 29
Catfish and Shrimp, 29
Chowder, Hearty Vegetable, 32
Gazpacho, 30
Gumbo, Seafood, 31
Hamburger, Hearty, 30
Shrimp, Catfish and, 29
Sweet Potato and Pepper, 31
Vegetable Chowder, Hearty, 32
Watercress, Tangy, 32
Spiced Ground Meat, 188

TURKEY
Barbecued, One-Day-Ahead, 82
Grilled, Fillets, 83
Herbed Peppercorn, Breast, 83
Lasagna, 84
Omelet, 182
Parmigiana, 84
Pasta Pie, Broccoli and, 85
Salad, Oriental, 86
Sandwiches, Pocket, 86
Steaks, Fried, 85
Spaghetti Sauce, Low-Fat, 87

VEGETABLES
Beans
   Baked, Carolina Treet, 97
   Green
      and Corn Casserole, 97
      Oriental, 98
Broccoli
   Canadian-Style Bacon and, 99
   Gourmet, 98
Cabbage
   Country Sweet and Sour, 99
   Steamed, with Cheese Sauce, 100
Casserole, 107
Cauliflower and Broccoli Toss, 100
Corn
   Casserole, Two-, 101
   on the Cob, Parmesan, 101
   Pudding, 102
Mushrooms, Oriental, 102
Onions, Herbed, 102
Peppers, Stuffed, 103
Platter, 107
Potatoes
   Country-Style, 104
   Party Casserole, 178
   Gourmet, 103
Squash
   Casserole, 104, 181
   Parmesan, 104
Stir-Fried, 106
Sweet Potato
   Candied, 105
   Casserole, Exquisite, 105
Tomatoes
   Baked, with Rosemary and
      Garlic, 190
   Marinated, 106
Turnips in Cheese Sauce, 106

MAIL ORDER FORM

Goodness Grows in North Carolina Cookbook

Name_____

Address _____

City/State/Zip _____

Number of Copies _____

x Cost $10.50 per book _____

Shipping & Handling _____
$2.00/book

Total _____

Make check payable to: **North Carolina Department of Agriculture
Division of Marketing - Cookbook
Post Office Box 27647
Raleigh, North Carolina 27611**

MAIL ORDER FORM

Goodness Grows in North Carolina Cookbook

Name_____

Address_____

City/State/Zip _____

Number of Copies _____

x Cost $10.50 per book _____

Shipping & Handling _____
$2.00/book

Total _____

Make check payable to: **North Carolina Department of Agriculture
Division of Marketing - Cookbook
Post Office Box 27647
Raleigh, North Carolina 27611**